NEOLIBERALISM FROM BELOW

RADICAL AMÉRICAS

A series edited by Bruno Bosteels and George Ciccariello-Maher

NEOLIBERALISM FROM BELOW

Popular Pragmatics and Baroque Economies

VERÓNICA GAGO

Translated by Liz Mason-Deese

DUKE UNIVERSITY PRESS

Durham and London

2017

© 2017 Duke University Press
All rights reserved
Printed in the United States of America on
acid-free paper ∞
Cover design by Matthew Tauch
Typeset in Minion Pro by Westchester Publishing Services

Library of Congress Cataloging-in-Publication Data
Names: Gago, Verónica, [date] author.
Title: Neoliberalism from below : popular pragmatics and baroque economies /
    Verónica Gago ; translated by Liz Mason-Deese.
Other titles: Razón neoliberal. English
Description: Durham : Duke University Press, 2017. | Series: Radical Amâericas |
    Includes bibliographical references and index.
Identifiers: LCCN 2017018618 (print)
LCCN 2017021285 (ebook)
ISBN 9780822372738 (ebook)
ISBN 9780822368830 (hardcover : alk. paper)
ISBN 9780822369127 (pbk. : alk. paper)
Subjects: LCSH: La Salada (Buenos Aires, Argentina) | Fairs—Argentina—Lomas de
    Zamora (Partido) | Informal sector (Economics)—Argentina—Lomas de Zamora
    (Partido) | Under-the-table employment—Argentina—Lomas de Zamora (Partido) |
    Neoliberalism—Argentina.
Classification: LCC HF5473.A72 (ebook) | LCC HF5473.A72 L6515 2014 (print) |
    DDC 381—dc23
LC record available at https://lccn.loc.gov/2017018618

Cover art: Woman shopping at a shoe stall in La Salada market, Buenos Aires,
Argentina. Photograph © Sub.coop.

CONTENTS

ACKNOWLEDGMENTS

My thanks are nearly infinite. First, to Iván and Diego Sztulwark, for their love. To Raquel Gutiérrez Aguilar, for many things that started with that walk between the Virgen de los Deseos and an apartment in the heights of Sopocachi. To Frida Rojas, Aida Göttl, and Ariadna Materia: my midwives. Without them, none of what was inside me would have managed to work its way out. To Silvia Rivera Cusicanqui, for the promiscuous rituals and conversations, in Buenos Aires and in La Paz. To Marta Malo, for the way in which she, in just a few blocks of Lavapies, explained the meaning of the sexual contract. To Josefina Ludmer, for the tricks for the weak. To the closest and most loving tribe, Rosana Fernández, Andrea Barberi, Alida Díaz, Lucía Scrimini, Paz Viano. To Natalia Fontana, my sister. To Ignacio and Juan, my brothers. To Daniel Gago, for the siren stories. To Sandro Mezzadra, for his complicity beyond measure. To Colectivo Situaciones, for the life in common. To Juan Vázquez and Delia Colque, from Colectivo Simbiosis, for their wisdom. To the laborious and persistent work of Tinta Limón. To the warm words of León Rozitchner. Also, to the crossovers, in one point of time or space, with Marcelo Matellanes, Saskia Sassen, Julián D'Angiolillo, and Hernán Fernández. To my *compañeros* from the University of Buenos Aires, Pablo Míguez and Ariel Filadoro.

The English version of this book warrants another round of connections and acknowledgments. Again to Sandro Mezzadra, who was the one who encouraged me to go forward with it—which would not have been possible without the careful and laborious translation of Liz Mason-Deese and the kindly help of Alicia Balsells. To Arturo Escobar for a generous and stimulating reading. This version benefited from some additions as a result of exchanges with Alexandre Roig (Universidad Nacional de San Martín) and Pedro Biscay (Central Bank of Argentine Republic). Thanks to Bruno Bosteels and George Ciccairello-Maher for inviting me to be part of this honorably titled series: Radical Américas. And, finally, to Courtney Berger, Sandra Korn, and Lisa Bintrim for all of their delicate revision effort.

Neoliberalism from Below

A Perspective from Latin America

Revolts against Neoliberalism

In Latin America *neoliberalism* has become a term seeking to remain attached to the past. As a keyword, it serves as a quick, widely understood diagnostic of a set of policies that altered the face of the continent (privatization, reductions in social protections, financial deregulation, labor flexibilization, etc.). A cycle can be seen in Argentina that corresponds to that of the region as a whole. During the 1990s, neoliberalism was expressed through structural reforms that originated during the last military dictatorship (1976–83); the period was characterized by paradigmatic reforms such as the Financial Institutions Law of 1977 and by state and paramilitary repression of popular and armed insurgency. An image suffices to indicate the imbrication of the state and the financial world: with this legislation, holding cells were installed in the headquarters of the Bank of the Argentine Nation that functioned alongside a clandestine trading desk (Biscay 2015). The 1980s ended with an inflationary crisis, leading to the privatization of public services, the closure of many private and state companies, and labor flexibilization corresponding to an opening to imports and general deregulation of production (Azpiazu and Schorr 2010; Basualdo 2000, 2006). Massive unemployment, after a few years of increasing rates of self-employment, caused poverty rates to soar. The unemployed workers of the country's interior cities (former oil workers) initiated the *piquetero* (picketing) movement in Argentina, which later spread throughout the entire country, adopting particularly politically radical forms in Buenos Aires's urban periphery. In 2001 the crisis erupted everywhere, provoking the organic collapse of the government and the banking system and shaking up the public stage by making social movements visible as determinant actors in the political conflictiveness.

In Bolivia as well, movements and popular uprisings occurred between 2000 and 2005 that ruptured neoliberalism's hegemony over the organization of life and production, opening a series of disputes over social wealth and political control (Gutiérrez Aguilar 2014). Community and neighborhood assemblies, rural organizations, and unions contested the privatization of public resources (water and gas) and overturned social relations of obedience, rejecting their normative and repressive structure. These forces of "plebeian democratization," as Raquel Gutiérrez Aguilar calls them, led to the resignation in 2003 of President Gonzalo Sánchez de Losada, a mining executive who had been president of the country for one term in the 1990s and who had begun a second term in 2002. Other countries in Latin America experienced similar developments, first Brazil and Venezuela, and later the recent protests in Peru and Chile.

Since the 1970s, after the defeat of the revolutionary movements, Latin America has served as a site of experimentation for neoliberal reforms propelled "from above," by international financial institutions, corporations, and governments. However, thinking of neoliberalism as a mutation in the "art of government," as Michel Foucault (2008) proposes with the term *governmentality*, supposes understanding neoliberalism as a set of skills, technologies, and practices, deploying a new type of rationality that cannot be thought of only from above. Moreover, this rationality is not purely abstract nor macropolitical but rather arises from the encounter with forces at work and is embodied in various ways by the subjectivities and tactics of everyday life, as a variety of ways of doing, being, and thinking that organize the social machinery's calculations and affects. Here neoliberalism functions immanently: it unfolds on the territorial level, modulates subjectivities, and is provoked, without needing a transcendent and exterior structure.

In this book, I would like to argue two points. First, we need to focus on the terrain of the resistant subjectivities that led to the crisis of this system of neoliberal regulations across the continent. Second, we must think about neoliberalism's persistence beyond its crisis of political legitimacy, looking at how it becomes rooted in popular subjectivities, resulting in what I call *neoliberalism from below*.

Thus, I intend to identify the revolts against neoliberalism as a crucial founding moment of its crisis of legitimacy in the region. Later, I will develop the notion of neoliberalism from below as a way of problematizing the reason why neoliberalism does not solely depend on its political legitimacy, at the same time as social movements have an agenda that imposes a kind of veto power on later governments. This requires conceptualizing the pragmatic that the popular classes deploy to adapt to, while also derailing, the unidimensionality of the neoliberal competitive norm, to complicate it and combine it with other practices and knowledges. Toward this end, I will detail the *strategic rationality* that the popular classes' vital perseverance brings into play. I analyze these popular frameworks as *baroque economies* in which the persistence of and confrontation with the neoliberal dynamic from above and from below are simultaneously negotiated. Finally, there is a second sequence, given by the emergence of a populism that is seeking to become the reigning ideology in accordance with a "return of the state," attempting to assert itself as synonymous with the "end of neoliberalism" in the region. The complement to this political argument is given by the developmentalist projects that are presented as the direct result of a new mode of state interventionism and that are supposedly in opposition to neoliberal logic. My argument will go in a different direction to show how neoliberalism and neodevelopmentalism are combined to give a particular character to state intervention, as well as to the very concepts of development and social inclusion.

The revolts during the crisis in Argentina in 2001 marked the breakdown of the political legitimacy of neoliberalism from above. In Bolivia the key moment was 2003. Those revolts are part of a continental sequence that caused the subsequent turn of the region's governments (see Colectivo Situaciones 2009), with significant events in the background of this sequence, such as the Caracazo. Ecuador lost its national currency in the crisis in 1999–2000, leading to the fall of President Jamil Mahuad. A year later, in Argentina, it was debated whether the departure from peso-dollar convertibility, which organized the productive and financial structure during the 1990s, would be carried out following the Ecuadorian model of the dollarization of the economy. In Ecuador, dollarization began as an emergency measure in a crisis situation (Larrea 2004) and has been maintained to this day, structuring a rentier economy through oil and remittances (Dávalos 2012). In 2002 a political crisis of great magnitude shook Venezuela: a coup attempt against Hugo Chávez in April and a national petroleum strike in December. What emerges in this sequence is the relevance of the rentier question in regard to the national currency and natural resources in the time of crisis.

The rentier question will be an essential element for understanding neoliberalism's persistence in Latin America and the connections between finance and neodevelopmentalism. However, I am interested in highlighting the crisis in the region as a milestone and as a perspective. The crisis is a privileged locus for thinking because there is a cognitive porosity; concepts are set in motion, and sensibilities express the commotion and reorganize the thresholds of what is considered possible and how it is expressed. One of liberalism's poisonous legacies is the projection of the social as a space made from above, without its own power or consistency. This has its correlative in the definition of the crisis: it is experienced as a return of barbarism, as a noncivil, prepolitical stage. Therefore, the crisis is conjured up through an enterprise that reinstitutes the political, where the social does not exist on its own but is produced by the political, which is understood according to its traditional institutions: political parties, the state, labor unions (as a way of translating Hobbesian theories about the relevance of a central sovereign authority and renewing them under the diffusion of populist theory). However, the crisis in Argentina in 2001 and the one in Bolivia in 2003 do not fit this image—nor does that in Ecuador. In the crisis, a properly political dynamic of experimentation in and of the social unfolded (or, in other words, a social protagonism was initiated). The celebrated "return of politics," a figure of speech created by progressive governments to make sense of the cycle, runs the clear risk of strengthening this division and freezing the social in place as that which is merely managed, as a territory of "bare life," which today returns as new social conflicts, unthinkable from a state-centric politics.

The social, when read as an instance of demands to satisfy, repair, and amend, reduces those collective dynamics to a passive position, denying their immediately productive condition. The consolidation of a (politicist) reading from above ends up failing in two ways. First, on denying the political elaborated from below, it loses information, a sense of opportunity, and even possible directions. Second, it is not effective in creating the illusion of an impossible consistency: the image of an omnipotent "above" for the state is primarily nostalgic but also an overly restricted reading of the present, where state action itself must adjust to a dynamic of governmentality and the "conduct of conducts," to use Foucault's terms. In addition, in this politicist schema, the popular, on being a concrete and motley complexity, displaces a strictly rhetorical figure. Only then can it be invoked to legitimate a power that repairs and unifies that which otherwise is condemned for spontaneity and multitudinous disorder.

Neoliberalism from Below

The progressive governments' perspective, which attempts to neutralize the practices from below while the governments present themselves as the overcoming of an era of popular resistance, closes off a more complex and realistic image of neoliberalism. It ignores the productive capacity of informal economies, and it ignores the ways in which migration propels a greater complexity in the territorial fabric. I will examine this productive capacity from the angle provided by a huge informal market on the outskirts of Buenos Aires, La Salada. As an empirical point of departure, this popular market enables me to develop a conceptualization of the popular economies that have flourished in so many Latin American urban quarters in the neoliberal age. Along these lines, when the governments do recognize these subjectivities, they do so under victimizing and moralizing forms. The progressive governments, despite their rhetoric, do not signal the end of neoliberalism. Further, they severely complicate the characterization of what is understood as postneoliberalism (for a debate: Brand and Sekler 2009). My thesis is that neoliberalism survives as a set of conditions that are manifested, from above, as the renewal of the extractive-dispossessive form in a new moment of financialized sovereignty and, from below, as a rationality that negotiates profits in this context of dispossession, in a contractual dynamic that mixes forms of servitude and conflict.

Therefore, *survives* is perhaps not the best term: understanding contemporary neoliberalism requires focusing on its capacity for mutation, its dynamic of permanent variation, especially looking at variations in meaning, at recursive, nonlinear time rhythms, at disruptions driven by social struggles—all of which reemerged with new aspects in Latin America in the context of the crisis of 2007–8.

In Latin America the increased participation of the state following the growth of mass consumption and the decline of neoliberalism's legitimacy has recently changed the neoliberal landscape: from the misery, scarcity, and unemployment of the early twenty-first century (and the forms of struggle and resistance that emerged then) to certain forms of abundance found in new forms of consumption, work, entrepreneurship, territorial organization, and money. The greater "promiscuity" of the territories of Latin America is increasingly presented as part of a series of baroque economies reconstructing a new political dynamic that overflows and qualifies neoliberalism itself.

To draw an initial topology: *from above*, neoliberalism recognizes a modification of the global regime of accumulation—new strategies on the part of corporations, agencies, and governments—that induces a mutation in nation-state institutions. In this regard, neoliberalism is a phase (and not a mere aspect) of capitalism. *From below*, neoliberalism is the proliferation of forms of life that reorganize notions of freedom, calculation, and obedience, projecting a new collective affectivity and rationality.

By *neoliberalism from below*, I am referring to a set of conditions that are materialized beyond the will of a government, whether legitimate or not, but that turn into the conditions under which a network of practices and skills operates, assuming calculation as its primordial subjective frame and functioning as the motor of a powerful popular economy that combines community skills of self-management and intimate know-how as a technology of mass self-entrepreneurship in the crisis. The force of this neoliberalism ends up taking root as a *vitalist pragmatic* in the sectors that play a leading role in the so-called informal economy.

This vitalist pragmatic means, on the one hand, that calculation is a vital condition in a context where the state does not guarantee the conditions of neoliberal competition prescribed by the ordoliberal model.[1] In these forms of doing, calculation assumes a certain monstrosity to the extent that popular entrepreneurship is forced to take responsibility for conditions that are not guaranteed. On the other hand, this imperfection is given as indeterminacy and organizes a certain idea of freedom, which, in its own way, challenges some of the most traditional forms of obedience. One of the questions that must be addressed is how this rationality does not coincide exactly with *homo œconomicus*, as if it were a perverse tracing.

The first point in this respect is that the vitalist pragmatic allows us to consider the fabric of *potencia* (power) emerging from below. Thus, it launches a new form of *conatus*, to use the Spinozist term: the neoliberal dynamic is problematically and effectively combined with this persistent vitalism that always attaches to the expansion of freedoms, pleasures, and affects.

Therefore, it raises the question of the relationships between neoliberalism and informal economies. In Argentina, as a result of the crisis, these economies became visible and acquired the scale of a mass phenomenon, owing to the intense demonetization experienced in the country.[2] A series of innovative economic institutions (of savings, exchange, loans, and consumption) spread, combining survival strategies with new forms of popular entrepreneurship and brutal forms of exploitation. The economic recovery of recent years—

associated at a broader scale with the cycle of progressive governments in the region—has not caused them to disappear. On the contrary, the economic recovery incorporated them and promoted their articulation with the rest of the economy as part of its drive toward development. In Bolivia, Venezuela, and Ecuador, they are also recognized at the constitutional level: as the "social and communitarian economy" (Art. 307, Bolivia), as part of the "popular and solidarity-based" economic system (Art. 283, Ecuador), recognizing forms of "self-management, co-management of cooperatives in all their forms . . . and other associative forms guided by the values of mutual cooperation and solidarity" (Art. 70, Venezuela).

In contrast to the interpretation of popular economies as victimizing, which sees them only as forms of exclusion, the informalization of the economy emerges primarily from the strength of the unemployed and of women, which can be read as a response from below to the dispossessive effects of neoliberalism. A passage can be summarized: from the providing father or breadwinner (the male figure of the waged worker, the head of the household, and its counterpart: the welfare state) to feminized figures (the unemployed, women, youth, and migrants) who go out to explore and occupy the street as a space of survival and, in that search, reveal the emergence of other vital logics. In turn, a new politicization is produced in that passage: actors who occupy the street both as an everyday public space and as a domestic space, breaking with the traditional topographical division in which the private lacks the street, lacks the public. These actors' presence in the street transforms the landscape.

There is a notable urban impact: cities are transformed by this new, predominantly feminine, informal wave, which with its bustle and transactions redefines the metropolitan space, the family, and women's place. It is inseparable from the migrant presence that also colors the dynamics of these economies. Its contribution is substantial since the initiatives of the informal economy constitute a fabric that makes popular life in cities possible and affordable (Galindo 2010). Neoliberalism exploits and takes advantage of the economy's new (micro)scale, but the popular classes, the city's poor, also challenge the city and often struggle to produce situations of urban justice, conquering the city and defining a new "right to the city."

That urban space becomes mottled because it hosts these very dynamic economies and also becomes more complex in terms of temporality. A worker's economic strategy can be informal at times (tied to the calendar of events, happenings, seasons, etc.) without giving up aspirations to formalization, which are also partial and temporary. In this respect, *discontinuity* is one of the hallmarks of the worker's economic strategy. Those strategies were (and are) part of a material fabric that, in the case of the migrant economy, made it possible for people arriving in a foreign country to obtain resources to settle, invest, and produce and that functioned as a material resource and social guarantee for a popular productive rationality. Years later, the state itself and a series of banking and nonbanking financial institutions would recognize and reinterpret this migrant economy. Similarly, we can point to the resolution (in the sense of management, not disappearance) from below of the employment crisis, due to the organizational capacity of movements of the unemployed, which seized resources from the state and promoted a series of productive activities with important social value in the moment of crisis. These would later be recognized by the state as well as the financial institutions descending into the neighborhoods. *There are two reasons for emphasizing their anteriority: to signal that these initiatives produced jurisprudence*, in the sense that they enabled the creation of rights and reopened the discussion about the scope of inclusion through citizenship, and *to show that during the crisis this social productivity was unrecognized, feared, and/or repressed* by state as well as banking institutions (although they awoke to an early desire for connection).

The idea of a strategic conatus can be projected over these economies, which are urban fabrics that are both stable and dynamic and that challenge the imaginary of classic developmentalism. Here I am inspired by Laurent Bové's understanding of the Spinozist conatus in terms of strategy: as a set of ways of doing that are composed to construct and defend the space-time of their affirmation. The body is a memory of those things that are useful for it, that nurture it and benefit it. That mnemonic trace, Bové says, provides the experience and memory of a determined, beneficial "amalgam": "The test of the real then correlates with the birth of a calculating reason that, following a more or less successful strategy, will continue the drive of the pleasure principle" (2009, 57). In this sense, calculating reason realizes the strategic dimension of conatus. One calculates to affirm.

The strategy of the conatus is, first, revealed as a political model defined by a practice: "the determination and the resolution of problems" (Bové 2009, 222). Bové's emphasis on strategy is doubly attractive from the point of view of my attempt to understand the vitalist pragmatic that characterizes popular economies. On one hand, Machiavelli, Lenin, and Foucault can be read from this Spinozist invective as espousing philosophies that put immanence and strategy in tension. Then, following this point, strategy becomes a sort of vital continuum that is required for constant updates. It is from there that the method of bodies—whether individual or collective—originates, as a modality that draws a "dynamic ontology of the problem" (322), which results in nothing more and nothing less than the real movement of the Real. With a Marxian echo that cannot cease to be felt in this formulation, the real movement of the Real is neither an individualist strategy of consciousness nor an omniscient state of rationality, but rather a confrontation with the multiplicity of forces determining problems and necessary solutions. Strategy, then, remains closely linked to the orientation of the dynamism of bodies, while they persevere in particular problems and ways of confronting them.

Second, strategy is implicated with resistance, and both are *sources of rationality*: "where there is resistance and strategy, there is then also necessarily rationality" (Bové 2009, 323). The "very movement of rationality making itself" ("the real process of the genesis of the Real and Reason" [323]), beyond guaranteeing its objectivity by means of an abstract consciousness, has a directly political dimension given by the strategy of active resistance and its potencia of problematization as a means of constituting the Real. The philosophical argument has a precise meaning here: highlighting the rationality of popular economies in terms of vital strategies, capable of disputing social wealth.

When Gilles Deleuze comments on the tenets of Foucault's microphysics of power (2001), he also lingers over his own use of the word *strategy*: "power is not a property but a strategy" (Deleuze 2014, 37). In *Discipline and Punish*, Foucault's definition of *strategy* is precise: "innumerable points of confrontation, focuses of instability" (1995, 27). That conceptualization also has another formulation: strategies are *singular* (Deleuze 2014, 38). This includes the definition of the relations of force as "relations between singularities." Strategies exist from the point of view of micropolitics rather than structures. These strategies are forms of alliance, practical combinations, to the extent that a society can be read by the constitution of the strategic alliances that make it function. Deleuze reiterates, "A society strategizes before it structures itself" (41). Strategy is a matter of hodgepodge, while structure refers to that which is stratified. Stratification and strategy have a specific and fundamental difference: their relationship to movement. In other words, "a social field is not defined by a structure; it is defined by its set of strategies" (42), hence the dynamic that Deleuze names as an *assemblage* (which I return to in the following chapters): "Social assemblages are hodgepodges. And they strategize everywhere. . . . Everyone strategizes" (44).

This idea of strategic conatus provides us with a counterpoint to a rationality conceived in terms that are as victimizing as they are individualistic.

Unlike the figure of homo œconomicus, neoliberalism from below is explained by the historical development of certain relations of force crystallizing in conditions that, in turn, are appropriated by the strategy of conatus overflowing the cold and restricted idea of liberal calculation, giving way to figures of individual and collective biopolitical subjectivity, in other words, to diverse tactics for living.

In her latest book, *Undoing the Demos* (2015), Wendy Brown contrasts the figures of *homo œconomicus* and *homo politicus* under the thesis that there is a fundamental antinomy between citizenship and neoliberalism. Reading Foucault's 1979 course, she aims to analyze how homo œconomicus functions in times of financial hegemony, identifying three differences with classic liberalism. First, the current "economization" of the subject radicalizes liberalism, according to Brown, turning us into *only* homo œconomicus: "Smith, Senior, Say, Ricardo, Steuart devoted a great deal of attention to the relationship of economic and political life without ever reducing the latter to the former, or imagining that economics could remake other fields of existence in and through its own terms and metrics" (24). Second, the form assumed is that of human capital, rather than those figures of exchange or of interest; therefore, homo œconomicus is far from that Smithian formula of "truck, barter, and exchange" and "from Benthamite pursuit of pleasure and avoidance of pain" (25). Third, the specific model of human capital refers more to financial capital than to productive capital (26).

Despite Brown's sharp analysis, it seems that, with the predominant image of neoliberalism as economization, the very expansion that allows for understanding neoliberalism as a governmental rationality is restricted to returning to the idea of neoliberal reason as a sort of hijacking of the political. On the one hand, it re-creates a distinction between politics and the economy that enables an "autonomy of the political," in that the political appears as a colonized field to defend, while the "reign of the rule" becomes the privileged space for the democratic deployment of homo politicus. I insist that, under this idea of politics (with its strong Arendtian imprint), those properly political moments in neoliberalism and, in particular, in the "operations of capital" that neoliberalism interprets remain unrecognized (Mezzadra and Neilson 2015). I am interested in thinking about a practice of politics capable of questioning neoliberalism without thinking of it as the other of politics; in that move, I aim to define it as a field of battle that is extremely dynamic precisely because it is already political. Even if Brown notes that "when everything is capital, labor disappears" (2015, 30), for her, the issue of labor does not manage to form a counterperspective for thinking beyond neoliberal common sense and disputing—and not only adapting to—the notion of human capital. In this respect, the opposition between financial and productive capital also removes the density of finance's properly productive dimension. Finally, when she says that neoliberalism directly "eliminates the very idea of a people, a demos asserting its collective political sovereignty" (31), what also remains unconsidered is what we could call the popular politics within, against, and beyond neoliberalism, at least as an ambivalent series of experiences, tactics, and languages, revealing the strictly Euro-Atlantic framework of Brown's conceptualization. Then, speaking of neoliberalism from below is a way of accounting for the dynamic that resists exploitation and dispossession and at the same time takes on and unfolds in this anthropological space of calculation, which is, in turn, the foundation for an intensification of that exploitation and dispossession. This hypothesis falls within a (thematic and conceptual) expansion of the very notion of neoliberalism and, therefore, within its implications for tracing the political map of these intensely expansive economies of motley Latin American cities (another way of reading Karl Marx's warning that the real is multiply determined: "The concrete is concrete because it is the concentration of many determinations, hence unity of the diverse" [1993, 101]).

Once we put it in these terms, it is difficult to believe that the end of neoliberalism depends on a few governments declaring that they have left those policies behind. It is difficult not simply because we have to distrust what they say but because neoliberalism is anchored in territories, strengthened in popular subjectivities, and, in organizational terms, expanding and proliferating within popular economies. It has to do with deepening the ways in which the government imperative is articulated with forms of invention, which are not reducible to, although not entirely incompatible with, the neoliberal diagram.

The dynamic axiomatic of capital, as Deleuze and Félix Guattari (1987) theorized, highlights precisely this tension between, on one hand, the flexibility and versatility of capture and exploitation by capital and, on the other hand, the necessity of distinguishing the operations through which that machine of capture subsumes social relations from the inventions that also resist and overflow the diagram of capture and exploitation.

Baroque Economies

To disassemble the definitions of neoliberalism that consider it only as a set of structural policies of the past, here I will make a precise use of Foucault's work insofar as it allows for an understanding of governmentality in terms of expanding freedoms and therefore for an analysis of the types of productive and multiscalar assemblages that contemporary neoliberalism implies as a mode of government and production of reality, and that also overflow that government. Neoliberalism is both a subjective and a structural mutation, organic and diffuse. However, a new fold is still pending: debating the modes of domination imposed by this new, "free" manner of government.

In Latin America, Foucault must be completed by rooting the critique of neoliberalism as a mode of power, domination, and dispossession in the experience of the revolts that have occurred in recent decades, while also debating the images and forms of political happiness implicated in diverse notions of freedom, which simultaneously compete and cooperate under neoliberalism.

Marx's presence must be emphasized when reading Foucault, for two reasons. First, one must start from the premise that subjectivities always have to do with practices, with structures that are articulated practices, and with discourses that are always a dimension of practice ("foci of experience"), and that, therefore, consciousness or rationalist spirituality does not play a privileged role in the constitution of subjectivity.

Second, the question of the production of value is central but not in an economicist sense or one that conceives of labor as a separate and restricted sphere of social life, even though capitalism's principal feature is its ability to reduce value to the economic. Using Marx, we understand value as the production of existence, which is made evident by the concept of labor power, in its failed and impossible commodification because it is impossible to suppress the gap between the potentiality of human praxis and effective work.

The expression "potentiality" here does not refer to a temporal feature of the productive process (which capital rationalizes as teleological); rather— above all—it characterizes the linguistic, affective, intellectual, physical, cooperative multiplicity, or: life, put to work by capital.

I must add one more point: the relationship between Foucault and Marx is illuminated by the rehabilitation of Friedrich Nietzsche's philosophy of values, which in Foucault, in contrast to Martin Heidegger, is not a realization of metaphysics but an opening to the contingency of material practices. The context of this problematic that originates with Marx is needed in the current debate around biopolitics inaugurated by Foucault.

It is necessary to find a political vocabulary that can be deployed in that problematic immanence without smoothing over the contradictions and ambivalences. This arises only from the practices that take place in variegated territory in cities. These practices open the possibility for understanding the transindividual dynamic of the productive forces that always overflow the neoliberal schema and anticipate possibilities that are no longer those of state socialism. In other words, this is a mode of social cooperation that reorganizes the horizon of labor and exploitation, of integration and progress, of the good life and good government.

Emphasizing the transindividual dimension is also a way of debating the hegemony of homo œconomicus, of its individualist frontiers that are no longer taken as a prescription for and invocation of an anthropology but are taken for granted in their application and delimitation of the borders of homo œconomicus. In this respect, the point of view of homo œconomicus is revealed primarily as abstract, because it hides the social dimension of value, its necessary dimension of collective cooperation, in order to be able to appear as a figure of individual utility.

If the constitution of the individual is the result of a process of individuation in which the composite character of the individual is actualized time and time again, every individual is always more than an individual. The notion of the transindividual is particularly relevant here. As Étienne Balibar (1997, 6–7) argues, discussing Spinoza, this notion has the power to take us away from the binary of holism versus individualism, because it also escapes the division between interiority and exteriority when referring to the human community. The idea of transindividualness is, then, neither metaphysical nor romantic. It is based on there being a "mutual interest" in commerce or exchange with others, which, even if it seems to reinforce the idea of a utilitarian individual, twists it in another direction: toward a noninstrumental rationality. Balibar states, "Spinozistic 'reason' is doubly utilitarian, but in a specific sense. It is utilitarian in as much as the very principle of virtue for each individual is to look for what is useful to himself and what he needs in order to preserve his *own* existence" (28). To return to an earlier point, the question of the strategic conatus could be raised as that of how to distinguish between a utilitarian reason associated with the alienated state of perception (the effect of commodity fetishism) and a figure of the subject as "autonomous-strategic," even as a figure of citizenship, capable of a *realism of potencia*. Is there a counterpoint between Marx and Spinoza, or could it be said that there is a way in which, as I suspect, they are entangled?

How do we think of a subject in a way that does not fall into the legal fetishism of individual or free will (that which carved out contractualism and which, reflecting on law, Evgeny Pashukanis (2001) radically critiqued as a fetishism analogous with that of the commodity) and that, nonetheless, would be a subject that does not give up on the issue of *freedom* as the "trend toward innovation," understood as the "tension toward autonomy" of the social body?

In this vitalist pragmatic, neoliberalism from below implies communitarian forms in a nonlinear fashion. This is where to root the question about what political forms would be adequate for postneoliberalism and the emergence of elements of poststate citizenship, to use Balibar's (2015) formulation. That neoliberalism, as governmentality, would be compatible with certain communitarian forms is not anecdotal data, nor evidence of a pure global tendency toward the ethnicization of the labor market, but the index of the emergence of this era that tends to reduce cooperation to new business forms, while it also proposes social assistance as the simultaneous counterpart of dispossession. Therefore, in Latin America the rebellions against neoliberalism in the region are the starting point for reassembling a critical perspective for conceptualizing neoliberalism beyond its permissive and diffuse logic—but also for going beyond an understanding of neoliberalism as the triumph of homo œconomicus by the suppression of the political.

I propose thinking of these assemblages—transindividual productivities expressed in a dynamic informality—as *baroque* economies to conceptualize a type of articulation of economies that mixes logics and rationalities that tend to be portrayed (in economic and political theories) as incompatible. Bolívar Echeverría (2000) has linked the baroque to an art of resistance and survival belonging to the colonial moment. Álvaro García Linera (2001) speaks of a "baroque modernity" to describe the productive model in Bolivia in that it unifies "in a tiered and hierarchical manner, the production-structures of the fifteenth, eighteenth and twentieth centuries" (2014, 212). It also brings back servile or semislave labor as an important, but not hegemonic, segment of transnational economies in capitalist globalization, which confirms that modality as a (post)modern component of the organization of labor and not as an archaic hindrance of a premodern or precapitalist past that has been overcome. In Latin America the baroque persists as a set of interlaced modes of doing, thinking, perceiving, fighting, and working; as that which supposes the superimposition of nonreconciled terms in permanent re-creation. But there is something of the present, of the historical moment of post-Fordist capitalism with its acceleration of displacements, that particularly recalls this dynamic of the multiple.

My specific use of the notion of the baroque refers to the strategic composition of microentrepreneurial elements, with formulas of popular progress, that compose a political subjectivity capable of negotiating and disputing state resources, and effectively overlapping bonds of family and loyalty linked to the popular neighborhoods, as well as nontraditional contractual formats. This relates to anthropologist Aihwa Ong's (2006) definition of contemporary spatiality as "baroque ecology": the city is located in the center of an ecosystem that is created via the mobilization of distinct global elements (knowledges, practices, actors) and their interactions.

I am interested in how Ong highlights the urban spatial dimension of the baroque that takes place today. However, from my analytic perspective, the baroque refers to two principles that are fundamental for understanding these economies:

1. The informal as the *instituting source* or the origin of reality creation. I define informality not negatively, by its relation to the normative definitions of the legal and the illegal, but positively, by its innovative character and, therefore, its dimension of praxis seeking new forms. The informal in this sense does not refer to that without a form but to the dynamic that invents and promotes (productive, commercial, relational, etc.) forms, focusing on the process of producing new social dynamics.

2. The informal as a *source of incommensurability*, the dynamic that puts the objective measurement of the value created by these economies into crisis. The informal thus refers to the overflow, by intensity and overlapping, of the heterogeneous elements that intervene in value creation, necessitating the invention of new formulas for measuring value and the production of mechanisms of institutional inscription and acknowledgment.

Against the Moralization of Popular Economies: A Vitalist Pragmatic

This book addresses three interconnected situations, and an important part of the investigation consists in trying to understand how the connections among those situations function (Haraway 1991). First, there is the massive market La Salada, described as the largest illegal market in Latin America, occupying over twenty hectares on the border between Buenos Aires and its urban periphery. It took off with the crisis in 2001 and has not stopped growing and developing since, drawing contingents of sellers and buyers from various countries across the continent. The market owes its initial impulse to a migrant (particularly Bolivian) circuit and the know-how associated with that circuit, which combined well with the moment of economic and political crisis in Argentina. In La Salada almost everything is sold at very accessible prices. It is a powerful place of popular consumption and commerce, with a transnational scope (people come from Paraguay, Bolivia, Uruguay, and even Chile, as well as from all the Argentine provinces). In turn, it is similar to other markets: 16 de Julio in El Alto, Bolivia; Tepito in Mexico City, México; Oshodi and Alaba in Lagos, Nigeria; and the Silk Market in Beijing (most of these are included on the U.S. Department of Commerce's list of "notorious markets").[3] Much of the clothing found there originates in the so-called clandestine textile workshops, where migrant workers produce clothing for major brands, as well as for selling in La Salada. The majority of these workshops are located in *villas*, or neighborhoods where migrants constitute a large part of the population. It is a genealogical sequence that also reveals a logic of mutual contamination, of permanent back-and-forth, of complementarity and contradiction. Trajectories are woven among the villa, the textile workshop, and La Salada, with the popular, religious, and communitarian festival serving as one of the elements connecting them. The villa, where the migrant population is constantly replaced, is a space in which a multiplicity of labor situations are produced, ranging from self-employment to small businesses, including domestic and community labor, and tied to convoluted dependencies. But it is also where the textile workshop is "submerged"; the workshop takes advantage of the villa as a space of community resources, protection, and favors, as well as the source of a workforce. In turn, La Salada is articulated with labor in the textile workshops but also with the opportunities it offers small-scale retailers and importers (for example, those who import lingerie from China via Bolivia to be sold in La Salada) and the sale of all types of services (including financial services). The popular market exhibits and publicizes the clandestine nature of the textile workshop in a complex way, as it combines a form of production that is not entirely legal and is sustained by conditions of extreme exploitation with the expansion of popular consumption and the promotion of a diverse employment reserve. It is an ambivalent reality, as is the way in which the villa exposes the unbridled logic of the informal real estate market combined with the possibility of expanding migrants' access to housing in the city center. The dynamic of the festival, which is both celebratory and ritual, mobilizes a good part of the resources and energies, the justifications and aspirations, that articulate the workshop, the market, and the villa with one another.

My goal is to explore the popular economy that has developed in Argentina, which also forms part of the regional situation, as it has been shown to have transnational connections with other cities and countries; it is strongly marked by the migrant presence in the modes of production, circulation, and organization of its collective dynamics. In this respect, La Salada allows for a broader analytic, to the point that it can function as a *mirror* of other urban forms and even of a specific form of "logistical urbanism" (Massidda et al. 2010), highlighting a mode of production of heterogeneity in the metropolises of the Global South. It also accounts for a broader transformation in the world of work, which calls for a fundamental rereading of categories such as development and progress, poverty and precarity, inclusion and consumption. If anything colors and characterizes this map of a nontraditional—and nonindustrial—economy, it is that it is both informal and subterranean, while also linked to transnational value chains and major local brands, combining conditions of extreme precarity with high levels of expansion. Thus, it allows for questioning the productive dynamics of consumption associated with new uses of time and money. At the same time, it also sheds light on what I want to discuss: *the current ways in which development and neoliberalism are combined.*

There is a fundamental ambivalence that must be emphasized: a productive network that articulates communitarian moments and moments of brutal exploitation, with migrants, workers, microentrepreneurs, and community organizers as the protagonists. This oscillation does not arrive at a synthesis. It is precisely that point of ambivalence that manifests the rhythm of political tension, that requires categories capable of grasping and expressing that same tension. In addition, it reflects the temporal dynamism that these practices and the subjects implicated in them imprint on a spatial construction that is changing greatly.

The category of ambivalence beats in a rhythm between innovation and negation, as Paolo Virno (2008) has written. However, in that contingent and conflictive space, he highlights a vital pragmatic that has the potencia to institute a new space-time and challenge urban dynamics, as well as the uses of money, transnational links, labor conflicts, and resistance to forms of confinement and the impoverishment of popular life. To return to Virno, this vitalist pragmatic relates to the idea of the "opportunism of the masses," in other words, the permanent calculation of opportunities as a collective mode of being.

With this perspective, a clear strategy can be traced that opposes seeing the popular sectors as victims. Such victimization, which also appears as moralization and criminalization, organizes a certain field of visibility for the issue of migrant labor and, further, suggests a type of link between the norm and the popular economy, resulting in the moralization (and condemnation) of the so-called world of the poor. In opposition to this focus on victimization, I propose an "extramoral" perspective of vital strategies, in which it is crucial to understand how these economies and the subjects that produce and transit them are articulated and are thought, how they assemble energies and networks, cooperate, and compete.

To say *extramoral* supposes abandoning the metaphysical register (in the sense of a Western metaphysics that repeatedly cleaves being into an active spiritual moment and a passive material instance to be known and governed) of morals (whether of work, good manners, or, in the ethnic version, the noble savage) to concentrate on the vital edge of what organizes strategies for existing, creating, producing value, ritualizing time and space, and making life into a force of perseverance that assembles dissimilar spiritual and material resources and decisively questions three fundamental notions for rethinking our era: *progress, calculation,* and *freedom.*

Self-management, autonomy, and transversality—what Deleuze (2014) calls the leftist problematic—can be understood, in a first phase, in relation to their *opposites*: progress, obedience, and the ghetto. Even so, the resistant forms, the tactics *within and beyond* these very questions, force us to complicate that inverse relation and to further complicate its temporal relationship, its internal dynamism. And to add a twist to our thinking: How does popular self-management reorient the idea of progress? How is autonomy able to negotiate partial forms of obedience and strategies of contempt? How does transversality need to confront the protective (and not only discriminatory) idea of the ghetto?

Populism as Statism

The end or overcoming of the neoliberal "nightmare" could be critically analyzed, on the one hand, from the angle provided by the framework of neoliberalism as governmentality and, on the other hand, via a refusal to limit the discussion to the assertion of the dichotomy between the state and the market, which would confine the intense debate around the possible significance of postneoliberalism in Latin America to a new autonomy of the political.

This perspective challenges the idea that neoliberalism's opposite is the *return of the state*, understood in terms of a (contractual or pure) autonomy of the state, as proposed by the theory of populism (cf. Laclau 2005a). Thinking of neoliberalism as more than a homogeneous and compact doctrine emphasizes the multiplicity of levels on which it operates, the variety of mechanisms and knowledges it involves, and the way it unevenly combines and articulates with other knowledges and ways of doing. Such plurality does not weaken it as a technology of governance. However, the pluralization of neoliberalism by practices from below allows us to see how neoliberalism is articulated with communitarian forms, with popular tactics for making a living, enterprises that drive informal networks, and modes of negotiating rights that rely on the workers' economic strategies to negotiate the expansion of those rights. The forms of resistance to governmentality that appear in this pluralization demonstrate—depending on whether it is a moment of stability or of crisis—governmentality's versatile or precarious face. Above all, these practices reveal the heterogeneous, contingent, and ambiguous nature of the dispute between obedience and autonomy in the interpretation and appropriation of neoliberal conditions.

The vitalism of these microeconomies, which draw a map of the region that is simultaneously the outline and the reverse of neoliberalism, has to do with their capacity to construct, conquest, liberate, and also defend space. I call these economies *microproletarian economies* to reveal a new landscape of the proletarian beyond its Fordist meaning and to highlight the different scales that make these economies function primarily as assemblages. Also, as I will develop further in the following chapter, I use this term to debate the concept of the deproletarianization of the popular world. This production of space (which involves a process of deindustrialization and the configuration of those proletarian microeconomies) implies and involves a specific temporality. The launching of baroque economies supposes a strategic deployment: a set of modes of doing composed pragmatically in order to maintain themselves and persevere.

I define it as a pragmatic to emphasize its experiential, and not purely discursive, character. It is primarily about thinking of certain foci of experience in a nonmoralizing way and going beyond the application of rationales that are outside of their own tactics. In this sense, *extramoral* refers to the Nietzschean method of understanding morals as a machine of capture with the goal of normalizing and governing expansive subjectivities.

In these baroque economies, while there are forms of exploitation and subordination linked to migrant labor, which capital situates as its "low" part and exhibits as exemplary situations of obedience, there is also an aspect of resistant and democratic invention involved in this migrant hustle and its incorporation into a city like Buenos Aires or São Paulo. This opens up the traditional imaginary of integration and puts the very notion of difference in tension, both as a capacity for autonomy (as ontological production) and as an (ethnicized) differential of exploitation (as the production of surplus value).

Foucault noted a necessary displacement from the theory of the subject to the forms of subjectivation constituting a pragmatic of the self. This displacement seeks to leave behind a purely abstract idea of the subject to focus on the processes of material and spiritual constitution of those subjectivities. The entrepreneurship of the self is one of those pragmatics. Foucault also fits migrants into this definition. What is interesting is that there are two sides to this conceptualization: on one hand, the possibility of escaping from the purely victimizing image of those who undertake a migrant trajectory and, on the other, (overflowing the strictly entrepreneurial definition) the possibility of the formation of human capital, without abandoning the idea of progress. Is it possible to think about the anxiety of progress outside of the neoliberal regime, defined as an array of individual rationalities ordered by profit? Is it possible to vindicate calculation beyond profit? Is it possible for the "opportunism of the masses," spoken of by Virno (2004, 86), to be a social dynamism, even if this is not often attributed to popular sectors? Finally, to add one more twist, is it possible to think of progress associated with another idea of modernity? It is easy to see that here I am addressing from a specific point of view a set of questions that have been at stake in critical debates for quite a long time now.

The hypothesis that I am going to develop in the following chapters is that the difference in subjectivation that these baroque economies stimulate lies in a will to progress that mixes the Foucauldian definition of the migrant as an investor in himself or herself with a way of doing that brings a communitarian capital into play. It is a vital impulse that deploys a calculation in which a neoliberal rationality is superimposed onto a repertoire of communitarian practices, producing what I call neoliberalism from below. However, in that jointly created lag between the communitarian element and the neoliberal-individualistic rationality, we see the beginning of a new interpretation of the vitalist pragmatic.

Let's return to time. This baroque mixture shapes motley zones that exhibit a temporal folding. This implies that labor categories become fluid and intermittent and allow themselves to be read as complex trajectories plotted with an extremely flexible urban calculation, from working as an apprentice, to engaging in microentrepreneurship, to combining the informal economy with the possibility of becoming formal, to being unemployed for a while. At the same time, the workers obtain resources through communitarian and social tasks and tactically transit, take advantage of, and enjoy family, neighbor, commercial, communal, and political relationships. In short, the motley quality that characterizes this economy—a key concept for the Bolivian sociologist René Zavaleta Mercado (2009) that has been reworked by another Bolivian sociologist, Silvia Rivera Cusicanqui (2010a)—reveals the plurality of labor forms and highlights the very borders of what is called labor.

In this regard, neoliberal reason, as I propose to use it, is a formula for showing neoliberalism as a rationality—in the meaning that Foucault gives the term: as the constitution of governmentality—but also contrasting it with how this rationality is appropriated, ruined, relaunched, and altered by those who are supposedly only its victims. But that reappropriation does not occur only from the point of view of direct antagonism, as a more or less traditional geometry of conflict would suppose, but rather starts from the multiple ways in which neoliberalism is utilized and suffered, based on recombination and contamination with other dynamics that pluralize the very notions of rationality and conflict.

The same idea of reason is a central figure in Pierre Dardot and Christian Laval's book *The New Way of the World* (2013), which argues against the idea that the global crisis of 2007–8 that marked Europe and North America was a crisis of neoliberalism. Their argument is that the nature of neoliberalism itself has been misdiagnosed; therefore, even the crisis functions as a scenario in which neoliberal premises, condensed as austerity measures, are strengthened. Here the contrast with Latin America is interesting, since in this region—as I have been showing—what emerges from the economic and political crisis is the crisis of the legitimacy of neoliberalism, which delegitimizes any discursive appeal to structural adjustment. Another important point in Dardot and Laval's work is the emphasis on neoliberal *rationality* as a historical construct and general norm of life (4). Like Brown, they point to competition, instead of exchange, as the general principle of the era. In this point, neoliberal citizenry is deployed as a permanent mobilization driven by that competition.

Following this line, Dardot and Laval's political conclusions underscore neoliberalism's cunning as "productive" of forms of existence, generalizing the model of the market and the enterprise precisely as a global *rationality*. The subjectivity that is perfected is one that is "accountable and financial" (15). However, I want to debate the idea that this reason becomes totalizing, abstract, and, thus, *homogeneous* in its effects. The difference in the use of the term *neoliberal reason* that I propose here has two lines: to include the resistance that heterogenizes the idea of reason itself and to include the way in which this heterogeneity challenges neoliberalism as governmentality.

The heterogeneously composed baroque logics that I highlight are dynamics that express a social-political-economic present, that recuperate long-term memories, while they are shown to be unabashedly flexible in making the city, businesses, and politics and thus display a dispute over the very idea of progress in its purely accumulative and linear sense. These baroque logics are the material, psychic, and expansive fabric that I analyze in certain popular economies, which make a recategorization of the productive forces in Latin American metropolises necessary. While they bring neoliberal reason to unintended areas, they also immerse it in logics that are shown to be unbeatable, and in these displacements paths of questioning and disobedience are opened up.

Neodevelopmentalism

Arturo Escobar (1995) has characterized development in Latin America as an "invention" in which a body of economic theories and their technical and political promoters constructed the entity of the "underdeveloped economy," which was translated into a series of policies aimed at reaching the objective of "growth," guided by institutions such as the World Bank, delineating in a paternalistic and colonial way a certain problematization of hunger, agricultural economies, women as subjects to be incorporated, and so on. But there is also an element of the developmentalist impulse that has an anti-imperialist tone, inspired by Latin American structuralism, mainly theorized by Raúl Prebisch and his team at CEPAL (Comisión Económica para América Latina y el Caribe-Naciones Unidas; 1970). These positions, emphasizing the categories of center and periphery as forms of structural hierarchies that are fully functional for the capitalist system and its international division of roles, also functioned as resources for perspectives of regional autonomy. Their fundamental policies were based on the formula of import-substitution industrialization, with a prominent role for what was then referred to as the national bourgeoisie (called to go beyond their dependent role as the "lumpen-bourgeoisie," as Gunder Frank [1972] named them), related to a protectionism capable of providing those countries with comparative advantages and negotiating social benefits for the consolidation of an integrated working class. The "Keynesian left," to use an expression of the time, considered that economic development could be driven by state intervention. Contemporary neodevelopmentalism does not strictly rely on any of those characteristics but attempts to relaunch the old premises in a context where the demands of the global market are completely different, where the role of productive transnationalization is a central fact. Neodevelopmentalism achieves a type of consensus that allows it to combine policies of social inclusion with an increase in imports and monetary stability. But the case of Brazil, in some ways the most successful country in the region, also encountered problems when the external demand for raw materials slowed down and the crisis of 2013 broke out, revealing that "the government's most important investments do not concern urban infrastructure intended for mass consumption but the infrastructure of ports and highways designed to foment an export economy that also implied a significant process of privatization of the country's major ports" (Domingos Ouriques 2013, 134).

How is this discussion about neoliberalism tied to the characterization of the current moment as a "return of the state" and its neodevelopmentalist possibilities? The neodevelopmentalism promoted in the region during the last decade is tied to a specific conjuncture: it results from the conditions imposed by the exit from neoliberalism's crisis of legitimacy. That crisis, whose impetus was the rejection of the policies of privatization and austerity synthesized in the Washington Consensus, generated a field of possibilities for reinstalling an idea of development whose axis would be a certain type of social inclusion. This conjuncture's regional character is decisive. It also adds a third element: the mode of insertion into the global market that situates Latin America as a provider of raw materials especially needed by China.

This neodevelopmentalist articulation has required (just as happened in the 1990s with the neoliberal strategy) a new type of activity by the state intended to create—not without conflict—apparatuses designed to capture a portion of the rent (mainly from agriculture, mining, and petroleum) and to promote, based on these flows of money, a politics of social inclusion through consumption (made operational by the promotion of social welfare packages, aid to cooperatives and popular ventures, credits, and subsidies), the nationalization of pension funds and expansion of retirement benefits, *paritarias* (direct wage negotiations between unions and companies), the renationalization of some companies that had previously belonged to the state, and an increasing concentration of agribusiness.[4]

There is a triple political effect: first, the revitalization of state intervention, seemingly with Keynesian features; thus, second, the projection of a common regional autonomy; and, finally, the displacement of North America by China as the hegemonic power. In contrast to the developmentalism of the 1960s (Gudynas 2015), the current neodevelopmentalism is not materially driven by industrialization. My hypothesis is that even if neodevelopmentalism evokes an industrialist imaginary, today its capacity for deployment is directly tied to the hegemony of rent. This assumes, and is based on, a decisive mutation in social inclusion: it is no longer achieved by expanding wage labor but rather by extending the capacity to consume to sectors that do not necessarily have what was traditionally known as inscription into the wage system (I develop this point further in chapter 5).

Neodevelopmentalism, as it occurs at the regional level in this cycle, becomes inseparable from a generalization of the production of rent and the financial mediation of the social. Meanwhile, at the level of rhetoric and the political imaginary, it is presented in opposition to the predominance of the financial. Such a gap generates a special role for the state insofar as it manages to combine and synthesize both lines. I want to underscore that, rather than thinking in terms of a falsehood of neodevelopmentalism, we must adapt the idea of development itself in order to understand the current modes of its realization.

In this perspective, tracing a consistent border between neoliberalism and neodevelopmentalism is not easy. Quite the opposite is true: the neodevelopmentalist strategy expresses a particular conjuncture with and considerable political effort within the structure of neoliberal reason.

This involves debating the argument put forward by the defenders of progressive governments that opposes a neodevelopmentalism founded on neoextractivist rent to the financial hegemony of the 1990s (García Linera 2012). My argument would be the opposite: the neoextractivist form of contemporary economies in the region has an organic relationship to finance. This hypothesis makes it possible to expand the concept of extractivism to go beyond its sectorization in raw materials (Gago and Mezzadra 2015).

Through this expansion, a space is also opened up for critiquing the notion of development.

It must also be noted that in this phase development has a way of being compatible with the discourse of *buen vivir*, while also boosting the extractive companies. Progressive governments have attempted to resolve this tension through conjunction, under formulas such as the National Plan of Development for Buen Vivir (2013–17) in Ecuador or the National Plan of Development: A Dignified, Sovereign, Productive, and Democratic Bolivia in Order to Live Well (2006–11). The role of the planner state reappears, after decades when the state was spoken of only in terms of its reduction or its modernization (in the form of its withdrawal), and it reappears in a way that aims to amalgamate a renewed version of development under formulas referencing the agenda imposed by social movements, synthesized in antiausterity policies and social inclusion programs.

Thus, one dimension of neodevelopmentalist strategy is the pacification of certain territories that become strategics. In the case of Ecuador, for example, the governmental discourse that promises a postextractivist objective depends on the intensification of extractivist industries as a way of financing that reality in the future. The researchers Cristina Cielo, Lisset Coba, and Ivette Vallejo argue, "Ironically, however, public funding for the massive investments necessary to move towards such a transformation depends on international financing and investments in natural resource exploitation. State policies since 2008 have extended petroleum and mining concessions, and as the intensity and extent of extractive enterprises has increased, so have social conflicts around these industries" (2016, 119). This type of state investment in infrastructure results in the reconversion of certain territories into spaces apt for exploitation. This dynamic does not simply pacify but also arms a new social conflictiveness, a new intensity of violence. And it does so not only in campesino territories, or in areas rich in natural resources, but also in the urban peripheries.

In many countries—as can be seen in Argentina, Bolivia, and Ecuador—the government's rhetoric uses the extractivist profile as a source for generating a diversified economy capable of producing value-added and scientific-technological development (in proposals ranging from ecotourism to the knowledge society).

Neoliberalism: From the Extensive to the Intensive

Let's interpret an image that has become hegemonic today: the consolidation of neoliberalism in the region during the 1990s appears to take the form of an external power capturing and instrumentalizing the state. In this view, foreign capital plays a revitalizing role in neoliberalism's capacity to expand by appropriating sectors of the national economy through privatization (of services, pensions, etc.). In the Argentine case, this process can be divided into two periods: that of peso-dollar convertibility (1991–2001) and that of postconvertibility (2002–12). As Alejandro Gaggero, Martín Schorr, and Andrés Wainer (2014, 18) note, this division shows that centralization and denationalization are first *extensive* (the acquisition of national public and private firms by foreign hands) and later *intensive* (structural differences and relationships with other fractions of local economic power). Paraphrasing David Harvey's (2003) formulation about "accumulation by dispossession," they propose, "It could be said that, until the resolution of the crisis of post-convertibility (2002), an 'extensive' *foreignization* by 'dispossession' predominated, while after that foreign capital largely expanded in an 'in-depth' or 'intensive' way" (2014, 81).

The developmentalist moment, if we no longer oppose it to financial hegemony and its colonization of the state in the last decade of the twentieth century, could then be seen as a moment of internalization of neoliberal power, which is boosted through rentier resources, intertwining elements that seemed contradictory (and that continue to be so according to certain rhetorics): rent and development, renationalization of companies and increased financialization, social inclusion and mandatory banking (the Bank of the Argentine Nation's most recent slogan is "Banking is social inclusion").

One of the keys to neodevelopmentalist effectiveness, however, lies in maintaining neoliberalism as an external enemy power, which is part of the discursive effectiveness of populist reason. The difference between the neoliberalism of convertibility and that of postconvertibility, to use the previously mentioned sequence, seems to lie not so much in a question of degrees of purity or harshness as in a "topological difference" (Fujita 2015). In important scenes from recent years, such as the renegotiation of the public debt and the confrontation with the so-called vulture funds, the transnational dynamic of properly neoliberal finance is again confined to the confrontation between the nation-state and capital, giving a new twist to the impossibility of analyzing the state's material and concrete modes, even though an effective alliance is reached between the state and capital, unlike in past decades. It also shows how transnational corporations expanded in concentrated sectors (such as energy and services), taking advantage of the recovery of the domestic market and export sectors "that have been deeply favored by the early and sharp decline in internal costs in dollars and the increase in international prices of raw materials and other commodities, all of which have resulted in higher margins of profitability" (Gaggero, Schorr, and Wainer 2014, 152).

The key point is to analyze how the current variation in the relationship between the state and capital originates from a certain popular politicization and, in turn, how it attempts to confine current forms of politicization to the neodevelopmentalist one. The hypothesis that I propose here is the following: *what is unique about the progressive governments in South America's form of management is their attempt to articulate rentier-financial mediation with the conditions opened up by the plebeian revolt* (a notion I return to in the following chapters), or, in other words, their attempt to weave together that vitality of revolt with the categories of political economy. In the case of these governments, therefore, financial mediation is inseparable from a politicization of that mediation.

Neoliberalism as Development

Raewyn Connell and Nour Dados (2014) propose a distinction between theories of neoliberalism and the practices that carry it forward: the former are homogeneous, while the latter refer to an always imperfect realization. It is, the investigators say, a difference of geopolitical perspective (120): in the North it is theorized; in the South it is experienced. But what particularly interests me in their argument is another idea: "neoliberalism as a development strategy" (122). They underscore neoliberalism as an institutional framework of state policies that came together in Latin America with the dictatorships and that reoriented the region from diverse attempts at import-substitution industrialization toward a pattern of extractive and financial economies: "What neoliberal policymakers had to attack worldwide, often using Cold-War tools, was *other development strategies*" (123). Even if they characterize the welfare states of diverse parts of the Global South (e.g., Argentina during Peronism, South Africa during apartheid) as "limited in scale," they want to challenge the idea that neoliberalism only dismantles development policies without proposing any alternative. As the authors indicate when discussing the neoextractivist articulation with contemporary neoliberalism, it is clear that "growth takes the form of rents extracted by predatory elites, who . . . are not a productive bourgeoisie" (125).

For my argument, it is important to take this point even further because the continent's dictatorships are where we see a *constitutionalizing* effect of neoliberalism. First, these dictators promoted legislation that has persisted even into the present moment, well into the rule of progressive governments (Nápoli, Perosino, and Bosisio 2014). Yet accounting for their true reach requires undoing the democracy-dictatorship pair at the level of the state to recognize neoliberalism as a specific mode of the dictatorship of finance over societies. Even more, and here is the second aspect: underneath the formal or legislative character of neoliberal power, the material or substantial character of that constitutionalization of society, with regard to subjects and subjectivities, appears. Through military terror—and, with it, financial power—the decades of the 1970s and 1980s established a neoliberal reason at the level of habits and affects. Once all the differences in terms of violence and terror are considered, it becomes possible to draw a parallel with the conversion of North American workers into shareholders to then theorize how profit has become rent, as described by Christian Marazzi (2011).

The 1990s, which portrayed the best-known features of neoliberalism, extended those policies through the interventions I mentioned earlier, including structural adjustment, privatization, and massive unemployment. Neoliberalism's crisis of legitimacy, with the emergence of social subjects who are the protagonists of a new antagonism, opens up a new governmentality. The following scenario is inaugurated: the political revolves around a national and popular will that aims to reverse the already delegitimized neoliberal policies, and neoliberal reason is reproduced and relaunched, taking the tenets of populist political theory as its premise, for the simple reason that this theory spreads its cultural hegemony over a neoliberal constitutional background— the government of finance—that it has not managed to change (Instituto de Investigación y Experimentación Política 2015). This phase in the region is much more open and contentious, and it tends to penetrate institutions, producing oscillations between very dynamic moments and times of stagnation that make neoliberal reason a true terrain of struggle.

CHAPTER I

Between the Proletarian Microeconomy and the Transnational Network

La Salada

La Salada in the Triple Frontier

The market La Salada is a space of intersection and movement, at the border between the city of Buenos Aires and the districts of Lomas de Zamora and La Matanza in the urban periphery. In its twenty hectares, numerous bustling transactions accumulate: food, clothing, technology, leather goods, shoes, music, and movies are bought and sold. In the early days, it took place only at night, always on the threshold between Wednesday and Thursday, and between Sunday and Monday. An area that was once a popular riverside resort during the 1950s is being renewed today as a transnational and multitudinous shopping zone. Each day more and more buses, vans, and cars from all over Argentina, as well as Uruguay, Bolivia, Paraguay, and Chile, arrive at the market.

La Salada has been characterized as the largest illegal market in Latin America.[1] It is divided into three sectors of warehouses: Urkupiña—in honor of the Virgin of Cochabamba: the Virgin of Urkupiña; Punta Mogote—referencing the traditional Mar de Plata beach; and Ocean, also referring to the seaside, reinforced by the feeling of oceanic immensity that is awakened upon seeing the market in all of its unfolding. Additionally, La Salada had an entire sector of open-air sales, called La Ribera, which was much more precarious. This sector has currently been suspended, although sections of it are sporadically assembled. It is the space subjected to the most pressure, because it has been the market's most informal and most conflictive boundary ever since the gendarmerie was moved in and held ready on the edge of the Riachuelo, as a border force for establishing order.

La Salada is a migrant territory because of its composition: it was founded by a handful of Bolivian women and men at the beginning of the 1990s.² Currently, the majority of vendors come from different parts of Bolivia, but there are also Argentines, Paraguayans, Peruvians, and, recently, Senegalese, who are responsible for selling *bijoux* (cheap jewelry). La Salada is also a migrant territory because of the circuit that its merchandise follows: buyers arriving from neighboring countries open routes of distribution and commercialization toward their countries, while many of the goods arrive from various parts of the planet. La Salada, in its apparently marginal character, is a node in an expanding transnational network and a privileged site for demonstrating the multiplicity of economies and heterogeneous processes of work through which the global economic system is materialized. This singular locality constitutes an assemblage, combining an anomalous and differential component (one that is capable of sustaining the hypothesis of popular globalization "from below") and dynamics of subordination and exploitation, indicating a modality that is characteristic of the postmodern phase of capitalist rule.

La Salada proposes—it exposes and invites—an epistemology that measures up to it (to its height and its overflowing width), a *border* epistemology, to use Gloria Anzaldúa's (2012) expression. This is a mode of knowledge that emerges from the displacements of territories, occupations, and languages. This requires paying attention to those trajectories and trusting that there is an expressive force, a vital promise, a knowledge of movement, a perspective capable of being elastic and generous with the tumultuous rhythm of what is taking place. How is La Salada a border zone? Why locate La Salada in the Triple Frontier?

1. *The border as the social space of the heterogeneous.* That the majority of its founders and current stallholders are migrants imprints a transnational character on La Salada that then disperses itself throughout Buenos Aires. However, it is not only a question of origin. It is also about projection: the merchandise of this megamarket crosses internal and external borders and remaps the circuits of commercial, political, and familial comings and goings. In turn, the replicas that La Salada sparks in different places (called *saladitas*, or little Saladas) expand its influence and, in their itinerant multiplication, demonstrate a capacity to rapidly conquer new spaces. Thus, La Salada is anxious to expand to other places or to directly invent them. It is a successful formula for a type of popular business at different scales. But, above all, it is a dynamic that is informed by procedures and knowledges articulated in an assemblage of highly variegated and dissimilar components (a contingent web

of routes, uses, and affects) that favor a series of what I will call *proletarian microeconomies*.

2. *The territorial border.* The spatial border is not only a metaphor but also a concrete location. La Salada is a *borderland*, in the sense of the intersection of jurisdictions situated next to the Riachuelo (Little River), as well as the border between the urban periphery and the capital city. It is also the limit and overlap between land and water: riverbank and cornice. Taking La Salada to other locations, placing it in other neighborhoods, cities, and countries, is also a way of relocating that bordering practice to other sites and producing a new cartography of transactions, travels, expectations, and ventures. In recognition of its border character (as in other urban territories), the national gendarmerie has been chosen as the security force that monitors it.

3. *The analytic bordering zone.* The market, as a mass phenomenon, concentrates a radical mutation of concepts and binaries, between center and periphery, marginal zone and scarcity, suburb and merchandise, small-scale economy and informal economy. In addition to the "inversion" of prices that takes place from the viewpoint of the real estate market—the extremely high cost per square meter in La Salada is on par with that in the wealthiest and most exclusive zones of Buenos Aires—we should also note the insinuation of growth and, thus, the perspectives on productivity distilled in market spaces (in the material plane as well as in the virtual plane through Internet sales). The velocity of the trajectories involved, the routes of vendors and visitors, situate the market at a spatiotemporal cross point: a laboratory of expanding popular economies that challenge (or explode) certain categories of analysis and force concepts to cross their own disciplinary borders.

Living Currency

Popular markets reached their peak during the crisis of 2001 with the massive experience of barter.[3] The multiplication of currency notes and the possibility of exchange under rules different from those of the formal-legal market are a decisive precedent for understanding the success of the megamarket La Salada. One moment, that of the crisis, when much of the country maintained itself through quasi-fake currencies, expanded modes of production and consumption that combine self-management with smuggling, piracy, and invention. In times of turmoil, currency becomes, to use Pierre Klossowski's (2012) beautiful expression, a living currency, because the norms of economic functioning reveal themselves, more than ever, as a "substructure of social affects" (17). In turn, La Salada's recent impact cannot be understood outside of the inflationary rhythm, another way in which a certain excess of currency (and its virtual falsification or devaluation) is again shown as "one mode of the expression and representation of instinctive forces" (17). La Salada opens the possibility for small-scale popular consumption and enables access to cheap goods and services at a time when consumption is becoming the quickest and most dynamic form of social inclusion, and it does so as an expressive space of a mode of baroque transactions.

La Salada was strengthened during the crisis of 2001, although, strictly speaking, it does not owe its origin to that decisive conjuncture. Nor was it weakened following the crisis; the recent economic recovery has not caused it to stagnate or decrease in size. On the contrary, the conglomeration of La Salada and the complex economic web connected to the megamarket have become key pieces of new political-economic articulations. If the market and its first breakthrough, linked to the simultaneous scarcity and multiplicity of currencies, are intimately connected to the conjuncture of crisis, it should be emphasized that market know-how becomes a way of permanently managing a greater crisis: that of the world of formal wage labor.

The crisis is revealed as the privileged locus of analysis, because it demonstrates the social dispute over obedience, through rules that enable and hinder accumulation, but also because it is a moment of collective experimentation with other forms of living, cooperating, exchanging, and protecting one another. La Salada thus becomes a sort of laboratory for new forms of producing, consuming, and constructing networks of distribution and commercialization, structuring itself as a quarry of new types of employment.

Textiles are the market's key sector, and their trajectory during the last two decades represents a prototype. If in the 1990s the textile industry was dismantled as the result of the massive influx of imports favored by peso-dollar convertibility, the industry was revitalized after the crisis, the end of exchange-rate parity, and the devaluation of the Argentine peso, although with a new base: the outsourcing of production to small workshops whose labor force is made up of sewing workers from Bolivia.

Proletarian Microeconomies

In La Salada the formal desalarization seen during the employment crisis is stabilized. It is clear that moments of economic fragility intensify hierarchical relations (Moulier Boutang 2006), but in La Salada we see a framework that exhibits these same problems in a space of strong prosperity and the creation of new modes of employment.

The contemporary situation is characterized by the emergence of new forms of dependent activities combining freedom from the regulations of Fordist dependency with new forms of servitude to market fluctuations in unprecedented forms (Virno 2004). In this way, the multiplication of labor realities is replicated as the multiplication of the levels, scales, and dimensions that make global space heterogeneous, crisscrossed by different migratory movements that transform the international division of labor (Mezzadra and Neilson 2013a). Thus, the current capitalist drive becomes competitive and dynamic by flexibly articulating itself with the practices, networks, and attributes that have historically characterized the flows of unpaid labor. This allows us to understand the labor market as a "pluri-articulated" assemblage where mixed and hybrid forms coexist (always as a counterpoint to a homogeneous ideal of wage labor).

This argument, capable of gauging the heterogeneity of the contemporary world of work, is especially useful for arguing against the unidimensionality of informality. Informality, if understood only in terms of deproletarianization, risks being reduced to the privileged source and space of violence and crime. By emphasizing La Salada as a territory marked by extreme and exceptional violence, while also marginalizing it, this discourse appraises in a strictly negative way that which in fact functions as a possibility for life (and not only survival and violence) for a massive portion of the population, as a space for highly innovative modes of coping with scarcity, violence, institutions, and consumption.[4]

All the vitality involved in the creation of a space of popular commerce and consumption, with its tactics and hierarchies, transactions and appropriations, comes undone if there are only victims (of neoliberalism, of unemployment, of mafias, etc.). This does not deny the violence of social relations, nor romanticize their transactions, but neither does it unilateralize them.

I call these economies *proletarian microeconomies* in order to show a new landscape of the proletarian beyond its Fordist definition and to highlight the question of the scales that make these economies function primarily as assemblages. Also, as noted above, I argue against the notion of the deproletarianization of the popular world.

In this respect, La Salada manages to combine a series of proletarian microeconomies composed of small and medium-sized transactions, while also serving as the base of a large transnational network of (mostly textile) production and trade. This occurs because of the development of small-scale commercial retail, enabling diverse survival strategies for resellers and opportunities for big business for small importers, manufacturers, and market sellers, as well as creating a space for mass consumption. Enormous numbers are managed in La Salada: with only two days of activity per week, in 2009 more money passed through it than in all the country's shopping malls combined (nearly 15 billion Argentine pesos as opposed to 8.5 billion in the shopping malls, according to the official data of the National Institute of Statistics and Census).[5]

La Salada and the textile workshops form a circuit in which labor categories are changing and intermittent: flexible transitions between dependent work and self-employment initiatives, ranging from engaging in moments of informality and never-abandoned aspirations of "going formal," to receiving state subsidies, to relying on communitarian networks, tactically transiting, using, and enjoying family, neighborhood, commercial, communal, and political relationships. In short, the border zones populated by this economy reveal the plurality of labor forms and call into question the very limits of what is called work.

La Salada is a territory of new regimes of submission and new places of social innovation. The question is how to also grasp the moments of seeking autonomy and freedom that function as "the permanent backdrop to processes of servitude and (internal and external) colonial hegemony" (18)? With his insistence on reading against the grain, Antonio Negri (2006) states that it is possible to understand migrant cultures and behaviors as constituent countercultures. This implies searching for a definition of labor in which the history of *slave-migrants* demonstrates a fundamental reality: they are entirely integrated within, but also remain outside of, capital. The potential for an independent political-social reality is at stake.

The Archaic as a Source of Innovation

La Salada exhibits a new composition of labor power—informal, illegal, precarious, innovative, and entrepreneurial—that has become notorious in postcrisis Argentina as the key element of an economic restructuring based on new forms of labor. It also demonstrates the decline of alternative practices challenging wage labor that had emerged from the most radical sectors of the movement of the unemployed.

La Salada and the textile workshops exhibit a singularity: the migrant composition of the labor force, which plays the lead role in this popular economy and is not restricted to a single nationality, brings out, in the extreme, forms of recomposition and transformation in the world of work that overflow its traditional coordinates (formal, waged, masculine, national labor, conceiving of the isolated individual, detached from his or her home and relations of reproduction).

A "communitarian capital" travels with Bolivian migrants and is reformulated, characterized by its ambiguity: it is capable of functioning as a means of self-management, mobilization, and insubordination but *also* as a means of servitude, submission, and exploitation.[6] However, the archaic is not confined to a traditional custom and usage that would contradict new forms of employment; instead, the operation is more complex: the archaic becomes the input for an absolutely contemporary recombination.

Hence, a unique form of entrepreneurship emerges, promoted by the informalization exploited by the textile workshops and continued in La Salada, which places value on domestic-communitarian elements, bringing dynamics of self-management into play and nurturing concrete political networks.[7]

A Vitalist Pragmatic

To understand the dynamic of the migrant labor force, I will focus on the power of decision making and will to progress that mixes the Foucauldian definition of the migrant as an investor in himself or herself with the utilization of communitarian capital. This is a vital impulse that deploys a calculus in which a rationality based on the desire for personal and family progress is superimposed onto a repertoire of communitarian practices. A second, complementary hypothesis is the specifically postmodern articulation of the communitarian with the post-Fordist productive world: its capacity to become a labor attribute, a specific type of qualification, for the migrant workers from the Bolivian highlands who have come to Buenos Aires. In being put to work, the communitarian becomes a source of a pragmatic versatility that crosses borders and is capable of adaptation and invention.

Anticapitalist premises cannot be attributed to that vitalist pragmatic a priori. However, it demonstrates a level of self-management in the production of social life that is organized without the political mediation of traditional institutions (from the state to the trade union, from the political party to social assistance). At the same time, it is also a principle of organization and expansion of popular life that knows how to pragmatically relate to and negotiate with those traditional institutions (which are declining or being refunctionalized in a new dynamic in which they are no longer the privileged mediators).

The vitality that I want to highlight, however, implies a fundamental political perspective: that the subjects of these baroque economies are not considered as victims. The systematic disinvestment in the state during the harshest phase of neoliberalism generates the space to interpellate social actors under the logic of the microentrepreneur and entrepreneurship. It is a way in which the politics of self-management appears to compensate for activities and services of reproduction that the state no longer takes responsibility for (from education and health care to security and transportation, and other forms of care work), so that workers are forced to assume the costs of their own reproduction. Thus, as Silvia Federici argues, "every articulation of the reproduction of labor power has been turned into an immediate point of accumulation" (2012, 102).

The Market and Production of Urban Fabric

However, what I am interested in investigating is the mode of growth associated with market dynamism and all the layers of activity that it organizes. The market is the space where part of the value of the merchandise produced in the workshops is realized, and it is simultaneously the prolongation of a traditional commercial center that has crossed borders and that includes techniques of sabotaging commercial forms or, at least, of using things in multiple ways (from contraband to knock-offs). Thus, an entire glossary of terms must be rethought based on their concrete meanings in La Salada: *illegal, clandestine, knock-off, fake, real imitation, real stolen merchandise, legal fake merchandise*, and so on.

The market proliferates and grows, upward and sideways, in warehouses and under the open sky, on the premises in Greater Buenos Aires and at an infinite number of points colonized by the saladitas. It also grows in terms of the services it provides (for example, the formation of a health insurance plan for the Urkupiña market) and the series of businesses that it enables. As an urban fabric, the market manages to combine a temporality of rapid and versatile construction (stalls are assembled and disassembled, while the infrastructure itself is increasingly stabilized and strengthened) with sustained and amplified progress over time.

In the social sciences it is common to associate the informal economy with an invisible and marginal economy. Even the moniker of an economy operating "under the table" (that is, outside of the legal parameters and tributaries of the formal economy) reveals that supposed character of the hidden economy: in the shadows.[8] However, these economies can no longer be considered marginal from any point of view, and even less so with regard to their capacity to relate intimately to metropolitan heterogeneity (the articulation of forms ranging from self-employment to illegal commerce, which, in neoliberal terms, negates what those fragments have in common and organizes them as segments). They also reveal cities' dilemma over the simultaneous visibilization and invisibilization of the productive function of these economies.

Increasingly massive and street based, these informal economies oscillate between hypervisibility and invisibility. In short, there is a debate between those who seek to eradicate informal economies and those who propose their recognition as part of contemporary urban dynamics. Meanwhile, these economies' visibility is full of dilemmas, in the form of stereotypes and prejudices, but also in the difficulty of naming practices that combine commercial circuits, family survival strategies, enterprises that appropriate knowledges of self-management, and an informality that values independence. The question brings us to the regime of visibility that the neoliberal city brings about and the ways in which it is subverted and reconfigured by certain popular practices. If relocation and displacement are the foundation of contemporary metropolitan heterogeneity, how do they become visible in the sense of valuing their productive capacity and their constructive capacity to make the city? These dynamics require a new way of seeing, capable of overlapping and contradictory logics.

Copy and Border

Let's examine one of these overlaps. Is there a relationship between simulacrum and border? John and Jean Comaroff (2011) argue that the global world's mobility supposes a growing market of forgeries that allow access to that movement: fake titles and marriage licenses, counterfeit passports, and the like. When governance is about apparatuses of control of flows, counterfeiting is a way of circumventing or sabotaging some links of those regulations.

This supposes that certain areas of the world would be destined to be, or would have a historical affinity with, a "counterfeit modernity," where everything happens as a copy, under the guise of a false object or apocryphal document. Peripheral modernity, in this sense, would be almost fictional (the insistent appeals to build "a serious country" would fall under this schematic).[9] Its counterpart, the reign of the original, would be the space dominated by legality. However, contemporary global capitalism reveals those spaces of homogeneous and regulated modernity (an original modernity) as spaces in crisis, since the (productive, social, ethnic, etc.) heterogeneity that they had maintained as a colonial outside is now immersed in and proliferating within their own interior. Furthermore, the South's supposed illegality is revealed as an adequate, and even constitutive, component of the new assemblages of power in the global economy, as Saskia Sassen (2008) refers to them.

The impact of neoliberal transformations is crucial here: they complexly weave together a growing web of informal activities with entrepreneurial dynamics (at a popular and business level, and with both acting at a transnational scale) in a context where rights are made flexible and taken away. Then, is the reign of the copy proliferating in fictive modernities a collection of experiences from which the principles of alternative modernities arise and are projected? Does La Salada propose a vernacular epistemology of the copy as the truth of things? In the megamarket La Salada, everything is a copy, and everything is real, simultaneously—hence its polemic power and its problematic charge. In any case, *forgeries* are called such for reasons that question the very notion of what is false. In addition, there are multiple categories and forms of the counterfeit in circulation. This is due to the mode of production of—mostly, but not exclusively, textile—items that are bought wholesale, by small-scale retailers, or for family consumption. The "clandestine" textile workshop stands out in that blurry production zone that gives rise to that immense node of transnational distribution and sales that is La Salada. A new paradox is opened up: La Salada is a space in which a type of production that is defined by its clandestine nature is publicized and expanded. Once again, the simple opposition between the two terms is complicated: the *original* is produced underground, and the counterfeit *copy* is openly distributed.

Between the workshop and the market, all sorts of brands proliferate: there is apparel without any sort of logo, other apparel with brands specifically produced for La Salada, and also apparel with brands belonging to well-known clothing stores, since workers for major brands often receive some of the merchandise as part of their payment. Or competition may force brands to hand over design patterns and cuts of fabric to various workshops in an informal bidding process in which the workshop that produces the item the fastest wins the contract. However, in this process more than one batch of garments with all the signs of the original is left free, displaced and available for the "parallel" market.

It is not a simple matter: workers who receive these items as part of their payment (or who appropriate them in a trickle-down method to complement their income) are responsible for inserting them as "original" branded garments into some segment of the market. That is, the same garments, removed from their legal circuit of commercial valorization, have to demonstrate that they have the same quality and design, even if the price is notably lower and even if, effectively, it is their very producers who guarantee that the objects are *identical*. But what does *identical* mean? Here that notion could be limited to the mode and material of manufacture. However, the notion of *authenticity* clearly demands other immaterial components of valorization, associated with a universe of belonging, images that make certain forms of life explicit to different segments of the public. La Salada puts those forms of life into debate, to the point of questioning, subverting, or pirating them. This modality of the post-Fordist economy—which for Maurizio Lazzarato (2006) refers to the creation of worlds as a central element of the current mode of the creation of goods—finds an ironic and challenging provocation in this experience of popularized piracy.

In any case, the task of reselling the merchandise of recognized brands, which finds a parallel channel in La Salada, reveals the ambiguity of the true brand that is only tautologically confirmed as such: when one pays a high price for something because it is the brand. However, once subtracted from the circuit in which that brand is valued as such, this garment—even when made in the same way, with the same materials, and often by the same workers— is multiplied in a popular and transnational chain of sales and commercialization, jeopardizing the value of exclusivity. La Salada is at the center of an important contemporary debate on this point: disputes around the appropriation of the immaterial, which translate precisely into battles around intellectual property and trademark rights.[10]

Copy and Control

Sportswear is the paradigmatic form of branded apparel, but all brands have a similar relationship with the idea of being original. Brands' antipiracy campaigns are confronted with a paradox: they must deauthorize garments made by the same people who make the so-called legitimate ones. As the garments are produced in the same way, the difference increasingly lies in the paying of a high price for a garment as the ultimate and true act of its effective and distinctive consumption. This is a difficult way for the brand to impose its authority. Even loyal customers, disposed to pay an elevated price as a form of distinguished consumption, when faced with the popular use of those brands proliferating in social sectors that originally did not have access, impact the garment in an increasingly ambiguous way: confirming the need to assert its originality even more, at the same time as the distinction requires greater immaterial resources, since the materials (preparation, fabric, labels) are not a reliable source of originality.[11]

The conditions of exploitation in the textile industry and its intimate relationship with fashion—which, following Jacques Rancière (2004), operates as part of the factory of opinion and as a place for elaborating social difference—also open up possibilities for the workers to boycott the brands, create parallel brands, and denounce the brands' tactics. The protests against the brands (mostly by the organization La Alameda between 2010 and 2013) were an example of this type of campaign, which sought to make visible an economic circuit that assembles legal and illegal parts but whose operation requires it to be invisible in order for consumption to be carried out effectively. These public allegations also sought to highlight the absurdity of the differentiation between expensive businesses and popular markets when they both sell the same merchandise.[12]

A woman working in a textile factory, which formally works for the large brands but also contracts out to clandestine workshops, recounted the following. The factory, where 80 percent of the workers are migrants, produces garments for major multinational sportswear companies. One of its commissions was to manufacture soccer jerseys for one of the most important teams in Argentina. The new jersey's launch was planned as a big event. In the workshop, one of the sewers takes a picture of the still brand-new, secret jersey with his cell phone, and this photo makes it onto social media, in a sort of clandestine anticipation for the team's fans. The image spreads, and the team and the brand see their scoop ruined, with concern and great loss of prestige, losing control over the launch and promotion of the premiere and, therefore, the profit. Retaliation hits the workers, who are then prohibited from having any communication device, any type of phone. The workers now suffer twice as much since, during their long workdays, cell phones were their way of knowing how their children were, coordinating their care, talking with them to hear their voices, and letting them know, for example, when they would be home.

The brand impacts the workshop, exacerbating its control mechanisms, as an abusive way of containing the image's secret, a key component of an item's promotional campaign. The sanction is the response to the workers' sabotage of that production secret (what was traditionally known as a trade secret), a sort of punishment for the workers' revenge, a revenge in which those who make the products become the first to enjoy and circulate them. Mass counterfeiting—with increasing levels of perfection—demonstrates the growing gap between the desire for globalized consumption and the political management of scarcity or exclusivity.

Mimesis and Heterotopia

Foucault used the concept of heterotopia in contrast to the idealist notion of utopia. The market, with its nooks and crannies, being mounted and dismounted, would have the status of an other space, capable of establishing a dynamic of varied transactions on the city's borders. As a rule, a heterotopia juxtaposes various spaces that normally would be incompatible in a real place. This overlap holds the idea of an alternative order, a critique of the existing order. In this sense, the market proposes a space of multiple uses and also an alternative, cyclical time.

At the same time, copying of brands produces a simultaneous effect of parody and devaluation.[13] La Salada's complexity in this regard comes from the expansion of consumption that originally would have been segmented by class (restricted access to brands), underpinned by a mode of production based on conditions of intensive exploitation of migrant workers. Can we infer a mode of subversion of market rules as we look at this mass counterfeiting, or is it, rather, the popular affirmation of these rules?

The consumption of counterfeit trademarked clothing disrupts the trademark's prestige as a sign of exclusivity, while it demonstrates how that exclusivity is predicated on a restricted classist exhibition. This supposes that as the brand is desired, used, and displayed by popular classes, its value is subverted or devalued. It is a way of producing the copy that devalues the original while exposing what they have in common, their semi-identical production, highlighting the dispute over the difference in an intangible and ever more decisive good: the construction of a way of life. As Hsiao-hung Chang (2004) signals, "fake" brands and the consumption of "superlogos" "could rewrite the whole theory of mimesis." Along this line, the false itself is dislocated in respect to the true-false distinction, while the *fake* "in 'fake globalization' means 'counterfeiting' as well as 'appropriating'" (233).

At a large scale, the fake constructs a heterotopic landscape: a meticulous but noninstitutionalized regulation of the traditional way of organizing open-air exchange. Neither its heterogeneous texture nor its expansion, nor its appearance and disappearance in the middle of the night during its early years, allows us to compare La Salada with other urban spaces.

Foucault speaks beautifully about markets, which he compares to the theater, as heterotopic spaces tied to time, following the form of a party. They are true chronic heterotopias that are built at cities' borders.

The reign of the transnational copy that characterizes the megamarket of the Buenos Aires urban periphery might be a pirated form of that anonymous, multiethnic, and mobile multitude that populated the ships that made capitalism a transatlantic enterprise. The market brings together, in its heterogeneous composition, a new type of proletariat, surely a fake one if compared to that which was established in modern times.

Can Stallholders Speak?

Despite its large migrant composition, La Salada has gained notoriety in the mainstream media through the voice of one of its Argentine leaders: Jorge Castillo. With him, market vendors also managed to join the official business delegation that visited Angola with President Cristina Fernández de Kirchner in 2012. The market's representation—its political and media voice—is Argentine, leaving the majority of its participants in the shadows. Here a central conflict is debated: Argentine work is identified as dignified work, while migrant labor is linked to the moniker *slave labor*. Hence, to echo Gayatri Chakravorty Spivak's (1988) controversial question, can the subaltern speak? Can migrants' voices be heard when La Salada is spoken about in public?

Castillo's frequent appearances in the press also reveal the expansive logic regarding the future promised by the market: on more than one occasion, the leader has revealed that he has already bought land in Miami to set up a branch of La Salada there, and, even more important, he announced the addition of food items as part of the market's offerings.

There is a double argument seeking to legitimate the expansion: on one hand, it emphasizes the increase in popular consumption, while it blames overpricing on corporate intermediaries (unions, retailers, etc.), an argument with even greater repercussions in a context of rising inflation. On the other hand, it reveals that the productive mode enabled by La Salada (flexible, precarious, supported by varied forms of self-entrepreneurship, etc.) is the basis for the majority of productive circuits and, therefore, is not exclusive to the market of markets. In the case of the future and promised food market, with the slogan "From the farm to the consumer," La Salada would launch one of the key aspirations of the social economy that was publicized during the crisis but that it failed to implement at a large scale.

Let's return to the voice: in this regard, the role of community radio stations, organic to the economy going from the workshop to the market, becomes central. We will talk more about them later, because it is through them that market participants are able to create their own site of enunciation.

Nevertheless, the traditional muteness with which the subaltern are represented—with its counterpart, invisibilization—in recent decades has given way, according to Beatriz Jaguaribe (2007), to a hypervisibility founded on a new "aesthetics of realism." This arises to narrate the metropolitan experience, the anonymous lives, in a global world saturated with media images. In the case of Brazil, analyzed by Jaguaribe, magical practices coexist with a carnivalesque imaginary. Yet these codes of realism, "as a narrative form of the everyday" (11), have nontraditional characteristics: they are not utopias, they are not supported by lettered cultures, and they have the dramatic intensity of a reality that is perceived as more vital.

In contrast to the realism of other decades, there is no aesthetic experimentation, but there is a willingness to dismantle clichés. The proliferation of images comes at the cost of "visual inclusion": it makes subjects and experiences visible that, based on the legitimacy of their testimony and their presumed authenticity, exploit a new capacity for producing images.

Could it be said, then, that the notions of *invisibilization* and *muteness* suffer from a certain anachronism when we are thinking about the subaltern worlds of Latin American cities? Jaguaribe argues that the trend of favela tours, for example, is due to the fact that, in contemporary capitalism, poverty, exclusion, and local violence are resymbolized as part of "authentic communities." The Brazilian sociologist makes a point in regard to the favelas that I am interested in testing in La Salada: are these the privileged spaces of dispute where ideals and imaginaries of modernity fail and are reinvented?

Do they, then, demonstrate the defeat of a normative and inclusive modernity while experimenting with forms of inclusion beyond the norm (something that Carlos Monsiváis (2006) also pointed to in regard to the sellers of pirated DVDs in Mexico)? Could it be said that much more than solely a cartography of exclusion remains to be understood? For example, the proliferation of other forms of consumption, the production of images and space-times of well-being from the ground up, the negotiation of rules, and the construction of a visibility announce another perspective.

On the Common

How does this economy articulate with the communitarian knowledges that are essential for producing and sustaining forms of intensely exploitative labor? Those knowledges also have diverse drifts, as repertoires of modes of self-managed territorial organization and of the constitution of a popular market that enables certain consumption at a mass scale. It is precisely that point of permanent ambivalence and oscillation, with the profile of an archaic and postmodern, democratizing and reactionary time, that matches as a flexible and variable form of communitarian, popular, and plebeian production.

However, on what base is that ambivalence produced? For Raquel Gutiérrez Aguilar (2011b), the communitarian reunites "operative principles," certain forms of "organization of social, productive, political, and ritual life" that have persevered from ancient traditions on our continent but that are also extraordinarily flexible and dynamic and have a capacity for contamination, expansion, and reinvention that constitutes the key to their timeliness. That communitarian social doing is based on an economy of reciprocity that "tendentially sketches an expansive web of circulation of material and symbolic goods, where, in turn, such goods tend to be increasing." This complex economy projects features of autonomy and self-determination, displays procedures of collective decision making, and also brings up a debate about wealth.

It is no accident that the perseverance of this communitarian social doing is today intertwined with an extensive political and theoretical debate about *the common* as a notion that goes beyond the classic liberal division between the public and the private and that provides a key to a type of production that is increasingly socialized and dependent on complex networks and levels of cooperation. Here there is another question: What is an operative notion of the common? The "equivocity," in Étienne Balibar's words, as the tension between opposite significations, the "ethical-political singularities" assembled in multitudinous social doing, which coexist with the appropriations of what Negri terms a "communism of capital" (in Curcio et al. 2010, 316), points to that terrain of dispute and ambivalence. However, the emphasis on the fact that today the decisive struggle occurs through the "construction and destruction" of the common (Reyes 2010, 503) cannot be ignored.[14]

I stress the notion of the *operative* demonstrated by these definitions, because therein lies the key: the capacity of the communitarian to exhibit and expand forms of doing. With this, I want to point out that when I speak of the ambivalence of the common, I am not using a rhetorical device or making a theoretical pirouette but emphasizing up to what point social forms of collective doing capable of constructing autonomy and appropriating social wealth are under dispute. Also, I want to underscore that we cannot ignore their weaknesses and perversions, their wrinkles and contradictions, if we want to understand their operative complexity. The point of departure is clear: in these modes there is a vital *potencia* capable of initiating and developing other logics, other times, and other spaces in respect to neoliberal hegemony.

In the economy going from the workshop to the market, the productivity and uses of the communitarian, capable of organizing forms of exploitation and business, of microenterprise and economic progress, are challenged. The ambivalence of the communitarian thus lies in its capacity to be intertwined with an opportunistic dynamic in the strict and not the moral meaning of the word *opportunistic*: as a propensity to capture the best option. As Paolo Virno (2004) has argued, opportunism and cynicism in post-Fordism express public sentiments because they constitute the ambivalent modes of being that correspond to processes of socialization of the labor force. Hence, the labor force finds itself precisely forced to be opportunistic in respect to contingency, and cynical with regard to universal and fixed rules, in order to be able to survive and prosper.

Communitarian Capital and Fractal Accumulation

In the particular case of Bolivian migration, which plays a leading role in La Salada and the textile workshops, a communitarian capital also migrates. This communitarian capital, as I noted earlier, is characterized by its ambiguity: it is liable to function in terms of self-management, mobilization, and insubordination and *also* as a mode of servitude, submission, and exploitation.

As noted, the communitarian aspects, with their flexible meanings, compose a landscape of a new migrant proletariat, which is simultaneously political, neighborly, familial, and delocalized. That heritage becomes capital in different ways, capitalizing on knowledges and practices considered to be archaic or premodern (or antimodern) as inputs for adapting and reinventing forms of production, circulation, and consumption.

Characterizing the communitarian element in this way demonstrates the problematic nature of the notion itself when it is made to work in the city (thus taking away its strictly rural connotations), involved in market transactions and practices (removing it from a closed circuit of reciprocity), and linked to migrant trajectories (displacing it from its purely territorial identity and anchor).

I hypothesize that there is a bonus for popular economies, in their skill of innovation and informality, that has to do with calling up modes that had been previously displaced or marginalized while the pattern of wage labor spread as the majoritarian norm. Nor can they be confined to a matrix of "solidarity," which, from the point of view of political anthropology, seems to be a weak category for understanding the complexity of what I call baroque economies as a composite of disparate practices.

"La Salada is a place of survival without rules," I was told by a financier who had started his business there. Yet it is the market itself that "provides a type of exceptional financial education: precisely by not having rules." The historical experience of Andean self-employment connected to the territory of the Buenos Aires urban periphery in the midst of the crisis is the space-time where financial versatility finds an opportunity for progress. In addition, what is revealed in these economies is the rationalization of diverse reproductive economies as immediately productive economies.

Going a step farther in the argument leads us to ask, what type of accumulation is this communitarian capital capable of? Following Gutiérrez Aguilar, it could be said that the dynamic of the popular-communitarian economy produces a fractal system of accumulation. This would mean that accumulation does not follow a linear and progressive logic but rather "associative M-C-M loops" (Gutiérrez Aguilar 2011a). If it could be diagrammed based on two mathematical models, we would say that there is geometric growth and exponential growth. Geometric growth could be thought of as the pattern followed by industrial accumulation, while financial capital tends to grow exponentially (without ever fully achieving this).

The hypothesis of fractal accumulation serves for understanding a mode of accumulation that, on reaching a certain point, displaces capital accumulation toward other associative nuclei (the family, neighborhood, friends), whose distinctive quality is their strongly relational character, thus abandoning the canonical form of geometric growth. This would explain a displacement of accumulation as the driving force of small- and medium-sized businesses, enabling small- and medium-scale reproductions. The mode of growth and proliferation marking La Salada's rhythm can be characterized in this way. Each point of accumulation would result in a new series that would be dependent at its starting point but, at the same time, would relaunch itself as a new point of departure. Accumulation, under the fractal figure, would not have as its unidimensional goal the growth and concentration of capital, but rather its multiplication, operating in a networked way and enabling a logic of scalar multiplication. We are left with the question of whether this strongly associative character as a dynamic of accumulation can become a counterpoint to the properly capitalist figure of "possessive individualism," classically described by Crawford B. Macpherson (1962).

This fractal geometry of accumulation, besides allowing for thinking about processes in terms that are not strictly linear, introduces a certain notion of circular temporality. This temporality, defined by each iterative loop in fractal reproduction, can break, however, unfolding and/or turning into a traditional dynamic of accumulation. It is crucial to investigate this transition, in which the state's contention for territory (the demarcation of La Salada's borders by the gendarmerie's force) and attempts to establish more formal enterprises within the market itself (for example, the construction of the new warehouse Tunari, which seeks to be neater and less market-like than the rest of the constructions) play a key role.

The fractal mode of accumulation that I am hypothesizing is a mode of proliferation that would work both to reinforce the dynamic border and to limit accumulation. Meanwhile, it is a modality that assures the regeneration of the labor market: it trains and organizes workers in a context of informalization and the transformation of state institutions, re-creating a logic of exploitation, already outside of any norm of traditional contractual work (opening a broad range of combinations of diversified waged and contractual forms), and enables a flexible labor flow from below that is articulated with communitarian dynamics historically associated with territories lacking welfare institutions.

Thus, La Salada produces welfare—or institutions of well-being—from below. This occurs because the zone of La Salada concentrates a productive know-how that unfolds as the rapid invention of economic forms, mixing production and reproduction, linked to tactics of the simultaneous resolution of issues of life and work, work and life. Fractal accumulation seems to coincide with what I noted above: from one point of view, the politics of self-management appears to compensate for a lack of activities and services of reproduction (such as education, health care, child care, security, and transportation), forcing workers to assume the costs of their own reproduction. However, when this thesis is immersed in that type of communitarian practice, it brings us back to the ambiguity of an autonomous drive capable of breaking down distinctions between life and work, not only as an effect of capital's dispossessive cunning, but also as a tradition of non-state-centric self-organization.

That simultaneity between the productive and the reproductive—which has broken with the modern distinction that divides political and civil life from reproduction as a natural social sphere (e.g., Hegel)—reappears under new forms. However, building on Gutiérrez Aguilar, the question is, how is the domestic-reproductive plane connected to the plane of the common? What defines the saturation point and the passage to a new nucleus of accumulation in the hypothesis of fractal accumulation? What internal rule fixes this measure or frontier? One hypothesis is that state intervention seeks to accelerate that saturation point when it territorially contains the space where fractal accumulation expands. What would happen if this limit did not appear?

In these situations, the question is, how does this productive molecularity coagulate, and how is it taken advantage of by a logic of servitude and capitalist (brand) exploitation?[15] To put these questions on a more abstract plane: how does this logic challenge the logic of capitalist accumulation? Would the logic of fractal accumulation encourage a dynamic of demonopolization or dispersal? Would it be internally linked to the very dynamic of migration?

Assemblages

These baroque economies' mode of functioning, in which La Salada appears as an especially experimental node, requires a high level of logistics, that is, the coordination of processes, resources, and actors (see Carmona-Rodríguez et al. 2012). In other words, logistics involves the problem of the articulation of segments. It is that management of contact between diverse elements, which also gives shape to the complexity of their informality, which, it bears repeating, should not be thought of as pure improvisation, transience, and simplicity. From the market's internal transportation service—cart drivers—to the transportation of vendors from the Argentinean countryside and neighboring countries, from the legal and nonlegal mechanisms of importation into the distribution network to the provisioning of merchandise and negotiation of space within the market, from the internal network of services and employment to the modes of tax manipulation and negotiation with government authorities, what we see unfold is a heterogeneity of articulations that requires rethinking the ways in which value is produced, the subsumption of that productive diversity to the power of capitalist rule, and ways of inhibiting, counteracting, and even resisting that subsumption.

This landscape, already characterized as a territory hosting multiple modalities of labor, like a leopard print, to use Virno's (2004) image, should be thought of as an *assemblage*. The notion of the assemblage highlights "inter-minable, contingent, and changing articulation of a set of highly heterogeneous elements (technology, territories, populations, modes of economic production) that are the base of the constitution of contemporary global capitalism" (Ong 2006, 180). On one hand, it systematically connects elements that are usually thought of as separate: local economies versus the global economy. But it does so in a way that focuses attention on the problem of the territorial, as well as extraterritorial, coordination of material and immaterial dynamics.

In opposition to the idea that globalization universalizes processes, the category of the assemblage allows for demarcating the gaze of unification and homogenization in order to dwell on specific articulations, with their par-tial and temporal connections and boundaries. In this respect, Sassen draws a fundamental connection between the decomposition of nation-state unity and the production of "particular types of territoriality" (2008, 386), where global and national elements are mixed, producing new types of articulation among territory, authority, and rights. These terms, when analyzed separately, denaturalize the idea of a national construction of territory, authority, and rights and allow, instead, for analyzing the different degrees of denationaliza-tion of each segment. Thus, the global and the national can be studied starting from concrete assemblages among these three key components (5). The disar-ticulation of the traditional territoriality of the national is produced by these new assemblages that (1) assemble global and national elements, (2) combine different spatiotemporal orders (velocities and ranges), (3) are capable of pro-ducing new zones of interventions for which there are no defined rules, (4) are also able to produce new actors, and (5) do so in such a way that existing capacities are re-created under new logics of organization (389).

Going into the analysis of territories thus enables rooting "a geography of strategic territories at the global scale" (Sassen 2007, 126) based on the cate-gory of place and processes of labor. Above all, it allows for understanding the global through its concrete articulations at the territorial level based on the connections between economies and places, trajectories and politics. Beyond the smooth and neutral idea of space, the assemblage enables a simultane-ous micro- and macroview, taking into account different segments that are put into contact, their discontinuous ways of generating processes, and, finally, the specific productivity of the parceled and mobilized form assumed by the production of value and the production of subjectivity.

Such a geography is thus converted into a *geo-economy*, crisscrossed by greatly differentiated lines that decisively include reiterated exits, escapes, or flights from the territory, since the vector of movement is a fundamental point for understanding the assemblage's logic. Thus, the process of decomposition or denationalization that Sassen refers to also requires making visible the movement or impulse behind the disassembling of the nation-state territory based on a dynamic of deterritorialization, or labor power's flight from territories, that forces, also in a new way, capital's flight and the creation of spaces, rights, and regimes of authority in keeping with those new velocities and mobilities.

The notion of the assemblage, however, assumes heterogeneity as the regime of existence of things. Therefore, it is necessary to continuously produce articulations, contacts, connectors. In this respect, *the assemblage is a relational (not substantial) logic.* Gilles Deleuze says that an assemblage "is a multiplicity which is made up of heterogeneous terms and which establishes liaisons, relations between them, across ages, sexes and reigns—different natures. Thus the assemblage's only unity is that of a co-functioning: it is a symbiosis, a 'sympathy.' It is never filiations which are important, but alliances, alloys; these are not successions, lines of descent, but contagions, epidemics, the wind" (quoted in DeLanda 2006, 121).

For Manuel DeLanda, the notion of the assemblage functions as a counterpart to the traditional conceptualization of organic totalities. In other words, "the rationale behind the theory of assemblages is, in part, to avoid discourses in terms of 'the power,' 'the resistance,' 'the capital,' 'the worker.' Thus it avoids reification in favor of demonstrating the logic of operation" (2008, 84).

Defined in this way, the concept of assemblage displays two dimensions:[16]

1. One is composed by two axes or poles called, at either end, *material* and *expressive*: these are variable roles and may be combined; that is, a component can play a mixed material and expressive role by exercising different capacities.[17]
2. Another dimension comprises variable processes denominated as *territorialization* and *deterritorialization*: an assemblage can have components that work to stabilize its identity and others that force it to change or even lead to the transformation of the assemblage itself.

I am interested in DeLanda's definition of processes of territorialization as "processes that define or sharpen the spatial boundaries of actual territories." At the same time, he also refers to "non-spatial processes which increase the internal homogeneity of an assemblage, such as the sorting processes which exclude a certain category of people from membership of an organization, or the segregation processes which increase the ethnic or racial homogeneity of a neighborhood" (2006, 13).

For DeLanda, assemblage theory avoids a taxonomy of essentialisms, but, above all, it shows that the identity of an assemblage, at any scale, is always the product of a process (territorialization and sometimes codification) and, therefore, is always precarious to the extent that other processes can destabilize it (deterritorialization and decodification). Thus, the "ontological status of assemblages" is always *singular* (2006, 28). In other words, it forms what is called a *flat ontology* (DeLanda 2006; Harcourt and Escobar 2005).[18]

La Salada, understood through the dynamic of the assemblage, can be seen as a "structure of spaces of possibilities," meaning that the possibilities of an assemblage are not given (unlike properties) but rather are precisely possible even when they do not actualize and emerge from interaction. La Salada is a structure of opportunities.

Assemblages are complex spaces, with *topological invariants*, that is, *universal singularities*, in the words of Deleuze: "Thus, while persons, communities, organizations, cities and nation-states are all individual singularities, each of these entities would also be associated with a space of possibilities characterized by its dimensions, representing its degrees of freedom, and by a set of universal singularities. In other words, each of these social assemblages would possess its own diagram" (quoted in DeLanda 2006, 30). From this perspective the divergence between micro and macro—or the choice between holism and individualism (Dumont 2001)—disappears. What is important is *the relationship between the micro and the macro* (DeLanda 2006, 32). These two notions have meaning in connection with variable scales and not fixed entities, with "a certain spatial and temporal scale" (DeLanda 2008, 81). If assemblages are logics of articulation of the heterogeneous, they enroll and simultaneously produce scales.[19] That is, they produce spaces and dimensions over which a map of actions, interdependences, connections, technologies, and politics is defined.

Neoliberalism and the Informal Economy

A system of microfinance did not develop in Argentina as it did in Bolivia, where the impulse toward microcredit formed part of the neoliberal policies that managed to capture and capitalize on an extensive network of popular micropractices linked to communal production, services, and commerce (Toro 2010). As part of the program of structural adjustment and privatization, Bolivian public policies promoted self-employment and the informal economy in a way that would have been unthinkable in Argentina, where the culture of work (historically central to Peronism) delayed and hindered such positive valorization of these dynamics even though there, too, neoliberalism dismantled the large nuclei of formal waged work and led to record unemployment levels.

In Argentina the informal economy was made visible and acquired the scale of a mass phenomenon owing to the crisis and intense demonetization that the country experienced in 2001–2002.[20] Since then new economic institutions (for savings, exchange, loans, and consumption) have nurtured strategies for survival, mixing a capacity to confront the crisis with new forms of popular entrepreneurship and intense forms of exploitation. The recent economic recovery has not made them disappear. On the contrary, it has incorporated them and promoted their articulation. The conglomerate that operates between La Salada and the textile workshops is part of that series.[21]

The expansion of this informal economy combines the small scale of family businesses with factories and small- and medium-sized workshops (which do not aim to change scale) and commercial circuits of import and export. This economy, as noted above, challenges the logic of the visible versus the invisible and is better understood as an alteration of the very regime of the visible.

Entrepreneurs, Businesspeople, and Citizens

"La Salada is Argentine!," states the cover of the first issue (October 2010) of La Salada's internal magazine. That phrase encapsulates a many-sided conflict. On one side are the complaints of various Argentinean business groups, united in the Argentine Confederation of Medium-Sized Enterprises (Confederación Argentina de la Mediana Empresa), who denounce the impossibility of competing with La Salada's conditions of production, sale, and distribution. The accusation that foreign workers (workshop owners, textile workers, and market vendors) are responsible for that competition is explicit, although the majority of that migrant web works for "Argentine" brands (although not exclusively).

A second position is represented by a certain rhetoric of political liberalism that does not condemn informality a priori since it considers it a sort of buffer zone for the poor. This defense of La Salada has been personally assumed by Alfonso Prat Gay, a former congressional candidate for the Coalición Cívica y Social (Social and Civil Coalition) and a former president of the Central Bank of Argentina, who was suggested as a candidate for minister of economics by more than one partisan force and was an official for J. P. Morgan during the crisis of 2001. His main argument is that those who participate in the megamarket should be considered entrepreneurs. He adds that if they are not included in the market, they could potentially become criminals: "If we continue discouraging La Salada, we will be strengthening drugs and violence in the villas." He relates this to the "informality of the excluded," arguing that "defining the informality of the vulnerable as illegal . . . is telling them that being poor is illegal, de facto criminal." His request is for strict neoliberal coherence: "It is impossible to be in favor of microenterprise and against La Salada."[22]

On the contrary, the Argentinean retailers argue that the government should defend them since they represent national industry. The Confederation of Medium-Sized Enterprises issued a statement refuting Prat Gay's argument.[23] The head of the organization, Osvaldo Cornide, noted, "All businessmen, entrepreneurs, and citizens who were concerned about the unfair competition generated by clandestine sales in organized commerce were more concerned after reading Dr. Alfonso Prat Gay's article, 'In Defense of La Salada and Its Entrepreneurs.'"[24] The title of Cornide's article summarizes the crux of the battle: "Clandestine Sales Are Not an 'Enterprise.'" Cornide attributes equal status to "businessmen, entrepreneurs, and citizens," excluding and drawing a border isolating those who populate La Salada, who Cornide believes are engaged in clandestine, illegal activities. In the Confederation of Medium-Sized Enterprises, they feel betrayed because that border is being diluted: "It is surprising that it would be the former president of an institution like the Central Bank who minimizes the ethical sense of what the culture of 'paying taxes,' 'respecting rights,' 'combating piracy,' and finding dignified job opportunities means for entrepreneurs on those grounds."[25]

The businessman requested that the government audit and regulate transactions in the market, contesting the characterization of La Salada as a productive organization. It situates the market as a mere effect of underdevelopment, employing a language of poverty (it speaks of market participants as excluded, needy, and vulnerable) to erase the entrepreneurial character of the market's doers, and it rejects the market as an economic alternative, noting especially its "indignity."[26] Jorge Castillo, administrator of the Punta Mogote sector of La Salada, responded to the business invective, saying that there is also a large amount of informality in downtown businesses. Thus, he highlights the informal condition as intrinsic to the whole economy and the entire city and not as an exclusive quality of marginal sectors and/or peripheral neighborhoods.

The market is revealed as a promiscuous zone. At the same time, it reveals the condition of the city as such. The promiscuity to which I refer—without a moral connotation—expresses the motley character of the market space. It is an effect of the confusion that emerges from the continuous recombination of commercial circuits, modes of family survival, enterprises appropriating knowledges of self-management, and an informality that values independence.

Informality is, above all, heterogeneity: self-employment, microenterprises, contraband, clandestine activities. However, informality cannot be thought of as the radically different other of formality. Today these modes are mutually contaminated and, primarily, are articulated with and complement one another. Therefore, rather than being regarded as conflicting options, they should be analyzed in their concrete assemblages. At this point, the traditional binary between visible economies and submerged economies is diluted, in favor of an articulation of more complex visibilities that both are exploited by the neoliberal city and exceed it.

Cartographic Notes

A multidisciplinary work carried out by the collectives Rally Conurbano and Tu Parte Salada (mainly composed of architects and urban planners) between 2005 and 2008, seeking to evaluate the "geopolitical evolution of this (sub) urban center" and the relations within the sequence from nonoccupation, to spontaneous occupation, and then to planned occupation of the space of the former riverside resort, indicates hallmarks from the viewpoint of an intensive cartography of the area (Massidda et al. 2010). One of these is that even if this market began with few resources and in an almost artisanal way, today "it operates in sync with global centers of nonhegemonic commerce": Los Altos in La Paz, Bolivia, or Oshodi and Alaba in Lagos, Nigeria, or the Chinese province of Guangdong, the largest production zone for goods in the global nonhegemonic system. La Salada is configured, then, as "the center of a network of regional markets and also as a node in a global network of informal commerce" (Massidda et al. 2010, 180).

They also underline its *absence* from the cartographic record (from commonly used guides and maps, such as those from Lumi and Filcar, as well as municipal maps). Thus, it escapes the usual logic of the planned use of the city:

La Salada as a market that, along with others, operates on the margins of the rigorous application of trademark laws and labor legislation, therefore, takes place on a contentious border with illegality and is not contemplated in the public cartographic record of the 1990s. None of the marginal phenomena in respect to state politics are registered: the slums figure as extensive parks, as part of the river, or as vacant areas. They are phenomena that are generated beyond the state system and thus are excluded from the official image of the city, from the model. Going even further: what is inscribed on the map in the market's place is not an empty space, nor any current civil function, but rather the last official use that the site had as a resort although it does not have any functional relation with the present. (Massidda et al. 2010, 190)

As when the villa is considered a *wasteland*, the representations that circulate about the city's densest spaces are notoriously opposite: they indicate empty, almost deserted spaces, whether barren or covered with water, deserts or swimming holes.

Last, a key issue: La Salada is an example of a "logistical urbanism" based on "experiments" rather than "projects." This supposes an essentially mobile construction, able to be quickly assembled and disassembled, capable of rapidly mutating and of being thought of as an intermittent yet lasting installation:

If logistics is defined as "all movement and storage that facilitates the flow of products from the point of purchase of materials to consumption, as well as the flows of information that get the movement underway," then La Salada would definitely be synonymous with movement, flow, point of purchase, point of consumption, flows of information, progress. All of these concepts also have their origin on the battlefield: contemporary logistics, focusing on commerce and determining production processes, is derived from military logistics, which defines it as "the practical art of moving armies, the material details of marches and formations and the establishment of camps and cantonments without becoming entrenched." . . . In La Salada's stalls there is not some merchandise on display and other merchandise in storage: everything that is seen is for sale, and all that is for sale is what has been produced for the day. It arrives, it is assembled, it is sold, and it is disassembled. Everything happens in one night. Still material, material in storage, is dangerous; it is a fixed, identifiable target, visible in the Google Earth of Santiago Montoya, director of the Tax Collection Agency of the Province of Buenos Aires. (Massidda et al. 2010, 197–198)

Hacerme feriante

La Salada was the object of a film released in 2010 entitled *Hacerme feriante* (Become a stallholder), produced by Julián D'Angiolillo. *Hacerme feriante* shows scenes from the riverside resort in its heyday in the mid-nineteenth century: robust families in crowded pools, the weekend as a space of well-deserved leisure. Those black-and-white pictures of happiness are then replaced by images of that place's reconversion over the last decade into another type of multitudinous space. The architecture that La Salada deploys is depicted here by a series of blueprints showing how poles, lights, tarps, and, as if it were a perfectly designed camp, an immense community of transactions are lit up in the middle of the night.

It shows continuous movement, displacements of thousands of people, an infinity of political, commercial, and relational articulations that enable that complex operation. "Become a stallholder" is a phrase that reveals that frenzy, that economy in motion, that putting oneself into a state of transience and, at the same time, of permanent consummation. The film narrates an immense landscape of occupation and appropriation of a space that was assumed to be abandoned (and that knew how to be so), which has been repopulated in an unexpected way and which governmental agencies are attempting to comprehend and capitalize on, although at a much slower pace and lagging far behind. In that hustle, the construction of a city that is not opposed to the neoliberal city unfolds. But it does challenge it. La Salada copies it but also sabotages it. It overlaps with it while opening the horizon of a different space-time.

What does it mean to produce images that take into account a mode of making the city that defies the neoliberal city's unilateral idea of the market? *Hacerme feriante* shows a city that is made of multiple scales, capable of articulating, in nonconventional ways, the relationships between the household and the neighborhood, between urban centers and rural towns, between the national scale and its increasing denationalization, between the festive dimension and the commercial one, between self-organization and the production of new authorities that reassemble territories that until recently had been considered vacant.

Hacerme feriante stages different apparatuses and moments of copying (for example, of DVDs). It itself, as a movie, would later be presented, copied, and sold in La Salada, as the copy of the copy of the copy, putting itself on a par with La Salada's own mode of production. The film's conditions of circulation are inscribed within what it shows, achieving an interiority with what it visibilizes and with the mode of proliferation of that form of visibilization.

In the film there are almost no voices. Above all, it avoids the off-screen explanatory voice. It is not that the images replace that voice. It displays an operation. *The film describes the movement of mounting, as if the maker of a film and the maker of a market in the end share something very similar: a skill of assembling, of montage, an exercise of composing materials with the capacity for exhibition, and a challenge to the image-brand as a stereotype, as a premade image.*

How do these dynamics affect the very landscape of the urban? *Hacerme feriante* presents the centrality of what is traditionally called the periphery. It disrupts the imaginary of the suburb as a space of restricted consumption to create room for an unfolding of objects, ceremonies, flows of people, and political, territorial, and commercial dynamics that connect that point, far removed from the city's center, to an infinity of other national and transnational geographic locations, in a network that clearly overflows the borders of the Buenos Aires neighborhood.

A view like that of *Hacerme feriante* is able to uncover popular (economic and political) institutions that definitively alter the landscape of what we understand as social doing. In this regard, the visual inclusion that the movie makes explicit is a becoming, an experimental institutionality.

What view would be immanent to these processes and capable of valuing what they already contain of the future city? *Hacerme feriante* visibilizes the market from a nonexterior position, incorporating the market dynamic, extending the film's folds, participating in and confusing itself with its mode of production and circulation. The leaders of La Salada have confessed to the director that the movie is currently being used as a "welcome letter" for vendors, besides being copied and sold in the market's stalls. The film maker is included in the first person in the title of the film, as an apparatus of visibilization. Thus, producing a view is producing a site of enunciation that allows itself to be traversed by a process, becoming a stallholder.

The Festival as a Moment of Market Consolidation

The festival is a mix of the stations of the cross and procession. The religious and dance festivals in La Salada consolidate that heterogeneous whole, composed of thousands of stalls; it is, however, not fully encapsulated in the union's celebration of Stallholders' Day (Día del Feriante). In La Salada, Stall-holders' Day is fused with symbols of Argentina (in addition to being concentrated in Punta Mogote, the only one of the three markets that is directed by an Argentine): a parade of gauchos, an enormous barbecue, a racecourse, and traditional music groups.

However, the best-attended festivals are the religious ones: those of the Virgin of Urkupiña and the Virgin of Copacabana, as well as Saint Michael the Archangel.[27] The festivals are held to win over customers and people passing by but also to obtain legitimacy in the media and in the neighborhood, displaying a novel cultural wealth, covering a big venture with festive signs, mixing expectations of progress with a fervent recognition of extracommercial orders. The Virgin of Urkupiña, the initial namesake of La Salada's first market, is also a figure of transactions and progress: Marta Giorgis (2004) calls her the "lending virgin."

For Silvia Rivera Cusicanqui, the festival organizes a "transnational neo-community": it renews and reinvents loyalties at the same pace as labor mobilities: "This forms an interweaving of opposing colors, a transnational neocommunity, whose contradictory identity and *ch'ixi* (motley) make the logics of accumulation and ritual consumption, of individual prestige and collective affirmation, coexist in permanent tension" (Rivera Cusicanqui 2010b, 15).

This does not preclude criticism of how the festivities operate, as Rivera Cusicanqui states, speaking of the Bolivian community organized in La Perla of Madrid, for example, as a chauvinistic space that, with "powerful icons of illusory welcome," manipulates and subjects migrant trajectories in a neoliberal way so that the festivity becomes "a belt of domestication of and disinfection from the Bolivian virus that has been introduced by so much migration" (quoted in Colectivo Simbiosis and Colectivo Situaciones 2011, 28).

The market forms part of an economy that internalizes it, and in that movement it diversifies and becomes more complex: later I will show how it functions as a gear in the textile workshop's prosperity. In addition, the religious festival is part of deciding to leave, of requesting help in the journey; it uses the language of promise, progress, and support in the face of adversity. It is also an excuse to come and go.

The Señor Santiago Bombori, or Tata Bombori ("the force of lightning"), is famous for granting miraculous healing and protecting against curses, and can be prayed to for progress. He is also someone who helps deal with crime and criminal law. In Buenos Aires his name is heard more and more, as the one entrusted with those who migrate—and with those who return if the destination point poses some severe problem. He is a saint who protects the one who leaves and also many times the place from where one comes. According to José Luis Grosso (2007), who has extensively investigated the matter, the cult is expanding, now ranging from Peru to the Buenos Aires urban periphery. But La Salada appears to have been its first stop. As Mario Vargas Ustares, a reporter for the newspaper *Renacer*, recounts, "[It is a] patron saint festival that was brought to Buenos Aires, specifically to the neighborhood of La Salada, by Iván Vargas and his wife, after all of their relatives had emigrated to Argentina, leaving the image of the saint alone and forgotten. At first, the festival was celebrated in La Salada market, but later the devoted reached an agreement to move it to the streets of the neighborhood."

The streets of some neighborhoods and villas, as well as the market and its surroundings, become provisional and operative temples, consecrating a route as an extraordinary space, leaving a wider area in the wake of the parade. By amply *financing* the celebratory economy, the textile workshop, located in both places (the slum and the market), seeks to not be exempted from that spatiality.

If time and space are qualified to the extent that they *give space* and *make time* for the sacred and its expressive forms, inclusion in the festival's dynamic also consecrates that clandestine economy, to the point of converting it into a legitimate piece of a spatial and temporal production of celebration. That spatiotemporality is a careful, reiterative construction. As the artifice of communitarian efficacy, it invents a mode of inhabiting space and signifying time. In the festival, time is shown in its qualitative dimension, state Hubert and Mauss (1964).[28] In other words, the material of its duration is intensity, hence its close link, its simultaneous definition, with festivals. In turn, there is an intimate relationship between the market and the festival: "The qualitative harmonies and discords of the parts of time are of the same nature as those of the festivals. Every fragment of the calendar, every portion of time, whatever it may be, is a true festival, every day is a *Fair*, each day has its saint, every hour its prayer." In short, the qualities of time are nothing more than degrees or modalities of the sacred: sinister or straight, strong or weak, general or particular religiosity.

Festivals mark discontinuity. They indicate intervals, dissect time as continuous, and inaugurate sequences of the coming time. Between the sacred moment and the following secular time there is simultaneously continuity and discontinuity. The festival segments time, divides it, while that secular prolongation is nothing other than waiting for the next festival, the time of its preparation. This will be, as Mauss (1999) says, "the law of collective rhythm, of rhythmic activity for social ends" (96).

The Ch'ixi as a Strategic Notion

Latin American cities, viewed from the perspective of this heterogeneous composition, with the market as one of their main points, are better understood as "motley urban centers," as Rivera Cusicanqui proposes. For Rivera Cusicanqui, this notion of motley involves a historical journey through the very notion of *mestizaje*, its ideological functioning, its internal tension and variation. In that journey, the *mestizo* becomes a simple, deproblematized term referring to the conjunction of elements.

She proposes denouncing and combating the multiculturalism that has been amalgamated in the state-supported neoliberal policies of the 1990s.[29] The neoliberal moment is contested by revolts in different countries across the continent, and multiculturalism becomes an official response as an ornamental and symbolic politics that, as Rivera Cusicanqui indicates, dramatizes the native condition and confines it to the past and the rural environment.

She highlights the mode of fallacious recognition that reproduces the legitimacy of the ruling elite while neutralizing the decolonizing, anticolonial pulse of indigenous vitality. The spatial and temporal confinement of the indigenous is another decisive point. For Rivera Cusicanqui, the enshrined stereotype negates the everydayness of indigenous people; it ignores their own project of modernity and forces them to accommodate themselves in the small boxes of minorities, as finally recognized noble savages. That confinement limits and flattens the indigenous to the occupation of rural space and to an "almost theatrical deployment of alterity"; in other words, they cannot escape a sort of "emblematic identity" associated with certain ethnic and cultural features (Rivera Cusicanqui 2010a, 59; also see Brighenti and Gago 2013). One of the most important political consequences that she warns of is that these mechanisms *deny the ethnicity of the motley urban centers*. In turn, this allows for complying with imperial requirements such as the forced eradication of coca or tax reforms against activities that are classified as contraband.

The widely propagated and celebrated notion of indigenous people (*pueblo originario*), in Rivera Cusicanqui's perspective, both affirms and recognizes, invisibilizes and excludes, the majority of the population of urban centers and networks of the internal market and contraband commerce: "It is an appropriate term for the strategy of disregarding indigenous populations in their majority status and denying their vocation and hegemonic potential and capacity to affect the state" (2010a, 60).

For Rivera Cusicanqui, the project of Indian modernity is a counterimage to the archaizing discourse of the native. The Indians are the ones, as motley collectives, that generate circuits of circulation that produce modern conditions. These motley collectives are a driving force of a long-distance internal market that is capable of guaranteeing capital's expanded reproduction. As a reversal or counterpoint, what is truly archaizing is the falsely modernizing discourse of nineteenth-century elites that operates as an "accessory tokenism" (Rivera Cusicanqui 2010a, 62) to the elites' rentier and feudal character and, as such, is conservative and supportive of successive processes of recolonization.

She concludes that the "insurgent potential of mestizaje" as a perspective rescues the space of colonial comings and goings that rebelled against the colonial levy, that *persevered in the modern national territory and resisted neoliberalism because it was capable of taking up the long memory of the internal colonial market*: the long-distance circulation of goods, the networks of productive communities (waged or not), and the motley and multicultural cultural centers.

On this level, motley urban centers are the space for the realization of projects of migration to the city nourished by successive generations' aspirations of "citizenshipization and metropolitanization" through "access to cultural, symbolic, and material goods that society strenuously denies the indigenous-campesino" (Rivera Cusicanqui 2010b, 107).

This migrant trajectory, along with the experience of economic circuits, organizes the motley composition of urban centers and their economies. On this plane, the concept of the ch'ixi, employed by Rivera Cusicanqui, especially thinking of Bolivia, expresses its conceptual and political power, giving that variegated space the charge of a completely contemporary political, cultural, and economic fabric that is capable of renewing anticolonial indigenous vitality. It is also useful, however, for thinking about it beyond Bolivia, in a space such as La Salada.

The ch'ixi is a reinterpretation of the concept of the motley that René Zavaleta proposed: "The notion of *ch'ixi*, however, is similar to Zavaleta's 'motley society' and proposes the parallel coexistence of multiple cultural differences that do not fuse but antagonize and complement each other. Each reproduces itself from the deepness of the past and relates to the others in a contentious way" (Rivera Cusicanqui 2010a, 70).

The ch'ixi, then, is the possibility of composing the motley lexicon of mestizaje as the popular world challenged by the demands of decolonizing practices. Rivera Cusicanqui continues:

> I consider this to be the most appropriate translation of the motley mixture that we so-called mestizas and mestizos are. The word *ch'ixi* has different connotations: it is a color produced by the juxtaposition, in small points or spots, of two opposite or contrasting colors: black and white, red and green, etc. It is that heather gray that results from the imperceptible mixing of black and white, which are confused in perception but are never completely mixed. The notion of *ch'ixi*, like many others (*allqa, ayni*), obeys the Aymara idea of something that both is and is not, that is, the logic of the included third. The gray *ch'ixi* color is white and not white at the same time, and is also black, its opposite. (2010b, 69)

The ch'ixi contains the strength of the undifferentiated, and "the power of the undifferentiated is that it combines opposites" (70).

Rivera Cusicanqui proposes contrasting the notion of ch'ixi (the motley) with that of *hybridity*, in an open debate with Néstor García Canclini and the decolonial theories that have used it. The hybrid, Rivera Cusicanqui argues, expresses the idea that from the mixture of two differences a complementary third emerges: "a third race or social group capable of fusing the features of their ancestors in a harmonic and heretofore unprecedented mixture" (2010a, 70). In this regard, the contrast with the notion of the motley, elaborated by Zavaleta, is clear: in the motley, there is no fusion of differences. There is antagonism or complementarity.

The similarity is deceitful and slippery in the letter and on the tongue. The heteronymous pair *ch'ixi-chhixi* is essential for restoring the contentious difference between the motley and the hybrid:

> its condition of being "stained," a dialectic without synthesis between antagonistic entities is the *ch'ixi* pole. The hybrid, insubstantial, and perishable mixture, the fusing and softening of the limits: the *chhixi* pole. Only a slight semantic twist, merely an accent, distinguishes the two. Yet in their opposition we can see alternatives and potentialities: on one hand, a decolonizing *taypi*, the possibility of a mestizaje conscious of its indigenous and Castilian (or Jewish, Arab, or Flemish) stains, with a syntax inscribed in the language itself and in the lived experience of contradiction. On the other hand, we see it as the model of an illusory mestizaje: the hypocritical

and median "third republic," which has made a *pä chuyma* language from softening and mutual seduction, a permanent process of duplicity, forgetting, and self-pity. (Rivera Cusicanqui 2010b)

Luis Tapia comments that Zavaleta, when he speaks of a motley social formation, is referring to a "disarticulated overlapping of various societies, that is, of different historical times, different modes of the production of subjectivity, of sociality, and especially different forms of structures of authority or self-government" (2008, 48).

This definition of the motley allows for evoking an image of the *contemporaneity of the noncontemporaneous*: as the overlapping of times, organizational and social flows, production of rules and visions of the world (Bloch 1995). In Zavaleta's usage, however, *overlap* mainly means *fracture*, the subordination of one temporality to another, even in temporality's disarticulation. Meanwhile, such disarticulation enables the parallel coexistence of certain forms of autonomy, the survival of resistances that do support pure adaptation or assimilation to a sole norm.

The motley society, by supporting that multiplicity of societies in the flesh, seems to prevent hegemony as an expansive totality without cracks. It is undermined by a partiality that affirms itself as such. Even if that partiality does not have the force to become a definitive interruption to hegemony, it imprints a nonclosed character onto that "disarticulated overlapping."

Following Zavaleta, but also going beyond him, the notion of motley has new uses and nuances today. If for Zavaleta it implies a negativity in that it expresses a level of disarticulation that he opposes to "the moment of epic fusion with civil society," which constitutes a "mass" (with a national-popular identity) (Tapia 2008b, 50), the recent mobilizations in Bolivia have promoted a reconsideration of the term. The motley goes from referring to a negative disarticulation to demonstrating a form of possible fusion in plurality. These types of struggles marked a new mode of transversality and convergence. Putting this concept in motion, as Tapia (2008) indicates, has to do with the very way in which the last cycle of radical mobilizations has been composed:

You can think of this set of mobilizations that has unfolded since 2000 as the emergence of this diverse and substantial political underground that has mostly been negated by the Bolivian state. In Bolivia it is said that a large part of society or of societies and of groups are organized; in other words, we have an extensive and diverse civil society with experience in self-organization, self-presentation, and, therefore, political action. Only in certain conjunctures does this become political and tend to dissolve the forms of discriminatory hierarchies and forms of exclusion in decision making and also question the economic model and state policies. I prefer to call this "savage politics." (50–51)

The overlapping of organizational forms, traditions, demands, and strategies of struggle with this new contemporaneity is capable of producing a novel form of articulation: "It is the oldest forms that have been renewed and moved to generate this type of condition of fluidity of the political, the social histori- cal, and the possibilities of change in the country" (49). What Tapia here calls *fluidity* we can think of as the current mode in which the contemporaneity of the noncontemporaneous can also be a positive form of mottling or a frame- work for a *savage politics.*

From a compatible perspective, Michael Hardt (2008) also highlights this meaning in relation to Zavaleta's theorization.[30] The motley would express—and enable the capture of—a double plurality: a "general heterogeneity of the forms of labor within capital" and "a cultural, racial, and ethnic motley" (42). A sec- ond disagreement with Zavaleta emerges here: his (also negative) conception of the multitude. While Zavaleta defines it as "something precapitalist, impotent, passive, like the mass and the crowd," Hardt (2008, 43) stresses the opposite: "For us, in change, the multitude form, as we have seen in recent struggles, is capable of autonomously transforming power, the world. And I think that this is the main challenge of the concept of the multitude for us: is it possible that in the motley society, either in labor or in the cultural ethnic sphere, the multitude would be able to organize itself and democratically, autonomously, transform the world, power?"

I will propose, however, a divergence from this division that Hardt makes between the use of the term *motley* to refer to a strictly cultural, racial, and ethnic plane and the use of *heterogeneity* to account for forms of labor. In- stead, I argue that those components become indistinguishable from the qual- ifications of labor, particularly migrant labor.

Promiscuity

I want to note another resonance: between the *motley* and the *promiscuous.* The notion of the promiscuous was developed by Colectivo Situaciones and then put in dialogue with Rivera Cusicanqui; they propose it as the tone of the era, as the logic of coexistence between elements of rebellion and capitalist hegemony. Thus, "ambiguity is converted into the decisive feature of the era and is manifested in a double dimension: as a time of crisis without an end in sight, as a scenario where heterogeneous social logics overlap, without any of them imposing their rule in a definitive way" (Colectivo Situaciones 2009, 9–10). The promiscuous has its own grammar; it is the territory of *and*s: everything fits, everything overlaps, and nothing seems to exclude one thing or another. In this regard, reality is characterized by "dynamics that coexist without a preordained meaning that could order the exchanges and flows or give coherence and stability to collective practices" (40).

A constellation of concepts account for heterogeneity as a complex and key notion of our time. On one hand, it is connected to the pluralization of labor forms and multiplication of subjective forms. On the other hand, it is also tied to how that heterogeneity, which in Latin America has been experienced and thought of as fracture ever since colonialism, today coincides with a mode of organization of post-Fordist capitalism, which expands that recombinant logic of the heterogeneous in a new way.

I am especially interested in tracing the current ways in which the heterogeneous becomes a mode of assembling anachronisms so as to result in a particular temporal regime and also a specific territorial composition.

Another level can be added: that mottling is fundamentally deployed in language. The "heteronymous pairs" that Rivera Cusicanqui (2010b) speaks of are an image, a use of language, that reveals the constant double face, ambivalence, contradiction, or reversal that organizes things not in a sharp binary but as a slippery border, a trembling edge, in which things are and are no longer, mutate, are reversed, or are contaminated in new relations, uses, and meanings. This heteronymity becomes fundamental in the language of heterodox thought and practices. It reveals a mode trained in ambiguity, in the cycles and transformations of things. For Rivera Cusicanqui, it is useful for understanding the "oblique and convoluted" (2010b, 14) modes through which Indian resistance took form.

Between the Ch'ixi and the Motley

One possible English translation of the notion ch'ixi could be "motley."[31] This is the adjective that was used to translate into English the way in which Karl Marx and Friedrich Engels (in *The German Ideology* [1998]) refer to the men and women expropriated by the English enclosures, classified as the "motley crowd" (Linebaugh and Rediker 2000).

Historians Peter Linebaugh and Marcus Rediker signal two meanings of the "motley crowd": first, a group that performs similar tasks or has a common objective (for example, those who worked in sugar and tobacco plantations or on ship crews) and, second, a sociopolitical formation of eighteenth-century ports or cities. The latter concerns the era of enclosures that Marx refers to in *Capital* (1977). The former takes the term to the more distant origins of transatlantic capitalism; "the 'motley crowd' in this sense was closely related to the urban mob and the revolutionary crowd" (Linebaugh and Rediker 2000, 213). Additionally, since the beginning of its usage, *motley* has also meant "multiethnic."

But Linebaugh and Rediker find another vein for the meaning of the word *motley*:

> In the habits of royal authority in Renaissance England, the "motley" was a multicolored garment, often a cap, worn by a jester who was permitted by the king to make jokes, even to tell the truth, to power. As an insignium, the motley brought carnivalesque expectations of disorder and subversion, a little letting-off of steam. By extension, *motley* could also refer to a colorful assemblage, such as a crowd of people whose tatterdemalion dress made it interesting. A motley crowd might very likely be one in rags, or a *"lumpen"*-proletariat (from the German word for "rags"). Although we write about and emphasize the interracial character of the motley crew, we wish that readers would keep these other meanings—the subversion of power and the poverty in appearance—in mind. (2000, 27–28)

The motley composition—in its multiplicity of meanings: the form of mixture, clothing, a capacity for sabotage, an ambivalence between what it is and what it is not—has to do with a way of denying the declassified, déclassé potencia of labor, while also making use of it. The motley composition is something like an *aleatory proletariat* that can be framed as a proletariat only by chance and in a discontinuous way. In other words, it could be said that it is precisely its random character that is a crucial fact for the successive reframings of men and women that capital captures and exploits as labor power. The composition of laboring forces is more closely associated with what Louis Althusser (2006) called the "materialism of the encounter." The materialism "of the rain, the swerve, the encounter, the take [prize]" (167) rejects need and origin, reason and cause, as explanations of events. The question is how something manages to become consistent and how that encounter can or cannot take place.[32]

The reference to an aleatory proletariat as an image that can be linked to a motley crowd attempts to emphasize the randomness of the whole and the contingency of its formation. Once the encounter has been produced, there is an accomplished fact, from which it is possible to derive tendencies, even laws, but it starts with the randomness of the encounter. Althusser cites Marx speaking of the mode of production as a "particular combination between elements":

> The elements do not exist in history so that a mode of production may exist, they exist in history in a "*floating*" *state* prior to their "accumulation" and "combination," each being the product of its own history, and none being the teleological product of the others or their history. When Marx and Engels say that the proletariat is "the product of big industry," they utter a very great piece of nonsense, positioning themselves within the *logic of the accomplished fact of the reproduction of the proletariat on an extended scale*, not the aleatory logic of the "encounter" which produces (rather than reproduces), as the proletariat, this mass of impoverished, expropriated human beings as one of the elements making up the mode of production. In the process, Marx and Engels shift from the first conception of the mode of production, an historico-aleatory conception, to a second, which is essentialist and philosophical. I am repeating myself, but I must: what is remarkable about the first conception, apart from the explicit theory of the encounter, is the idea that every mode of production comprises *elements that are independent of each other*, each resulting from its own specific history, in the absence of any organic, teleological relation between these diverse histories. This conception culminates in the theory of *primitive accumulation*. (2006, 198–99)

Like Deleuze and his concept of *agencement*, Althusser emphasizes the aleatory nucleus and the dynamic of reciprocal determination of the elements in play, signaling their independence from one another. This raises the machinic enigma or the chance of deviation of the combinatorial moment in which a certain (primary) accumulation takes place, that first moment of the launching of a new era of accumulation.

The Market as a Motley Social Space

The market is a thick space, with multiple layers, meanings, and transactions. It is a motley space that simultaneously cherishes traditions and is heretical in respect to many of them, that serves as a celebratory environment and a space of disputes, as a moment of encounter, consumption, and diversion but also an intense place of work and business, of competition and opportunism. It is maintained and develops as a massive business based on kinship, neighborhood, and friendship networks. It is also an economy of diverse languages: of costumes, dances, promises, meals, and excesses. The motley here is not, however, a cultural trait or a colorful difference but rather the sustenance of the immeasurability of these economies.

La Salada, while confined to a symbolic and geographic border territory, also has a proliferating dynamic that replicates, in other neighborhoods and cities, in Argentina and beyond, both the merchandise and the market form that characterizes La Salada. In turn, it represents a model of an open-air commercial center that challenges all the classic economic categories: informal versus formal, legal versus illegal, and so on. It works in harmony with similar spaces in other parts of the world, which could be classified as nuclei of nonhegemonic commerce.

I define this as a transnational network supported by multiple proletarian microeconomies. Therefore, as I have noted, it is revealed to be a privileged space for analyzing how the informal economy is primarily constituted by the strength of the unemployed, migrants, and women, which could be read as a response from below to the dispossessive effects of neoliberalism.[33]

Its urban impact is decisive (even though it is not marked on maps): a city like Buenos Aires finds itself transformed by this new, informal, predominantly migrant and feminine tide, which, with its hustle and bustle and transactions, functions as an agent for restructuring capital and urban space.

La Salada is a multitudinous web producing nonstate welfare. With the new project of becoming a food market, La Salada achieves, in a paradoxical and diverse way, what many experiments in the social economy proposed to do in the culminating moment of the Argentinean crisis of 2001: to cut costs, eliminate intermediaries, and contribute to massive popular consumption. It is a decisive intervention during times of high inflation, like the current moment.

La Salada displays great versatility and flexibility in terms of political organization, through multitudinous assemblies, leaders, and thousands of stall operators who organize the day-to-day of the market and connect it to other spaces like the slum, the workshop, and the festival. An image of unregulated open space gives way to a complex coordination of an infinity of flows. Festiveness and mysticism (virgins, saints, miracles, ekekos) accompany the bonanza. Ultimately, it is a mode of urban progress that escapes plans and blueprints. Migrant labor, in particular, allows us to question the idea of a normalization in the world of work, that is, a pattern of strictly wage labor and a workforce composed of Argentine nationals.

The market, as part of a complex assemblage with the economy of the textile workshop, is an especially productive territory for thinking the ambivalence of the common: that is to say, the multiple uses, conflicts, appropriations, and reinventions of a communitarian capital that is capable of functioning as a resource for self-management, mobilization, and insubordination but also, with no less intensity, as a source of servitude, submission, and exploitation, which rightly points out that the communitarian experience is a key moment of the social wealth under dispute.

Baroque Economies

A baroque economy like La Salada has, then, a similar logic to the bricoleur discussed by Claude Lévi-Strauss (1966): a capacity to bring together elements that at first appear to be dissimilar or to correspond to incompatible regimes, a heterogeneous composition of fragments and dynamics that do not resist an analysis of purity but, on the contrary, reveal a plurality of forms in an uneven meshwork. Armando Bartra (2005) notes this characteristic for certain domestic peasant economies: wagering on various activities without making the economy depend on one unique and specialized activity.

I call them *baroque economies* because the baroque refers to the *hodgepodge*. In La Salada this baroque style also has to do with imitation, the reign of the copy. "Every imitator is a manufacturer, a polytechnician," Rancière (2004, 30) says in regard to a fundamental topic: "imitators are responsible for a particular production," that which "reproduces and falsifies the image of the necessary." Imitators' power is their general power: "the power of the double, of representing anything whatsoever or being anyone whosoever" (10). Imitation or counterfeiting allows for overturning the stipulated consumption, places, and roles. Suddenly, anyone can consume anything. Products that are supposedly ranked by cost and brand start being consumed by anyone.

Additionally, in the market, those who migrate find the possibility of changing jobs, professions, aspirations. From there arises the strength of progress as the possibility of a transition, a change. Balibar says that only the prospect of "unlimited progress, that is, the idealized collective desire to effectively arrive at equality of opportunity for everyone in society, could maintain the pressure that tended to curtail privileges and hold perennial forms of domination in check, enlarging the space of freedom for the masses" (2014, 19); in other words, pressure is the motor of social citizenship. In migrant trajectories, this idealized collective pressure-desire for expanding rights is revived under that formula of the "antinomy of progress." However, unlike that amalgam between progressivism and statism that for Balibar characterizes the limits of nineteenth- and twentieth-century socialism, the aspiration of progress is no longer completely fused into the statist horizon but rather evokes—as Rivera Cusicanqui notes—a poststatist communitarian horizon in fully urban contexts.

When applied to popular economies, the baroque refers to the heterogeneity of productive forms: it is sufficiently flexible to combine and mix family workshops, home work, informal enterprises, and kinship networks with highly consumed brands, exportation networks, and transnational transactions. In its own way, it reissues a "baroque modernity" in Bolivia, as Álvaro García Linera refers to it, by unifying, "in a tiered and hierarchical manner, the production-structures of the fifteenth, eighteenth, and twentieth centuries" (2014, 212). It is also the repetition of servile or semislave labor (from the maquiladora to the textile workshop) as an important, but nonhegemonic, segment of transnational economies in capitalist globalization, which confirms that modality as a (post)modern component of the organization of work and not an archaic remnant of an overcome premodern, or precapitalist, past. The Universal Exposition of production forms that Virno (2004) talks about in defining post-Fordism is a different image, but one that is in dialogue with the baroque: the simultaneous coexistence of modes that, by means of forms that tend to be ever more modern and "free," challenge the linear narrative of progress and overcoming.

This baroque effect is translated onto the city. The dynamics led by the migrant labor force in Argentina give rise to a spatial reconfiguration through "new cross-border geographies of centrality and marginality" constituted by these territorial processes (Sassen 1999, 141). Understanding geopolitical processes in this way destabilizes the center-periphery division as it was understood thirty years ago: as a segmentation based on distinctions between nation-states. The market is a laboratory where many of these changes are expressed and where a new form of *making the city* is anticipated.

In this regard, La Salada is a singular space in which the categories of *territory* and *labor power* are juxtaposed, two categories that, as Sandro Mezzadra (2008) notes, are fundamental coordinates for explaining the *heterogeneity of global space* as a result of (a) the *explosion* of nation-state geographies and (b) the *implosion* that forces certain territories and actors into unexpected connections that enable processes of production and labor exploitation. A perspective emerges from La Salada for understanding how the borders between entrepreneurship and politics, between community and exploitation, between tradition and innovation, are being diluted.

Past Futures

A series of conditions that were previously considered superficial or external to the world of work paradoxically become key for expanding and politicizing the concept of work itself. I am particularly interested in two orientations that stand out. The first is the properly postcolonial orientation, which includes the ethnic-racial-national dimension, and the second is the micropolitical perspective, which includes the phenomena of sexual desire, struggles related to gender, and the refusal of family traditionalism. Félix Guattari's (2004) concept of "integrated world capitalism" allows for understanding capital's "response" to the rebellions in 1968 as *deterritorialization* of the nation-state's authority and also *transnational* integration, through a project of polycentric control: the world market. Such integration produces supplementary state functions, which are expressed in specific ways through a network of international institutions. Thus, the political cartography of exploitation at the global scale must record both planetary expansion and the molecular infiltration of control mechanisms, understanding them as attempts by capital to translate all life sequences into exchange terms (to quantify them economically and dominate them politically). It is necessary to understand them as a whole, since "in accumulation it is possible to establish a close link between the ways of organizing contracts governing property, sexuality, nationality, and racial, ethnic, or civil belonging, and the control of waged workers in the process of accumulation. Hence the violence of the confrontations in these terrains that are seemingly far removed from the economy and 'wage' struggles" (Moulier Boutang 2006, 43).

Both of these lines restructure struggles by expanding them into a terrain that encompasses diverse dimensions of (individual and collective) social life. Many authors have denominated this terrain of conflict as *biopolitical* (Foucault 2007; Negri 2006). In other words, today the governability of the labor market requires including the government of dimensions that increasingly overflow the limits of the workplace. Or, to phrase it in a positive formulation: the workplace includes in an increasingly direct way dimensions that must be governed as internal to labor power. It could be said that it has always operated in this way (even if it was not always read and made visible as such). The paradoxical dimension of domestic work as a source of absolute rent while it is denied as such would allow for establishing a concrete history of the incorporation of knowledges, uses, and forces that were simultaneously exploited and considered to be external (or directly disregarded) into the system of capitalist valorization. However, there is something new: to produce is increasingly to produce social relations, and, in that regard, production increasingly lies in the production of men and women as such.

Then the question is, how has the workforce become more intensely dependent on vital dimensions that up until three decades ago still had a chance of, even if only formally, being perceived and analyzed as external to the workforce's qualification? From the problem of the *great fixing in place* of the labor force to the exploitation of *differentials of mobility*: this could define a *continuum* of governability that has varied and experienced diverse forms of the subsumption of labor. In turn, this line expresses an extension of the vital variables to governing, since the production of value increasingly depends on a subjective intensity put to work and less on the repetition of a set of dry efforts and gestures.

How is what has occurred since the end of the 1970s a new *great transformation*, to use Karl Polanyi's (1944) classic expression? Posing the question in this way can mitigate the different viewpoints from which "change," its "intensity," and its relationship to the crisis (understood in positive or negative terms) are considered, while it also allows for reevaluating the whole lexicon that appears to have been enshrined as common sense during the Fordist period. Thus, setting concepts in motion emerges as a requirement of the very question to be addressed: how do we understand the history (or histories) of labor today?

Looking from today (simultaneously toward the past and at our present moment), we can see the sequence of anomalies that characterized the development of labor, thus allowing a key nonprogressivist historical critique. In turn, it is essential to have a global perspective that goes beyond the nation-state as the privileged axis of political, social, and economic organization, without thereby abandoning the need to discover the current forms of reconfiguration of state authority and its procedures of entanglement with the increasing globalization of capital. Last, the struggles plaguing labor today cannot be understood without a political valorization of the meaning of precarity as an existential, social, and anthropological condition. Determining what type of organizational strategy to produce depends on it.

The Contemporaneity of the Noncontemporaneous

Using Virno's words, the question is how to characterize the historical time that appears to *simultaneously* expose the universal history of labor that unfolds like a spotted and uneven print. This synchronous character that Virno points to is decisive, not because it erases hierarchies nor because it flattens time. Quite the opposite: it folds over the present in a way that complicates and makes us wary of any remnant of linear history. For this reason, he highlights another concept: "the contemporaneity of the noncontemporaneous" (2015b, 140). If Universal Exposition traces a spatial axis, an extensive plane, the *contemporaneity of the noncontemporaneous* is the axis of temporal intensity.

Originally used by Ernst Bloch (1995), this expression attempts to account for the overlapping logics, elements, and circumstances that, at first glance, do not seem to have a temporal adaptation. As if it were an erroneous or incongruent overlap, what is dissimilar in chronological terms is brought together again on a new common surface. The temporal dislocation thus refers to a challenged order: the norm according to which that which no longer was does not have a reason to return and that which exists does not have a reason for coexisting with that which occurred in another moment. The notion of progressivism—as succession and replacement, as improvement and advance—is profoundly questioned. After critiquing progress, a second step remains: What temporality is expressed in this possibility of simultaneity?

Virno proposes radicalizing the formulation in the following way:

What is meant by contemporaneity of the noncontemporaneous is, first, the coexistence of thought and execution, the potential "before" and the action "later," nonchronological past and determined present, that characterizes any historical moment. Since it consists of two diachronic elements, the most simple cell of temporality has a hybrid or *anachronistic* nature. The contemporaneity of the noncontemporaneous originally manifests in the fact that the immediate and indivisible here and now, besides being perceived, is also remembered as it is being experienced. If we do not recognize this fundamental anachronism, which supports all historical moments, we will not be able to understand the countless empirical anachronisms (the barter economy, the tenacious traditionalism of the Chinese family working in software, etc.) that sometimes appear in a particular historical moment. As for capitalism, it is true that it promotes the contemporaneity of the noncontemporaneous. Yet, in contrast to a litany repeated for decades, it is not about the coexistence of atavistic superstitions and technology. The crucial point is the theatrical exhibition of the juxtaposition of potential and act, an undefined "then" and a datable "now." The concomitance of the diachronic finally becomes explicit. Late capitalism . . . is the time when it emerges to the surface, with the relief that corresponds to a very concrete phenomenon, the radical anachronism on which the very historicity of experience depends. (2003, 149–50)

Empirical anachronisms is a suggestive way to name that proliferation of labor modes—which today are modes of life—that coexist in a new temporal unit. It is also a philosophical reference to the temporal disjunction that, for Virno, is the key to the historicity of experience: the gap between potential and act. It is a constituent disjunction for understanding labor, insofar as it is the central gap between labor power and the concrete act of labor, the heart of the Marxian explanation of surplus value.

Following Virno's argument (2003, 2015), we can conclude that historical time and potencia are necessarily intertwined notions. In other words, potencia and the act are temporalizing notions. As virtual and actual, they are concepts of human experience. The act situates in *cronos* that which potencia involves in a virtual way. A word, a labor operation, a loving gesture, and a political revolt are situated in time and shape it, but only to the extent that a potential of language, a power of labor (that is, potential), an aptitude for love, and a capacity for political rebellion are already acting as a condition of possibility for the act. It is true that the act excludes the potential. Executing a linguistic presentation, saying a word, also implies the preexistence of language as a faculty of the power of speaking, and supposes that when some words are stated, a sentence, for example, all other possible words and sentences remain radically not said.

I want to emphasize the following: potential and act are remade; they occur and they exclude each other. That the potential preexists the act should not be understood based on a chronological representation of time. On the contrary, the chronological presentation depends on this precedence. The potential precedes the act only because potential has the form of a past in general, a nonchronological past, a past that was never present and will not remain behind as present that has been. The past of potential is strictly contemporary with the now of the act. Virno's complex reasoning (on the real-virtual) is the result of an elaborated reading of Henri Bergson. Deleuze also took up a reading of Bergson in order to think a noncontrolled, nonnormalized time. Deleuzian philosophy incorporated Bergson in a point that it is important to return to: the idea of potential cannot be understood in the Aristotelian tradition according to which potential is teleologically marked by the act, nor is potential realized in the act. Thus, the unfolding of an open virtual, in continuous differentiation (what Bergson calls *duration*), is the basis for a *philosophy of difference* that seeks to provide us with essentially dynamic concepts of a folding, differentiating time.

Anachronism and Postcolonialism

Thus, anachronism is postulated as epistemology: as a paradigm of historical interrogation, it supposes the intrusion of one era into another. Virno, referring to images, argues that it is a temporal mode capable of capturing the excess, the complexity, and overdetermination that simultaneously operate in that which occurs. The procedure that he proposes is, then, that of a montage of dissimilar times that trace an effective history to the extent that it is a history "of discontinuity."

For Georges Didi-Huberman (2006), anachronism, a nodal piece of an impure way of narrating time, is related to notions like symptom, malaise, and ghostly and cursed survivals—in short, all names of that which prevents the closure of history, its canonical repetition, its conclusive tone. These resources, on the contrary, propose a method of imagination, quotation, unconscious and cryptic memory, and the poetic, procedures that exhibit a special affinity with "anachronistic historicity" and "symptomatic significance" (13).

Like Virno, this perspective centers the present as the privileged moment of a time in which the discontinuous, the nonlinear, becomes the organizational key to capitalism. The discontinuous and nonlinear are no longer features of a marginal experience but the dominant mode of our *present*. Our present is a moment in which the differentials of time move to the forefront as the organization of the real. If the modern experience privileged the homogeneous and continuous, anachronism remained relegated to the cursed part of history. In post-Fordism—another way of naming the crisis of modernity—it is the heterogeneous as a spatiotemporal experience that appears to respond to the dynamic of the strictly present.

Mezzadra (2008, 14) speaks of "differential inclusion"—as a new twist in the extensive history of this concept—to define the features of contemporary capitalism that operate through a logic of connections and disconnections, which fragments and unifies at the same time. Yet what differentiates this logic of articulation of differences from how the international division of labor has always been composed? For Mezzadra, it is about making room for a "postcolonial view" that, without losing sight of the divergences and hierarchies between places, regions, and continents, allows for understanding the heterogeneous fabric of productive regimes, temporalities, and subjective experiences associated with labor.

The postcolonial, in this open usage proposed by Mezzadra, becomes a "postcolonial condition," accounting for the implosion of the map that assigned clear and distinct borders between the center and the periphery and, therefore, assigned minor roles to Third World countries, negating their role in *constituting* modernity and therefore the so-called First World, as well as initiatives that were creating a corpus of experiences and texts of an *alternative* modernity.

The idea that the decolonial perspective is predominant in Latin America has been widely disseminated, but it must be confronted in a critical frame. The first Spanish translation of postcolonial debates was published in Bolivia in the 1990s in a compilation edited by Rivera Cusicanqui and Rossana Barragán. It was framed within a long history of political and conceptual problematization that Rivera Cusicanqui had engaged in since the 1970s around internal colonialism and practices of indigenous insubordination. She has made the most radical critique of the decolonial lexicon consecrated by the North American academy, aspiring to forge an academic canon. That critique has various levels; some of its main features can be summarized as follows:

1. For Rivera Cusicanqui, it is not simply about "inverting the hierarchy without touching the dualism (Guha dixit)" and using the catchphrase of Eurocentrism to construct new, clean binaries. This declassifying movement that she outlines is what allows for understanding even the "processes of whitening as survival strategies: there you must look at who appropriates force and not who wallows in pity or ceases to be pure" (Gago 2015).

2. "The postcolonial is a desire, the anti-colonial is a struggle, and the decolonial is a neologism of unsympathetic fashion." This formula synthesizes the nonhomogeneous or nonexchangeable use of the three notions. In this respect, Rivera Cusicanqui argues that to radicalize alterity, "difference must be deepened and radicalized: in, with, and against the subaltern" (Gago 2015). It is a mode of presenting the

question that also allows for circumventing the perverse relationship that is constructed when the structure is "indigenous resentment and non-indigenous guilt," the affective basis of populism.

3. Finally, the proposal is a "political economy" of knowledge that distances itself from the (multi- and pluri-)culturalist and purely discursive foci.

CHAPTER 2

Between La Salada and the Workshop

Communitarian Wealth in Dispute

The migrant presence of Bolivian women and men in Argentina produces a resonance between the conjunctures of the crisis of neoliberalism in the two countries. This is expressed in a series of political-economic articulations that expose a world of new popular institutions and transactions. The dissemination of communitarian elements, in this regard, is inseparable from both internal and transnational migrant movements. The effects of these displacements spread and disperse organizational elements that are recombined as forces and resources of a new popular economy and innovative forms of social organization. This communitarian dynamism contrasts with accounts that cast it in essentialist and purely stabilizing images.

As I said earlier, the informal economy in Argentina became visible as it grew massively as a consequence of the crisis at the beginning of the twenty-first century and the intense demonetization that prevailed at the time. *The notion of community plays a fundamental role in the conjunction of the informal economy and neoliberalism.* Although community is traditionally characterized as a premodern form of social organization, displaced and violated since the formation of nation-states, its timeliness, on the contrary, has to do with its ways of persisting in the midst of capitalist globalization, linked to the partial denationalization of the state itself and to the assemblages that I discussed in the previous chapter.

Mutation and Persistence

Community persists only insofar as this persistence serves to highlight community's *forms of mutation*: What does community mean when confronted with precarious labor? What types of resources does it imply for transnational migrant economies? What social articulation does it provide faced with weakening nation-states? Situating and submerging these questions in the comings and goings of the migrant economy can *account for the existence of the communitarian with markedly ambiguous characteristics*: versatile, self-managed, and a vehicle for exploitation and new forms of servitude.

Communitarian traditions and knowledges, primarily originating in the indigenous history of Bolivia, present themselves in Argentina today as double-sided: *as a resource for taking advantage of a cheap workforce disposed to being extremely flexible and at the same time as a resource for self-managed neighborhood organization*. This experience is translated into the terms of *communitarian capital*, which is ambiguous in that it is simultaneously exploited by the clandestine textile workshops and by experiences of urban self-management. The *flexibility of community belonging* becomes a key element for the articulation of a specific migrant workforce, the construction of urban settlements organized by multiple belongings and relationships, and (national and transnational) brands' exploitation of that ethos: the communal training and know-how, which the global economy's assembly lines can turn to their own advantage. Thus, migrant trajectories coming from Bolivia take advantage of an extensive production of imaginaries and subjectivities connected to the communitarian and a prolific weaving of (familial, festive, commercial, etc.) networks. The strategic relocation of such a communitarian ethos to forms of transnational urban economy permanently opens two levels of analysis: in its disruptive operation regarding the disciplinarian logic of the city itself and in its functionality for a servile type of exploitation.

In this way, community is a key concept for analyzing the problems traversing the economy, because it expresses a level on which the collective itself is defined by a set of common practices—language, customs, relationships, values, and so on—rather than by state sovereignty's effective configuring intervention. Along this line, we can explore how the communitarian functions as the language of the economy of migration in certain circuits, as well as a concrete form of the appropriation and redefinition of space (the emergence of a communitarian dynamic indicates a moment of reconfiguration of a collective composition that is already recognized by the juridical order). The questions can be summarized as follows: What type of temporality is supposed by the community? What kind of urban space can it construct? Is there a community value?

Crisis and Community

The *communitarian dynamic* does not have an immutable essence to cling to; therefore, there is no purity to turn to or defend. In other words, *it depends on concrete spatiotemporal assemblages.* The communitarian functioning I explore here is inscribed in the coordinates of post-Fordist capitalism and, more specifically, within the challenge to neoliberalism posed by the crisis in 2001. My hypothesis is that the communitarian mechanism has an *intimate relationship with the temporality of crisis.* It provides resources for self-management when confronted with widespread institutional dissolution. It assumes forms of exchange and social relations that do not have an institutional consistency a priori. It delimits a space of meaning in the face of generalized emptiness. The community, therefore, is a mode of interaction of bodies without a natural historical substrate outside of that game. It is an eminently political form of self-constitution.

After 2001, a cycle begins in Argentina with the crisis as its permanent virtuality. This means that many features of the crisis—especially the exhibition of instability and precarity as dynamics of the social—become the premises for all collective, institutional, para-institutional, or noninstitutional action.

To be more precise: the communitarian mechanism articulates modes of doing, saying, and seeing that are linked to migrant trajectories. It is a technology that connects diverse territories and reorganizes urban space. Yet it also exhibits a new composition of the labor force that has become especially visible in recent years. That new social composition bears the crisis of neoliberalism as an indelible mark.

In this regard, the emergence and popularization of new forms of informal, illegal, or precarious labor, especially since 2001, and the subsequent decline of the challenges to wage labor arising from the most radicalized sectors of the *piquetero* movement, made the migrant workforce visible as a crucial element of the economic recomposition based on new labor forms. It does this in various ways:

a. as the public exposition of certain expanded and *exceptional* (in terms of contracts, working conditions, pay, requirements, etc.) employment conditions;

b. as the other side of the refusal of work insofar as migrant labor is advertised with the equation: *profitability for submission*;

c. as the incorporation of self-management into the service of new popular business dynamics articulated with the logic of transnational companies and brands;

d. in coexistence with a political discourse at the government level that emphasizes the *national* possibilities of recovery from the crisis and of the political system;

e. in tandem with a reframing—and reactive moralization—of the mass subsidies that go from being unemployment subsidies to becoming compensation for "work" (later I will discuss up to what point these subsidies are in fact oriented toward *consumption*);

f. as a disciplinary element for decreasing the price of labor by devaluing the currency, which incorporates this price at the transnational global scale of competition (in this regard, as Yann Moulier Boutang [2006] argues, the maximum decrease in the cost of migrant labor puts a [material and symbolic] limit on the decrease in wages that national workers can assert themselves against);

g. as the advantage, both for the market and for the political consensus, of the consolidation of a new segmentation of labor, which received a boost following the impact of the crisis;

h. as the explanation for the appearance of forms of urban marginalization and poverty centered on work and not unemployment, giving rise to new class formations.

Let me be more specific about the relationship that I am proposing between the recomposition of labor, migrant economies, and communitarian practices. What is the connection between the emergence of so-called slave labor in the clandestine textile workshops located in Argentina and the expansion of this communitarian dynamic as the economic force of migration? What relationship is there between slave labor and the feminization of work? How are the feminine and the communitarian linked?

There have been forms of *affinity* and overlap between slave labor and women's labor since the beginning of modernity, as well as between the ways in which their resistance to exploitation has been organized. A few common points can be indicated—the historical foundations of such analogies (the production of a certain value form, a subordinated position in production, specific characteristics of their exploitation)—to conjecture that the *emergence of forms of slave labor in the local textile industry at the beginning of the twenty-first century is related to the crisis in 2001 and to a tendency toward the recomposition of labor that takes on the structural modifications proposed by neoliberalism.*

Informalization and Feminization: Toward Slave Labor?

The informalization of the economy reintroduces the categories of home and community as important economic spaces and reinterprets them to its advantage. In Argentina the crisis of neoliberalism led to the widespread use of subsidies as a way of getting through this crisis in the world of work. The logic of the enterprises promoted by these subsidies can be categorized as a drive toward initiatives based in the household and in the community.

This means that social assistance is articulated, particularly in times of crisis like 2001, based on domestic-communitarian economies in popular neighborhoods. The crisis was a moment when so-called domestic labor (of care, feeding a neighborhood, etc.) moved to the forefront because it was massively articulated with unemployment subsidies and in many households became the only source of income. Since then, the social protagonism during the crisis has also led to a political reshaping of public assistance: the distribution of food, traditionally a domestic task, was a fundamental moment in the formation of movements and enterprises that, in many cases, demanded autonomy from the state, appropriating its resources and collectively redirecting the use of those individually allocated benefits. In the crisis of 2001, social reproduction became independent from employment relations, in turn showing how the notion of *employment* is distanced from that of the (biopolitical) production of social value, capable of sustaining forms of socialization in crisis.

In itself, neighborhood-territorial organization requires domestic knowledges, and, at the same time, it projects them onto a public-political space in a very special way when the crisis is simultaneously a crisis of political representation and of the mediating function of institutions in general. This supposes that in popular experience there is a capacity to reappropriate an instrument of governmentality that, since its origins, has represented the state's onslaught against alternative forms of socialization in order to, after producing dispossession, restatize the social (Hirsch 1996). It is worth remembering that since its beginnings public assistance was (1) a decisive moment in the statist relationship between workers and capital and in the definition of the state's function; (2) the first recognition of the *unsustainability* of the capitalist system, which rules by hunger and terror; and (3) the first step toward the reconstruction of the state as the guarantor of class relations, as the supervisor of the reproduction and disciplining of the labor force (Donzelot 1979; Federici 2004, 84). What is being debated now is the possibility of the appropriation and tactical use of these resources that were originally distributed as social assistance.

I want to highlight how public assistance is entangled with the management of the crisis of wage labor in order to bring new elements into the debate over a politics of *governance* of the social. Maurizio Lazzarato (2006) argues that the languages of assistance and the labor market are today intertwined. The hypothesis is that both operate by managing scarce labor and, therefore, promoting the artificial creation of employment, but under a logic of the subsidy. The passage from the unemployment subsidies of the Plan Jefes y Jefas de Hogar (Heads of Household Program), which were used massively in the midst of the crisis, to their reconfiguration into the Plan Argentina Trabaja (Argentina Works Program) exemplifies this tendency in a literal way.[1] This dynamic simultaneously occurs in the proliferation of informal, multifaceted forms of work.

The Feminization of Space: The Community and the Home as Inputs

The feminization of these economies is inscribed within the framework of the crisis of wage labor, weaving the fabric through which the community and the home become essential for thinking about wealth. Dora Barrancos classifies this relationship between women's protagonism and crisis in broad terms: "There are countless historical settings in which 'feminine nature' is forged, not as an incardination, as an eccentric outside, but rather as an element that is immanent to the crisis" (2013, 253). She puts particular emphasis on Argentine history from the Mothers of the Plaza de Mayo to the *piqueteras*: "I will insist on the upheaval in standards, norms, and expectations of gender that emerges from crises, and on the hypothesis that the greater the severity of the damages, the more expressive is that which I call feminine visibility in the agora. Women loosen the chains and defy the normative restrictions that restrain them as subjects of private meaning" (2013, 257).

The feminization of labor involves a twofold process: on one hand, women's public presence increases, positioning them as important economic actors, at the same time as tasks undertaken by men in that same informal economy are feminized. On the other hand, it transfers characteristics of the economy of the household or the community, usually understood in neighborhood terms, into the public sphere. Some questions arise from highlighting this perspective: how does this feminization of the economy alter domestic and labor hierarchies? To what extent does such feminization of the economy refer to a tendency that cannot be reduced to the quantity of women that become part of it but rather is a qualitative modification of labor processes and forms of exchange?

According to Saskia Sassen (2003), women combine two different dynamics. On one hand, they integrate an invisible and powerless class of workers in the service of strategic sectors of the economy (they have no chance of unionizing or constituting a labor aristocracy). At the same time, access to an income, albeit small, feminizes the commercial opportunities produced by the informalization of the economy and transforms gendered hierarchies.

Certain subsidies, organized under a logic of microfinancing of enterprises and self-managed initiatives, allow the neoliberal perspective to be compatible with popular and communitarian forms of livelihoods. The know-how involved in domestic-reproductive labor, along with a complex repertoire of communitarian practices and knowledges, created a web of multiple economies in the midst of the crisis that enabled thousands of people to survive, while it displayed the powerful political capacity of popular self-management.

There are affinities between the feminine and the communitarian that categorize these economies in a particular way: the ability to work at microscales, confidence in the value of the affective as a productive moment, experience of the minoritarian as a specific *potencia*. The historical character of these features has to do with a dense history of subjectivities associated with reproductive labor, historically relegated to a functional and highly *productive* marginalization, as Christian Marazzi (2011) indicates under the concise image of the subjective history that is hidden in "the place of the socks." In moments of crisis like 2001, those qualities take on a directly political profile and begin fulfilling strategic functions in social organization while they also nourish neoliberalism's capacity to develop as governmentality.

If neoliberal premises "seek to strengthen or establish women as self-employed workers in small enterprises that are modeled upon capitalist enterprise" (Gibson-Graham 2005, 147), it is also necessary to see their other side: the moment of subjectivation and autonomy represented by these economies, which, as such, pose a challenge to hegemonic economies. Along this line, the feminist J. K. Gibson-Graham theorizes what they call "diverse economies" as "producing a language of economic difference to enlarge the economic imaginary, rendering visible and intelligible the diverse and proliferating practices that the preoccupation with capitalism has obscured" (133). For these feminists, the language of economic difference is inspired by some crucial counterdiscourses: research about domestic labor as unpaid and invisibilized labor in countries' national statistics, studies of informal economies and their integration into North-South transactions, as well as the language of *Capital* (Marx 1977) about economic difference when it is not captured by historical stage theory and developmentalism, according to a systemic conception of the economy.

The *language of economic difference* becomes a way of detecting other processes of becoming, paying special attention to their situated character, which is the importance of the category of place: "In more broadly philosophical terms, place is that which is not fully yoked into a system of meaning, not entirely subsumed to a (global) order; it is that aspect of every site that exists as potentiality. Place is the 'event in space,' operating as a 'dislocation' with respect to familiar structures and narratives. It is the unmapped and unmoored that allows for new moorings and mappings. Place, like the subject, is the site and spur of becoming, the opening for politics" (Gibson-Graham 2005, 132).

The idea is not simply to oppose alternative economies to capitalist domination but rather to unravel certain economic practices in terms of their difference and to reintroduce contingency into thinking about the economy. But it is also to remove this economic diversity from the frameworks in which it was traditionally thought: as economies that were traditional, based in the family, backward, in opposition to the modern. Thinking with a logic of economic difference, according to Gibson-Graham's list, is a challenge that requires materializing the different types of transactions and ways of negotiating commensurability, the different types of labor and ways of compensating them, and the different forms of enterprises and ways of producing, appropriating, and distributing surplus. These criteria can serve to displace the communal from its precapitalist connotation, but also to avoid projecting it as a utopian-redemptive modality, as a savior from the commercial world. I aim to use this concept in relation to its ability to account for other economic logics based on their undisguised heterogeneity.

Community economies are not a celebration of the local. They are a way of accounting for a new combination of scales, capable of assembling dynamics, productive modes, knowledges, and circuits that at first appear to be incompatible. In this sense, place refers to a situated singularity. Again, community must be removed from its conception as territorial circumscription that risks becoming a form of confinement. On the contrary, the communitarian is simultaneously a form of rootedness and projection that, nevertheless, cannot be enclosed as a cliché of a prefabricated "alternative economy" or a type of ideally re-created solidarity. In this regard, the communitarian becomes operative to the extent that it is capable of opening an analysis of the terrains of economic experimentation beyond "formal markets, wage labor and capitalist enterprise" (Gibson-Graham 2005, 137).

The empty, nonprescriptive character of what they understand as community economies rests on the meaning of being in common as an always political invention: "To begin to think about this is to embark upon another kind of language politics, one that involves what we have called the 'community economy.' But rather than the proliferative fullness we see in the diverse economy, the community economy is an emptiness—as it has to be, if the project of building it is to be political, experimental, open and democratic" (Gibson-Graham 2005, 142).

The Eternal Irony of the Community

A certain Nietzschean perspective allows us to point to a relationship between the feminine and a form of the common that goes beyond the effective existence of a community. It would be a feminine common that consists of the capacity to "eternally" satirize the community (to use—also ironically— G. W. F. Hegel's phrase: the women are "the everlasting irony of the community" (1977, 288)). Or, in Friedrich Nietzsche's words, the "eternal feminine" could name that which opens a void within the community, unfounding it and blurring its boundaries. Precisely what this feminine mode has in common is a (virtual-actual) potencia: that of demystifying the community each time that it is presented as a totality, as a form of truth.

The feminine then functions as irony, deconstructing the stability of that which is presented as unified (Braidotti 2011; Gutiérrez Aguilar 1999; Precarias a la Deriva 2004). It also satirizes the widespread idea of politics according to which there is strength in unity. If there is another economy of forces that is affirmed as pluralism and dispersal, the force of the feminine common is its multiplicity; it is a stranger to unity and rather inclined to waste forces. This statement, however, calls for a method capable of assessing it, of showing its movement. In an attempt to address the matter, I will develop three methodological points: Why do Hegel and Nietzsche link the feminine to the eternal? A point of departure is to treat the feminine as the insistence—without bottom or end—on a becoming that desubstantializes the common, that makes it incapable of being attached to a ground, a language, or a land. The eternal feminine in Nietzschean language can be read as that territory capable of offering stateless forms of democracy, which do not require loyalty or belonging, in opposition to the substantial community. In the Hegelian allusion, the feminine indicates a negativity: that which casts doubt on the community in regard to its own seriousness, its own governability. In this context, I will draw on some feminist texts to understand that same indication in a positive sense.

Hegel wrote that women are the "everlasting irony of the community" (1977, 288). On Hegel's phrase, the Italian feminist Carla Lonzi, in the manifesto "Let's Spit on Hegel," states, "Wherever woman reveals herself as the 'eternal irony of the community,' we can at all times recognize the presence of feminism" ([1971] 1991, 44). After the deconstruction of the community, that is, after putting it in "more than one language," there is something of the feminine that becomes decisive in that multiplication, precisely because women are the "sex" that is not "one" but multiple.[2]

Women as a paradox in the discourse of identity is a point of departure for the critique of the metaphysics of substance structuring the subject.[3] Judith Butler (1999, 14), following a deconstructionist perspective takes up Luce Irigaray's critique of phallogocentric language of "univocal signification," in which women are "linguistic absence and opacity" as they are the unrepresentable, the nonrestrainable, the nonassignable. This raises the question of a (sexual-linguistic-affective) economy that escapes the significant phallogocentric economy (and its conceptions of the other, the subject, and lack). What other economy is accounted for by the feminine?

Let's return to Lonzi, for whom *difference* is not a juridical argument to oppose or replace equality but rather women's existential principle against (revolutionary) patricentric political theory. One key to this existential dimension is precisely that of giving value to unproductive moments (recharging that word with an *eternal irony*). This "form of life proposed by woman" is one of "women's contributions to creating the *community*, undoing the myth of this subsidiary industriousness" ([1970] 2010, 53) It could be said about sewing, as a departure from the idea of feminine labor as complementary or subsidiary, that the unproductiveness claimed as the feminine mode is a way of satirizing the community as the pure coordination of efforts, as a space of accumulation.[4]

When Nietzsche speaks of the "eternal feminine," he refers to the singular mode of that which "has no depth"—as Nietzsche characterizes woman—and that, at the same time, is not "superficial."[5] It is a certain amphibian characteristic that is simultaneously a *no longer* and a *not yet*. This is how the states of transition are characterized, and the eternal feminine seems to play with that image of interrupted transition, as the extreme part of an antiessentialism that draws forces toward an emptiness of origin and definition. The relationship between the feminine and the eternal serves, in this regard, to enable us to conceive of an ever open, nonwhole configuration of the world.

Therefore, the idea of the eternal linked to the feminine curiously appears in Hegel and Nietzsche as distrust: as irony, as eternal war, toward the community, which is always presented as complete and unified (Jacques Derrida would say fraternity). However, that idea of the eternal in Nietzsche can also be linked to his definition of women, whom he describes in *The Gay Science* as those capable of exercising "action at a distance" (1974, 123). This can be translated as a deterritorialized and timeless influence, capable of a paradoxical effectiveness: *extracommunitarian*.

Thus, the possibility emerges for understanding women's (ironic, distant, eternal, unproductive) force as stateless: that which does not allow the communion between community and identity. Therefore, the perspective of the feminine appears to go beyond all nostalgia: there is no lost community, and, thus, no community to recover (invoking the model going from Jean-Jacques Rousseau to Hegel and later resumed by the Romantics).

Is it possible to understand this unproductive economy in the profoundly ironic sense of the term *unproductive*, which links the eternal to the feminine and its potential to speak ironically about the community, as a way of distinguishing forms of social reproduction from the reproduction of capital?

From the Community to the Social Factory

A particular feminist perspective of the 1970s sought to debate the community, demystifying it and relating it directly to the factory, its supportive other. In their classic text *The Power of Women and the Subversion of the Community*, Mariarosa Dalla Costa and Selma James state, "The community therefore is not an area of freedom and leisure auxiliary to the factory where by chance there happen to be women who are degraded as the personal servants of men. The community is the other half of capitalist organization, the other area of hidden capitalist exploitation, the other hidden source of surplus labor. It becomes increasingly regimented like a factory, what Mariarosa calls a social factory where the costs and nature of transport, housing, medical care, education, police, are all points of struggle!" (1972, 11).

They indicate and anticipate a fundamental relationship: the community becomes the mechanism for what the tradition of Italian *operaismo* would theorize as the *social factory*. That is, the community is one of the elements incorporated into the sphere of valorization when this includes a set of connections, affects, and forms of cooperation that expand and reclassify a form of production that is no longer confined within the factory walls.[6]

Within feminist thought, this possible declination of the communitarian (as know-how, technology, affect value) is anticipated as a new chapter of capitalist valorization. Returning to the feminine figure as subverting the community—the Hegelian warning radicalized by feminism—James, in the introduction to the book she co-authored with Dalla Costa, traces a relationship between home and community: "Mariarosa Dalla Costa considers the community as first and foremost the home, and considers therefore the woman as the central figure of subversion in the community. Seen in this way, women are the contradiction in all previous political frameworks, which had been based on the male worker in industry. Once we see the community as a productive center and thus a center of subversion, the whole perspective for fully generalized struggle and revolutionary organization is re-opened" (Dalla Costa and James 1972, 20).

Community and women, then, function as the axis of a new form of valorization and, at the same time, introduce a new type of conflict. On one hand, they decenter the subject of the white male industrial worker from its privileged status of producer, and, on the other, they make visible the productive materials that from the beginning are foundational for capitalism while being invisibilized and devalued: the labor of reproduction, the constitution of social relations, affective cooperation. Women's relationship as producers of labor power directly connects them to capital and also puts them always on the verge of the possibility of subversion: "Women's relationship with capital is fundamentally that of producing and reproducing the current and future labor force, on which all capitalist exploitation depends. This is the essence of domestic labor and this is the labor for which the majority of women are prepared and with which all women identify" (Dalla Costa and James 1972, vii).

The identification of feminine labor as invisibilized labor has a direct relationship with its condition as unpaid labor in terms of wages, which minimizes it as subsidiary to male wage labor, while ignoring the intrinsic connection between the two. The "patriarchal wage," however, marginalizes and subsumes not only women's work but also peasant labor. Dalla Costa and James were writing in the context of an international struggle for wages for housework—not only to incorporate housework into the wage regime but also to break away from the idea of housework as strictly naturalized and free feminine labor. Deployed in this way, the feminist perspective does not simply introduce a specificity; it does not imply a particularism. Instead, it opens up the notion and the composition of the working class itself. In this regard, the authors put their struggle in conversation with that of blacks in the United States, noting a fundamental relationship between women and blacks. It is worth quoting at length:

> This process of development is not unique to the women's movement. The Black movement in the US (and elsewhere) also began by adopting what appeared to be only a caste position in opposition to the racism of white male-dominated groups. Intellectuals in Harlem and Malcolm X, that great revolutionary, were both nationalists, both appeared to place color above class when the white left were still chanting variations of "Black and white unite and fight," or "Negroes and Labour must join together." The Black working class was able through this nationalism to *redefine class*: overwhelmingly Black and Labor were synonymous (with no other group was Labor as synonymous except perhaps with women), the demands of Blacks and the forms of struggle created by Blacks were the most comprehensive working class demands and the most advanced *working class* struggle. (Dalla Costa and James 1972, 8)

From this perspective, the passage from the community to the social factory can be thought of as a movement of politicization (demarginalization and visibilization) of the experience of unwaged labor. Driven by the struggles of women, blacks, and peasants—in the feminist retelling—this movement problematizes the notions of class and labor and makes visible the multiple layers of value that the wage seeks to homogenize, monopolize, and command. The wage as political command over a multiplicity that exceeds it is contested by the insubordinate emergence of subjectivities that open up the very concept of exploitation.

The Social Factory as Method

The capitalist social factory, the expansion of exploitation over the whole of society, is the (inverted) correlative of the capacity to—ontologically—produce worlds and, therefore, an enrichment of cooperative capacity. It is *inverted* because that increasing cooperation occurs as the intensification of exploitation, obedience, and mystification of the world. Thus, the "inversion" (formerly in an idealist sense, now in a materialist one, as Karl Marx would say reading G. W. F. Hegel) that we require "puts things on their feet" and allows us to break through the deeper rationality of the present state of things. The *social factory* is, above all, and even as a condition for the functioning of capitalism itself, an image of the totality of a system of valorizing resonances, at the level of being itself. The problem of philosophies of community (Zibechi 2010) is that they intellectually—although not in reality—disconnect the community from its productive machinic context (and horizon), that is, from the factory, the valorizing movement of the whole. This separation is artificial but motivated by an understandable need to strengthen communitarian resistance to the becoming capitalist of the world, that is, to the—global—capitalist social factory. This gives rationality to sovereign institutions and political forces of emancipation that work against them.

The social factory then becomes a methodological perspective (and its variation founds an ontology of variation) that enables a critical point of view, from below, of the subsumption of life by capital, where the communitarian critique plays an important role, as demonstrated by a certain feminist philosophy. The categorization of feminine labor as "personal service" is one of the ways of not classifying it as work, by locating it beyond capitalist relations of production (outside of the investment of capital, according to Marx) and thus downplaying its specific productivity and dehistoricizing its function.

If, "in respect to women, their labor appears to be a personal service outside of capital" (Dalla Costa and James 1972, 32), the separation between reproduction and production condemns the former to a nonvalorizing, nonretributive sphere, subordinated to the definition of the wage in negative terms (as nonwaged activity). It is no coincidence that Paolo Virno (2004), when speaking about the multitude, returns to associating manual and servile labor with the source of the performative, as does Marx.

Slaves versus Wage Laborers

Following Dalla Costa and James, Silvia Federici (2004) argues that with the devaluing and invisibilization of women's work, domestic labor is created as a way of sharply separating production from reproduction. This enables a capitalist use of the wage to command the labor of the unwaged. However, Federici directs the force of this argument to thinking about the dispossession of feminine labor as the core of capitalism's primitive accumulation.

In this respect, she argues that with the privatization of land (enclosures)—the most well-known nucleus of theorization about primitive accumulation—women become the "communal goods." This means that their bodies and labor are mystified as *personal services and/or natural resources*. They are a territory that can be utilized because they guarantee social reproduction and provide common services:

> According to this new social-sexual contract, proletarian women became for male workers the substitute for the land lost to the enclosures, their most basic means of reproduction, and a communal good anyone could appropriate and use at will. Echoes of this "primitive appropriation" can be heard in the concept of the "common woman" which in the sixteenth century qualified those who prostituted themselves. But in the new organization of work every woman (other than those privatized by bourgeois men) became a communal good, for once women's activities were defined as non-work, women's labor began to appear as a natural resource, available to all, no less than the air we breathe or the water we drink. (Federici 2004, 97)

Women's historical defeat, in this respect, was the feminization of poverty. Federici argues that through a new patriarchal order, the masculine "primitive appropriation" of feminine labor was enforced, "reducing women to a double dependence: on employers and on men" (97). Thus, women's *enslavement* to reproduction poses an analogy to slaves in the Americas in the same movement of capitalism in its violent beginnings:

> While in the Middle Ages women had been able to use various forms of contraceptives, and had exercised an undisputed control over the birthing process, from now on their wombs became public territory, controlled by men and the State, and procreation was directly placed at the service of capitalist accumulation. In this sense, the destiny of West European women, in the period of primitive accumulation, was similar to that of female slaves in the American colonial plantations who, especially after the end of the slave-trade in 1807, were forced by their masters to become breeders of new workers. . . . But despite the differences, in both cases, the female body was turned into an instrument for the reproduction of labor and the expansion of the workforce, treated as a natural breeding-machine, functioning according to rhythms outside of women's control. (89–91)

Procedures for making domestic labor *natural* and *servile* are renewed as figures of mystification while they operate by classifying this labor in a certain way. The popularization of prostitution has to do with the theft of time and the creation of the figure of the housewife as a family enclosure for producing the labor force. Hence the importance of her methodological warning: women's wage labor, housework, and (paid) sex work cannot be studied separately.

Labor: Beyond the Distinction between the Modern and Nonmodern

The way in which postindustrial capitalism produces new combinations of elements of the servile economies with elements of postmodern economies should no longer be analyzed by looking at the hegemonic (or hegemonizing) tendency of *free* wage labor but based on the expansion of a new feminization of labor that implies the increasing valorization of attributes that permanently classify labor as nonfree. As an improved and expanded new type of colonial condition, the current feminization of labor principally suggests a great ambiguity: one through which a new capitalist drive becomes competitive and dynamic by flexibly articulating itself with practices, networks, and features that historically characterized the flows of unpaid labor.

It is necessary to highlight that the slave or servile mode is not the other of modern labor but rather its constitutive counterpart, as Susan Buck-Morss (2009) conclusively demonstrates through analyzing the simultaneity (and imbrication) of Enlightenment philosophies and the slave economy starting in the seventeenth century.[7] The colonial condition of the world has since characterized that double economy: nonmodern economies and modern economies—as an apparent dichotomy between servitude and freedom—functioning in a coherent manner in the same mode of production.

Carole Pateman writes, "The comparison of wives and slaves reverberated through the women's movement in the nineteenth century. Women were very prominent in the abolitionist movement and they quickly made the connection between the condition of slaves and their own condition as wives" (1988, 120). The same could be said of indigenous people, who—in another economy— share, along with slaves and women, a regime of labor with characteristics of *nonfree* labor. They share demands of loyalty and availability, and the fact that there is no (waged) *measure* of their labor. These are common requirements— although in different ways—of the domestic economy, the slave economy (of sugar production), and the economy of the *mita*, the *encomienda*, and the *pongo* (characteristic of the mining economy).[8] This supposes that feminized subjects—in a reactionary version of feminization—remain on one side of the *modern* line that divides servile labor from free wage labor. A series of binaries are imposed: wage labor versus subsistence, the distinction between labor force and ownership of persons, free choice versus force or captivity. This argument is even extended to sexual expropriation and expropriation of underage minors—often linked to the impossibility of having one's own name—that removes the possibility of locating a will in these subjects and also serves as a mode of reactively feminizing them, of severely victimizing them.

Thus, the feminine refers to a weakness that is foisted onto certain paradigmatic attributes—those who are supposedly underage minors, those who are under the sexual ownership of another, and finally, those who engage in a type of labor that is not formally governed by the rules of modern wage labor. Thus, the feminine or the feminization of a subject—by tone of voice and body position, but also in a determined relation to production and property, and in certain relation to the anonymous and the collective—implies a way of naming the subaltern. This naming implicitly carries a distinction that opposes a passive body, reduced to pure biological reproduction, to an active body with the power of producing meaning and language, in which the passive is tied to the feminine or to that which is feminized.

It is possible to propose another meaning, a variation, of feminization. It is a distinction of terms (political power versus biological-adaptive power), yet these are not mutually exclusive but rather affirm their difference without being set against one another; it is not a logic of opposites. Thus, disjunction is the dynamic of a separation; however, I want to distinguish between disjunction that excludes one of its terms and that which enables the affirmation of both, maintaining their differences.[9] The latter image can be linked to that conceptualization of woman as "being on the borderline," between *zoo* and *bios*, as analyzed by Julia Kristeva (in Clément and Kristeva 2003, 13). According to Kristeva, the feminine body expresses—in a dramatic way—a "strange intersection between *zoo* and *bios*, physiology and narration, genetics and biography" (14), and it is precisely the porous border between "biology *and* meaning" that familiarizes it with this being in transit. It is the fixation on some type of "naturalness," however, that encloses her as a "being on the borderline" while it marks a clear space of exclusion.[10]

The Feminine as an Economy

These modes of disjunction, then, differentiate between, on one hand, the feminine as an economy of production, use, and circulation (of goods and speech) that expresses conducts of rebellion and, on the other, the feminine that functions by naming the exasperation with or fixation on features of a submission that impedes language, or reduces it to lament as the naturalization of the sexual condition, making it inoffensive. This fixation or unidimensionalization of the feminine operates by making the voice a—semantic and somatic—record of submission or of the lack of authority to speak. However, it has another use: the feminine voice is that which breaks down the division between the public and the domestic by using language as a space of the heterogeneous, while it is also capable of a strategic efficacy of silence and language, in both cases as the organized and secret voice of mutiny or rebellion. This involves challenging or dismantling the attributes previously discussed in their pure negativity.

Through analyzing the migrant discourse and experience in Peru, Antonio Cornejo Polar (1996) develops the category of *migration* for reading segments of Latin American literature that are distinguished by their "radical heterogeneity." Migration, as a category, does not allow the exclusive opposition between indigenous and metropolitan identities (and, therefore, the dislocation of the terms *center* and *periphery*); it avoids the flat figure of the subaltern as the victim and, at the same time, perceives modes of repetition in difference: for example, how certain productive forms that migrants use—"reciprocity, economic operability of the extended family or simple godparenting"—are implanted in the cities in a nonlinear way in respect to the capitalist norm.

This idea of migration as "nondialectical heterogeneity" enables a particular reading in respect to possible alliances and subjects: if the subject is undefined by its experience of migration, its identity is not dissolved but multiplied to the point of making each subject a plurality of ongoing processes of subjectivation. Some feminists have theorized this type of relationship as a *coalition:* the concept of an "uneasy alliance" used by the Bolivian feminist group Mujeres Creando raises the challenge of a heterogeneous composition as a fundamental dilemma of activism. This kind of coalition, since it is practiced by affinity and not by identity, displaces the binary categorizations of constituted and fixed subjects: outside the community and literate as opposed to native and nonliterate, or even subaltern versus non-subaltern.[11]

Language as a Common Place

The experience of migration constructs "common places" in speech and song, spaces that dissolve the rigidity of the inside-outside or interior-exterior distinctions characterizing alliances of constituted subjects. Ángel Rama argues that the oral register adheres to communitarian norms and makes use of true common places (1996). Pierre Clastres's definition outlines the same relationship between language and a common place: what creates society in societies without a state is "the enjoyment of the common good that is the Word" (2010, 188). This immaterial territory of speech is capable of producing society when it is situated as a (nonsynthetic and nonstate) foundation of the common. Perhaps that is why the experience of stateless societies that Clastres speaks of can be understood today based on a contemporary relationship: the migrant experience disassembles the symbolic and territorial unity of the state *from below*. Situated in that constellation is also the argument developed by Virno (2004) about "common places" as linguistic forms and logics of general value (in a plus-minus relation; a relationship of opposites; a category of reciprocity) that today become important resources for the species as possibilities for orientation in the face of the disappearance of substantial communities like the nation-state. Virno speaks precisely of these common places as the experience of the foreigner who has only those common references to move about in a place that they do not know. Language, with the ability to turn to those common places, is a space of protection from spatial movement, that sensation of not feeling at home that, however, enables the simultaneous experience of disorientation and movement.

There are *common places* between the migrant experience and the experience of the feminine when feminine voices give rise to border situations: the experience of a nonexclusive divergence of itineraries, that enable other trajectories to linguistic, affective, and intellectual resources, which coexist as the multiplication of territories.

There is a displacement: migration in its spatial sense—which Cornejo Polar speaks of—is also the multiplication of meanings, histories, and temporalities from which one speaks and functions, unfolding into the present moment itself. The practice of the border (and the possibility of a border epistemology) that I hypothesize to understand feminization does not have a strictly spatial meaning. However, there are possible links between migration and feminization. First, there is an ambiguous relationship, not exclusive or directly simultaneous, between different levels of memory, narration, and meaning in a context where biopolitics operates as a machine of segmentation and imposition of hierarchies on modes of life. Second, it is difficult for that ambiguity to be read in purely identitarian terms (whether woman or migrant), and there is debate over its strategic functionality. Finally, there is a nonprogressivist temporality, as Gloria Anzaldúa summarizes: "for this Chicana the guerra de independencia is a constant" (2012, 15), which in turn enables a sort of expressive and productive montage.

There are some (abstract) features through which that feminine voice differentiates itself. On one hand, it is capable of activating the difference—or disjunction—between religion as a figure of resignation, domination, and consolation and a feminine atheism in a double sense.[12] It invokes an atheism that makes it so that speaking or silencing oneself is always a strategic action of distrust and confrontation with the "religious" voice as the authorized voice; this is an atheism that—in the same sense that Hegel positioned women as "the irony of the community"—utters heretical, damned enunciations. On the other hand, that atheism is also materialized in the way of taking on an action's meaning without reference to an abstract and larger totality: hence the concrete and immediate character with which their actions are colored, from which they derive meaning, and thus they shelter a distinct form of politics.[13]

The prelinguistic functions as the sensory material that is articulated with language and that makes it go beyond the strictly communicative-logical: the voice that is feminized appears to open to other logics of speaking and listening, in which affective materials have a fundamental place. According to Suely Rolnik (2001), singing—"the reserve and memory of affects"—is what allows the body to connect itself with its sensible states. Singing actualizes a series of "memories" in the body, as extralinguistic resources, that qualify the tone of voice. Finally, an invisibilized economy that is made visible in song and the heat of revolt is nothing more than bringing another productive and distributive logic onto the scene. Therefore, the subversive character of the feminization of the voice encounters its sexualization as a reactive response: a way of confirming a distribution of tasks and places that confines the feminine in a subordinated status, devoid of politicization.

In some way, these features that I point to as the feminization of the voice are in contrast with the habitual ways in which subaltern subjects are feminized, since this operation tends to involve—and indicate—their weakening or submission. A positive reading of feminization can be opposed to reading it as reactive, by locating it in other attributes: precisely those that make feminization (and its correlative of becoming childlike) an experience of collectivization, such as in song, which is not linearly homogenizing; in the link between the affective and the sacred, which is not necessarily religious; and, finally, as an economy that implements other strategies of production, circulation, and consumption that find a way of becoming visible in public rebellion—and of not simply being refunctionalized in the market economy.

The feminine becomes crucial to a permanent conflict around a number of issues: (1) an economy of discourses, tones, and narratives; (2) politics and uses of the body; (3) a determined link to wealth production and the property regime; (4) a relationship with authority and authorization (or a relationship with the law); and, finally, (5) a definition of one's own condition as a subject and of the ways in which alliances and relationships with others are understood.

To Make an Origin by Moving

What is brought to light in these accounts of migration, in the ways of capturing and converting forms of doing, thinking, relating, in the continuity of religious, festive, and culinary rituals, is an enormous capacity to make community belonging flexible, to the point of redoing it, redefining it, and creating new possibilities for the communitarian, as an effect of movement. Is it a deterritorialization of the community? It has to do with a way of constructing a territory that *makes the move its origin*. In other words, the creation of a new territory (that involves more than travel) is the effect of a long journey that re-creates the very idea of origin. That is, the move is woven into accounts of misfortune, hardship, and pain, and also into the narrative of an enterprise of progress, a decision to seek better well-being, and the inauguration of a life in an unknown city.

How is community regenerated in its uprooting? What communitarian elements travel and are suitable to being relocated? Does a community without territory work? How is a new territory constructed? Finally, what are the elements that turn the communitarian into a social mechanism with the capacity to mobilize, relocate, transform, and re-create itself?

The stereotype is that the community is a homogeneous, stable figure that, above all, is rooted in a territory. Let's explore another side of this figure, one that allows for reconnecting the communitarian question with migration. That is, the core of the issue is the community in movement, the community displaced from its stability and yet persistent. Its current condition is constructed in that paradox or ambivalence.

The Flexibilized Community

According to Álvaro García Linera, the labor force's capacity to make community belonging flexible "beyond blood kinship, the negotiated adoption of foreigners, using them to maintain a flow of products from distinct ecological zones, the formal and controlled commercialization of communal goods, products of labor," in order to "sustain and preserve the communal order of land access, their productive forces and cosmovision, and so on" is a strategy for confronting the colony, against which communities "deploy a tenacious and persistent resistance of reproducing themselves, of persevering in their internal logic and dynamic faced with colonial-mercantile unbecoming" (1995, 19).

Yet is it possible to think, in contrast to García Linera's argument, that in the neoliberal era, the community, rather than "unbecoming," is capable of mixing and reinventing itself under a new logic?

This assumes that the community, as a compendium of knowledges, technologies, and temporalities, enters into a complex system of variable relationships with different moments of capitalism in its also diverse (post)colonial phases. Community organization returned to the scene as a resource for social mobilization during protests in Bolivia in the twenty-first century. That organization demonstrates its flexibility again in terms of the mixture of elements, folding over the communitarian in diverse levels:

> The majority of the communities-ayllus that have sustained the mobilizations are productive, cultural, and family structures that combine modes of traditional organization with ties to the market, urban migration, and deliberate processes of internal social differentiation. Land ownership mixes forms of property or family possession with the communal; rules of territorial possession are meshed with political responsibilities within the community-ayllu; labor systems in the household maintain noncommercial forms of the circulation of labor power and of collective industriousness for planting and harvesting; the system of rituals and local authorities links each family's rotating responsibilities to the exercise of labor union authority and the cycle of local celebrations with the legitimacy and continuity of family ownership of lands for cultivation and pasture and basic productive technologies, which are directed by cultural patterns of reproducing communal unity. (García Linera 2001, 309)

Communitarian modes—of organization, authority, labor, and so on—find a new compatibility with the post-Fordist world, the disarticulation of the nation-state, and the weakening of large labor centers. In this sense, the communitarian also becomes novel and important as a mode of "deterritorialized collective action." Let me highlight two ideas: the communitarian transformation toward deterritorialization and, as such, its capacity to become an organizational resource for a new social reality, characterized by a transversality of problematics that simultaneously respond to the decomposition of the world of Fordist labor.

Also speaking of the place of community in the Bolivian history, Sinclair Thomson argues that it is a *form of political organization that is simultaneously changing and persevering.* His perspective "works against stereotypes of the community as a unified, discrete agent that simply resists, re-creates itself, or breaks down in the face of hostile external forces" (2002, 10). From this position, Thomson studies the political mutations of community organization in the southern Andes during the eighteenth century, while hypothesizing their temporal transversality.[14] Thomson states, "The events of 1780–1781 affected not only colonial society and imperial reform in the late-eighteenth-century Andes but also the nature of the independence process and subsequent nation-state formation in the nineteenth century. Two centuries later, the insurrection has acquired potent symbolic significance in national political culture and popular movements" (8).

Thus, its influence reaches the political-labor struggles of the 1970s and has even more of an impact on the cycle of uprisings that began in 2000 and continued at least until 2003. The flexibility of the community, or the dissolution of its stereotypical presentation as unified and homogeneous, is a key point for putting a long-standing concept in movement.[15]

Thomson makes a second point that is crucial in the discussion of the poststate communitarian horizon: *the perspective of the community in Latin America is a language and an organizational form that has been parallel to and politically effective against the rhetoric of citizenship.* For Thomson, the pan-Andean insurrection falls outside of the paradigm of the revolutionary Atlantic, which assumed that "the ideals and examples of liberation swept like a tidal wave from France and North America throughout the rest of the Atlantic world" (2002, 6). This map of the revolutionary Atlantic should be expanded, Thomson suggests, to "native American peoples [that] nourished their own ideals of liberty and self-determination." He continues, "While indigenous communities did not mobilize with 'democracy' as their aim, their struggles against the domination of an Old World empire brought about effective and enduring practices of communal democracy and sovereignty that differed from Western liberal principles" (276).

In this respect, Thomson remarks that the project of Túpac Amaru and Túpaj Katari was not undertaken in the name of republican ideals, as they did not reject monarchical sovereignty to vindicate a modern political project (7). Their revolts made demands in the name of "ancestral, hereditary, territorial, and communal rights, rather than of abstract and ostensibly timeless notions of human rights and individual citizenship" (2002, 7).[16]

Finally, community is *a name used by certain attempts at democratic radicalization.* Another aspect of the fundamental singularity of the anticolonial insurrections of 1780–81 is that "unlike [the other revolutionary struggles of the time], it was a movement against colonial rule and for self-determination in which *native American* political subjects made up the fighting corps, held positions of leadership, and defined the terms of struggle" (Thomson 2002, 8). They were the ones, Thomson says, who fought, led, and defined the struggle. They were also the ones who imagined forms of emancipation and spoke of a moment in which "they alone would rule" (10). In this regard, democratic radicalization was not a horizon toward the future; it already existed in the "lived forms of communal, decentralized, and participatory political practice" (7). Thus, the community is reconfigured as anticolonial practice and imagination (276). Taking Thomson's hypothesis a step further: communitarian vitality is encouraged and expressed in moments of external, as well as internal, tension and conflict.

The Motley Community and the Global Market

Speaking of community today can be an oscillation between a form of substantialization of a diffuse subject and a way of naming the motley. In either case, it has to do with comprehending the meaning of community in post-Fordist capitalism and not a way of referring to precapitalist practices or pure relationships of solidarity. Let's return to the variegated as a feature of the motley crew of contemporary workers. In this respect, Silvia Rivera Cusicanqui (2010b) projects her ch'ixi perspective to conceptualize the movements of the indigenous diaspora in the global market:

> The transnational communities of Aymara migrants thus travel in a postcolonial *thaki*, made up of cyclical ebbs and flows. In their displacement,

they articulate modes of recuperated traditions, invent genealogies, and reinterpret myths, staining the fabrics of global industry with their cougars and suns, transforming their large trucks into altars of saints and devils. The scene of the Aymara labor diaspora thus contains something more than oppression and suffering: it is a space for the reconstitution of subjectivity, as surely are all—even the most brutal—settings of domination, if we are capable of going beyond the figure of the sacrificial victim.

The community appears in its versatility: a movement capable of the same voracious cannibalism as is global capitalism, with the capacity to turn scenes of dispossession into spaces of diverse appropriation. The key is to take seriously the subjective figures that appear when one avoids the all-encompassing pretense of victimization. Clearly, it is not about simple romanticism or naïveté. Rather, it has to do with recognizing subversive capacity on the same plane as capitalist globalization. There is a reverse principle in Rivera Cusicanqui's language, which is also methodological: "The reversed performance of the contemporary *takis-thakis* transforms the rhythm of neocolonial capitalist machinery, creates intermediary spaces, reappropriates the methods and practices of the global market, at the same time as it asserts its own circuits, its repertoire of social knowledges, and the advantages and devices that allow it to confidently confront that unequal situation and its violence" (Rivera Cusicanqui 2010b, 15).

The challenge lies in thinking about those variable forms of a community that is simultaneously crossing national borders, constantly moving, mixing economies, and precisely managing a communitarian know-how and wealth that is in permanent tension with the exploitation and reinvention of the popular.

The Textile Economy

It is no coincidence that around textiles and fabrics there lies an entire economy to be unraveled, as forms of *weaving*. Tracking the concept of weaving does not have a purely allegorical meaning. It is an attempt to recognize its political dimension in a double sense: on one hand, the art of weaving as a discourse about the art of governing; on the other hand, an understanding of the textile industry as a crucial vector in the history of capitalist development. This problematic can be traced, even in its discontinuity and diversity of scales and temporalities, from the slave fields producing cotton to the nineteenth-century English workshops analyzed by Marx, the textile tributes imposed on women weavers in the colonies, and textile workshops in contemporary China and Argentina.

Adrienne Rich demands that this analysis be brought into the present moment:

> An international female proletariat of textile workers continues today, as it has since the industrial revolution. As we reclaim metaphors of women weavers and spinners, and the word *spinster* itself; as we sing the "Bread and Roses" anthem of nineteenth-century Lawrence, Massachusetts, mill girls; as we search with awe and pride into the flare and authority of women's imaginations translated into quilts, and study the histories secreted in colors, stitches, materials; as we write our elegies for the women burned to death in the Triangle Shirtwaist Fire, let us not fail to be aware of the history still being played out by "the nineteen year old Filipino woman sewing the difficult side seam along the denim cloth of a Levi's blue jean pant leg in a new industrial zone outside Manila." (1994, 151–52).

That feminized (although not majority female) proletariat has also nurtured a certain reconstruction of the local economy thanks to the proliferation of textile workshops, fundamentally supported by Bolivian women and men, that supply the large brands, manufacture for export, and also create their own lines for sale in informal markets. Such circuits allow for reassembling a multilayered transnational map: migration from Bolivia to Argentina, the migrant population's settlements in Buenos Aires and its surroundings, the construction of a whole network of (family, commercial, etc.) travel that permanently sustains this economy, the transnationalization of a political-economic force in a particular moment on the continent, and the incorporation of feminine and communitarian know-how into a series of a strategies of production and commercialization that are included in the global assembly line of contemporary economies.

Putting it more schematically, analyzing the national economy requires a denationalization of the variables to be taken into account, including (1) migrant labor; (2) clandestine or illegal work; (3) the construction of networks of commercialization and distribution that mix large brands and illegal markets, Argentinean cities and those of neighboring countries; (4) the politicization of said activity; and (5) the feminization of this economy.

Image Weaving

There are various citations of and allusions to the art of weaving in philosophy. They tend to function as a *constructivist* evocation. From Plato to Benjamin, it is an image that refers to the operation of creating bonds. Particularly in Plato's Statesman, weaving is a paradigm or model of politics and is differentiated from other figures that compete with politics to occupy the same role of caring for people, such as the shepherd (the statesman as the "shepherd of the human flock"), the doctor, the celebrated ship pilot, the military strategist, the persuasive rhetorician, or the judge.[17] The art of the politician (become weaver) is constituted through the link between the affairs of the city and the characters of the people who constitute it. First, it starts with "taking the eternal element of the soul and binding it with a divine cord, to which it is akin." It is an intertwining of opposing virtues (from which arises a "more than human race"). Second, it connects "then the animal nature, and binds that with human cords" (marriages) (Plato 2002, 71).

The work of this weaving reveals the entire project of political philosophy: the search for the midpoint between virtues such as bravery and prudence, between the "temperate natures" and the "brave," in order "to weave them together, like the warp and the woof, by common sentiments and honors and reputation, and by the giving of pledges to one another; and out of them forming one smooth and even web, to entrust to them the offices of State" (Plato 2002, 73).

The virtue of Platonic discourse lies in proposing a unique compatibility, starting from the supreme art of the polis, between the concrete historical materiality of the political and the disciplinarian orientation of philosophy, based on the nomination of a suitable surface for interweaving souls and bodies, in accordance with divine inspirations and knowledges.

In the case of Walter Benjamin (1969), it has to do with finding an affirmative image in history's discontinuities for broadening his theological philosophy of messianic disruption: we weave in the present with the threads of tradition, lost for centuries. The quality of Benjaminian metaphysics opposes and refutes the Platonic political philosophy based on messianic eruption. It is about undoing the Platonic weaving to remove its "divine threads," tainted by the metaphysics of measurement (the midpoint as the exact point, not as Aristotelian moderation) and the Idea—and recuperating the bodies woven there, this time in another art of weaving, repairing interrupted pieces, old shreds neglected by the idealism of Western history.

There is another twentieth-century thinker who has taken the weaving metaphor seriously, though in its feminized version. Sigmund Freud signals this art as women's only contribution to the history of civilizing inventions (Fiorini and Abelin-Sas Rose 2010). It is a feminine art that is a "copy of nature" (in Fiorini and Abelin-Sas Rose 2010). Nature and femininity are constituted, again, as an analogous pair. In this case, the art of weaving does not belong to the political sphere but to the feminine condition; at the same time, it is extremely close to prepolitical naturalism.

At the same time, Freud says, women weave to cover up nature's defects. There is a double operation: it is part of nature and, at the same time, hides nature. Therefore, it hides *itself*. The art of weaving would seem to be a rite of passage: it likens us, as women, to nature, and at the same time it gives us the tools to hide our own nature. A nature that denies itself: this could be the definition of woman that emerges from such an image of weaving.

The French feminist Luce Irigaray subjects Freud's observation to criticism:

Woman can, it seems, (only) imitate nature. Duplicate what nature offers and produces. In a kind of *technical* assistance and substitution. But this is paradoxical. Since Nature is all. But this "all" cannot appear as no thing, as no sex organ, for example. Therefore woman weaves in order to veil herself, mask the faults of Nature, and restore her in her wholeness. *By wrapping her up.* In a wrapping that Marx has told us preserves the "value" from a just evaluation. And allows the "exchange" of goods "without knowledge" of their effective value. By abstracting "products," by making them universal and interchangeable without recognizing their differences. (1985, 115).

Irigaray expands the question of value: What is that which is hidden, whose knowledge is expropriated, and what is that which negates difference in favor of universal exchange? The basis of commodity exchange finds its parallel in the operation of the universal-patriarchal exchange of women. Irigaray continues:

Whence the need for weaving to shield the gilded eyes from the possible incandescence of the standard. . . . Into a mobilization, monopolization of sexual value for the production of cloth, tissue, or text which abscond with its inner prize, its inner fires (l'en jeu, l'en feu), and put them into the checking account of a proper name, very often. One is referred, or turned back, to the standards governing the possession of discourse, to God, the paradigm of all proper names/nouns, who (re)produces himself in a virgin through the intercession of the word. Meanwhile woman weaves to sustain the disavowal of her sex. (116)

Weaving is impregnated with muteness—or with the mystification of language, even when its materiality is that of what can be read: in a text, a fabric, or a weaving. If Plato's weaver deploys the art of mediation (and therefore, we can assume, speech), Freud's weaver is confined to the tasks of camouflaging (she is and is not nature) and muting her labor (her public-political value is removed). Thus, she weaves her own economy of submission and concealment, as a feminine ghetto.

If Irigaray questions the economic infrastructure that dominates the conception of the role of women in Freud, it is because she recognizes that there "misogyny can be understood as *an ideological bond that bails out* the current regimes of property," the monogamous patriarchal family. Only by taking for granted the context of family exclusion can Freud understand feminine labor as women's "weaker social interests" and "social inferiority" (Irigaray 1985, 120).

Weaving as Language

For Rivera Cusicanqui, the notion of identity as territory is masculine. In contrast,

> the notion of women's identity is similar to weaving. Far from establishing property and the jurisdiction of the nation's authority—or the people, or indigenous autonomy—feminine practice weaves the fabric of interculturality through practices: as producer, retailer, weaver, ritualist, creator of languages and symbols capable of seducing the "other" and establishing pacts of reciprocity and coexistence between territories. Women's seductive, acculturative, and enveloping labor allows for complementing the homeland-territory with a dynamic cultural weaving that unfolds and is reproduced until it encompasses the bordering and mixed sectors—the *ch'ixi* sectors—which contribute with their vision of personal responsibility, privacy, and individual rights associated with citizenship. The modernity that emerges from these motley arrangements and complex and mixed languages—which Gamaliel Churata called "a language with

homeland"—is that which builds indigenous hegemony upon realizing itself in spaces created by the invading culture—the market, the state, the union. (2010b, 9)

The question is, how can a theory and practice of the common be formulated that is not a new form of excluding others in the name of community?

CHAPTER 3

Between Servitude and the New Popular Entrepreneurship

The Clandestine Textile Workshop

Orientalism

"In Bajo Flores we make clothes and put tags on them that say 'Made in India' or 'Made in Thailand.' Therefore, no one thinks that they are buying something made by Bolivians in Buenos Aires, in clandestine workshops. They think that it comes from the Far East." This analysis by a former sewing worker clearly summarizes the textile workshops' supposed clandestine condition. There are more than fifteen hundred of these workshops in the city of Buenos Aires and its periphery.[1] They manufacture for large brands, as well as for circuits of informal textile sales, and they are the hidden mechanism behind the sector's reconversion and growth in Argentina. Disassembled following the massive growth in imports facilitated by peso-dollar convertibility, the industry was relaunched after the crisis with new foundations, based on outsourcing of production (cutting and sewing) to so-called clandestine workshops.[2]

According to the current leader of the Argentine Industrial Union (Unión Industrial Argentina), José Ignacio de Mendiguren (former vice president of the Argentine Apparel Chamber [Cámara Argentina de la Indumentaria]), 78 percent of the apparel produced in the country is manufactured through illegal circuits. This includes outsourcing of apparel production to clandestine workshops, to which an intermediary delivers the cloth (which can be cut or not) to be sewn into garments.

During the 1990s in Argentina, textile workshops were usually started by Korean migrants, who employed Bolivian sewers (Kim 2014); over the last decade, these workshops have become more widespread, but now the owners are also Bolivian. This is a decisive change, and it allows for recognizing a *communitarian capital* as the basis of their growth. That capital functions as a differential labor attribute for recruiting workers based on bonds of trust and kinship, and combines modes of life and labor that exploit communitarian wealth.

From the *Maquila* to the Textile Workshop

The clandestine textile workshop can be thought of as a variation of the paradigm of the *maquila*, not because it is situated on the geographic border or because it employs only women or uses sophisticated technology, but, rather, because it constitutes a *prototype*, a formula for the organization of labor that goes beyond the textile workshop; it is replicated in other fields and innovates forms of precaritization and transnationalization of productive processes. Another common element is the utilization of migrant labor, with the urban calculations and expectations that it mobilizes. The maquila, an assembly industry, and the textile workshop are both part of a global assembly economy.

Additionally, although not the hegemonic mode of production in Argentina, the workshops exhibit an extreme form of certain features that today characterize precarious contemporary apparatuses of exploitation, which increasingly rely on the government of life rather than the regulation of modes of employment. Finally, they share the transnational structure in which both the maquila and textile workshops are inscribed. In this regard, the dimension of territory assumes a decisive role: these are border zones, both because of the migrant composition of the workforce and because of the production of *an exceptional zone of accumulation* that precisely delimits one boundary of the exceptionalism of the production of value.

Thus, the textile workshop shapes the nucleus of the migrant economy and, in that dynamic, is interwoven with the economy of illegal markets and legal commercial circuits, as well as with the villa as an also exceptional city space. To the extent that the space of the textile workshop is connected to the market and the villa, the production of a specific space is organized in this web. It produces a zone, a zone that amalgamates an economy that exceeds it, and, at the same time, an economy that sustains it as an exceptional place.

Urban Calculation

The maquila, Alfredo Limas Hernández (2004) says, formats a city: *the maquiladora industry* in Ciudad Juárez *makes the whole city into a maquila.* It is the expansion of a productive form into a city form. Thus, that urban

center—a desert dotted with maquilas—urbanizes injustice. That urbanization exploits thousands of young women from the Mexican countryside,
who, even so, find new possibilities for consumption, entertainment, work,
and life in the maquilas. The uprooting that populates the city is the source
of disobedient urban experiences. Yet it is also the surface on which an
apocryphal citizenry of women workers without rights is settled, women
who are sacrificed and killed (Segato 2013). The result is a successful transnational economy: in the 1990s, Ciudad Juárez had the lowest unemployment rate in all of Mexico. In a broader sense, Sergio González Rodríguez
demonstrates how this industry mixes control and technology in an intensely hierarchical way, with the "person as the cybernetic arm under
increasingly vertical control in exchange for meager pay" (2002, 31). The
maquiladora industry becomes an industry of femicide, in that it enables
"idiosyncratic hate, misogyny, class hatred" and exploits "disposable bodies." González Rodríguez says that Ciudad Juárez is a geography-territory of
migrants "who accept the uprooting and abandonment of the communitarian memory that expelled them" while it replaces that memory "with a *new
urban calculation that is developed between exploitation, survival, and hope*"
(87; italics added).

I will use the idea of urban calculation to analyze the rationality that organizes a metropolitan experience that assembles highly exploitative jobs that
have a high turnover rate with forms of access to consumption, entertainment, and possibilities for experiencing the city. In the case of Ciudad Juárez,
it is migrant women from the country's interior who bring this calculation into
play. This calculation promotes a nomadism with risks, suffering, and danger,
but also with aspirations for progress, expectations and projects, and the search
for independence.

Some Hypotheses

My hypothesis is that the dynamic of the migrant labor force must be understood as a force of determination and will to progress that mixes the Foucauldian definition of the migrant as an investor in himself or herself with
a decision that brings communitarian capital into play. It is a vital impulse
deploying a calculation in which a neoliberal rationality is superimposed onto
a repertoire of communitarian practices.

My second, complementary hypothesis is that there is a specifically postmodern articulation of the communitarian in its ability to become a job at-

tribute, a specific qualification for the migrant workforce from the Bolivian highlands in Buenos Aires. *In becoming labor, the communitarian becomes the source of a pragmatic, transborder polyvalence, capable of adaptation and invention.*

Along these lines, I can make a third hypothesis related to the *reproletarianization* of the labor force, not in the sense of disciplining that would classify the labor force only in regard to its predominant form, but rather identifying how the sectors forming part of a diffuse and greatly heterogeneous proletariat expanded and were reconfigured after the crisis, according to increasingly less uniform modes of labor. This hypothesis places migrant labor in the center of a process of reproletarianization that questions a "normalized" discourse and imaginary of labor, that is made visible as the flip side of the previous decade's economic recovery and also of the one-dimensional understanding of the popular classes under the idea of deproletarianization.

The situation of the clandestine textile workshop, however, could be presented as exemplifying the nuances with which the term *proletarianization* should be understood. As Shahid Amin and Marcel van der Linden indicate, "developments in the so-called 'Third World' can be understood only if these intermediary forms of wage labor (indicators of partial proletarianization) are taken seriously" (1997, 4).

This supposes a nonprogressive linearity between modern labor and nonmodern labor forms, and, above all, a way of reading the global articulations of the segmentation of the labor force. Therefore, I want to argue that the use of the term *proletarianization* must be framed from a perspective that prioritizes the heterogeneity of working men and women in contexts of profound transformation and that, above all, redefines the very notions of ambiguous identities, precarious situations, and peripheral contexts, which, at the same time, become central for understanding broader changes in the labor force.

But that proletarianization puts the workshop economy in tension with the productivity and uses of the communitarian. When Raquel Gutiérrez Aguilar speaks of the "communitarian web," she is referring to multiple forms of the production and reproduction of social life "under diverse standards of respect, collaboration, dignity, care, and reciprocity, which are not completely subjected to the logic of capital accumulation, although they are often attacked and overwhelmed by it" (2011b, 13). According to Gutiérrez Aguilar, the term refers to diverse collective subjects and "has the virtue of not establishing its foundation within the very heart of the production of capital, for example, in the economic sphere of capital, but rather attempts to emphasize the multiform, versatile, and demanding reproduction of life as such, in the form of a bond that is established (communitarian, focused on the common) and the specific purpose motivating it. In this sense, it is based on 'that' specifically human element that overflows capital time and time again, which expands over diverse terrains of what used to be called the 'sphere of natural social reproduction,' in contrast to the 'civil sphere' and the 'political sphere'" (14). Here I want to suggest this notion of communitarian webs as a counterpoint, with different connotations, capable of organizing forms of exploitation and business, microenterprises and economic progress, and, in turn, of not being completely removed from those "diverse standards."

From the Recovered Brukman Factory to the Clandestine Workshop

Brukman, a textile factory primarily occupied by women, presents a counterpoint. I use this extreme example to propose an initial dualism that I will, nevertheless, later dismantle and problematize. Brukman was taken over by its workers, mostly women, only a few days before the beginning of December 2001. It was a textile factory that mostly produced suits, and its owners had left it in complete bankruptcy. Its experience of self-management served as a role model during the crisis and as an emblem of the recuperation of factories by their workers during the country's complete political and economic collapse. The factory's clothing was turned into images for stencils and wandered through international art shows, while the words of those seamstresses who had taken their machines onto the streets were heard and circulated by hundreds of people (Moreno 2011). At first glance, the clandestine workshop presents the opposite: it lacks a public, is run by a boss, and is quasi-invisible.

If Brukman's experience demonstrates the positive side of the crisis by showing that the political means of addressing the lack of work cannot be pure acceptance through submission, the workshop appears as a brutal form of subordination and confinement of mostly Bolivian male and female sewing workers, removing those conditions from public visibility. The workshop's seclusion is part of a biopolitical and racist articulation that spreads across society as an extreme but exemplary image.

I am interested in the comparison of these two images: if the exhibition of the broken relationship between a certain form of capital and labor, in the paradoxical occupation of factories after they had been emptied and abandoned by their owners, politicizes that relationship insofar as it reveals the contingency of any order and the collective ability to problematize it, the workshop's seclusion depoliticizes it because it removes the moment of domination from public discussion, making it abstract and mystified and justifying it with culturalist arguments. What is the basis for this concealment, this claim of removing it from the work "scene"?

The designation as *clandestine* refers, in a nondefinitive way, to various angles. On one hand, it alludes to conditions of irregular documentation (ranging from complete illegality to precarious documentation; those with the latter are referred to as "the precarious"). On the other hand, it refers to irregularities in the workshop owners' tax situation (although there is also a range of situations between authorization and infraction, between illegality and parallel arrangements with control and monitoring institutions). More broadly, their inscription as clandestine refers to an ambiguous, undefined space when it comes to conceptualizing and differentiating between legal employment and illegal, informal, and under-the-table work and the like. Additionally, many of the workshops are facing allegations of human trafficking from the legal system because of their labor exploitation.[3]

How, then, is the designation of clandestine determined in the case of the workshops? As I noted above, the framework that characterizes the workshops as such is neither clear nor one-dimensional. According to Ariel Lieutier, "usually, the clandestine workshops are enrolled in the AFIP [Federal Administration of Public Income] and give invoices, and very few workshops have been found that are authorized or with authorization in process, and where workers were reduced to servitude" (2010, 24). Other workshops rely on having some workers registered as self-employed. These are workshop-dormitories, where people live and work. But providing housing is not illegal in and of itself and is not a reason for being considered clandestine a priori, hence the nuances of characterizing that condition in an absolute way. Framing the employed workforce under the figure of "reduction to servitude" enables intervention through human trafficking regulations, allowing for legal action.

In a general sense, when the workshops are spoken about, the term *clandestine* is used to designate the juxtaposition of a series of extremely precarious working conditions that mix, in a context of (formal as well as informal) economic growth, *irregularities* from the perspective of the regulation of formal, contractual labor with *illegalities* from the strict legal perspective, in intense situations with no distinction between conditions of life and work, employment and servitude. Features of these *labor forms* are already spread throughout the labor market in general as concrete forms of precaritization, but they reach an extreme level in the workshop, highlighting its simultaneously *exceptional* and *general* character.

Then, if the language of regulation refers to a world of work where the conditions of production need to be legislated, the notion of the clandestine exposes a management of the workforce that exceeds legal parameters and includes vital spheres within the expanded governance of the worker's body and subjectivity. The management of this excess occurs in two ways: (1) as a type of exploitation beyond flexible labor legislation and (2) as the valorization of communitarian life. However, in the workshop, it enables the reemergence of servitude in a developmentalist context—that is, the context of a certain recovery of the national economy—in postneoliberal conditions.

An unexpected overlap complicated the image of the textile workshop even further. In 2007 a clandestine sewing workshop was found operating in the former clandestine detention center Automotores Orletti, an old mechanic shop used as a site for torturing the detained and disappeared from Argentina and other South American countries under the last dictatorship's repressive continental strategy Plan Condor.[4] The deranged overlapping of clandestine conditions further disturbs the public discourse around the textile workshops.[5] What does the persistence of clandestine spaces of confinement mean in a moment when former detention centers are being turned into public spaces dedicated to remembering? That the same site, which still maintains the ruins and traces of its functioning in the hands of state terrorism, would be rented out and utilized as a clandestine manufacturing workshop turns that confinement into an image that is symbolically saturated and that involuntarily connects radically different historical moments. The form of confinement does not refer to political persecution, with its tactics of kidnapping, torture, and death, but rather to the fixing in place of a migrant workforce, which is managed as labor power in renewed conditions of exploitation.

From the Street to Work

The crisis of 2001 and the subsequent decline in challenges to wage labor that emerged from the most radicalized sector of the movement of the unemployed (Colectivo Situaciones and Movimiento de Trabajadores Desocupados (MTD) de Solano 2002; Svampa and Pereyra 2003; Zibechi 2003) allow us to put the migrant workforce into perspective and make it visible as a crucial element of the recomposition of the world of work with new labor forms. The fact that the majority of men and women working in the textile workshops have a migrant background reveals and enables an analysis of key elements of that recomposition. Or, as I noted above, it demonstrates the characteristics of an ongoing reproletarianization. While migrant labor in the clandestine workshops exposes certain exceptional employment conditions, it also reveals a common model of employment in postcrisis Argentina. In this respect, the conditions of migrant labor exacerbate and broaden a debate about working conditions in general and their current constitutive heterogeneity (Mezzadra 2011).

The case of the textile workshops concerns an *organizational formula* that is not confined to the workshop but rather is replicated in other branches and areas of work. The proliferation of the textile workshop beyond the workshop allows for it to be understood as a paradigmatic situation of a precaritization or informalization that continues to expand and change, as a chromaticism within the diverse world of work. At first glance, the migrant workforce encapsulates the flip side of the refusal of work or, at least, its problematization as it was experienced in Argentina with high unemployment levels and the emergence of a broad spectrum of movements of the unemployed that politicized, named, and debated the employment crisis. I say the flip side since the meekness of migrant labor is advertised as the key to its productivity. In this equation, migration's impetus in a decision and longing for new horizons is forfeited or denied, preventing a conceptualization of forms of migrant labor based on something other than culturalist explanations.

It must be noted that this situation coexists with a macropolitical discourse that increasingly emphasizes the national possibilities of economic and political recovery from the crisis, which corresponds with a parallel rethinking of unemployment subsidies, which are changing from policies that combat unemployment to policies that aim to restore work under new forms.

The gap between, or, better, coexistence of, a neodevelopmentalist discourse at the macropolitical level and these labor forms is fundamental for understanding the complexity of their relationship. In an article in the Bolivian newspaper *Renacer*, titled "Variable Policies with Textile Workshops," Jorge Vargas connects the workshops to the growth of local industry and does not regard them as a threat to it, as is usually thought, because of the Fernández de Kirchner government's relative protectionism:

> Another type of government, for example, a neoliberal government, would open up to the free import of apparel, and then we would see how much

the workshops could produce, when an avalanche of garments at bargain prices flooded Argentinean stores and markets and forced the workshops to close and transformed the economic sector. But that is not this government's orientation. Although it has errors and shortcomings, there is a general policy of protecting, strengthening, and developing Argentinean industry and production. And the textile workshops in Buenos Aires and its suburbs form part of this industry, despite the fact that the documentation of many of the owners and workers indicates that they were born in Tarata, Potosí, Achacachi, or Oruro or that they danced the *saya* in Los Yungas.[6]

The Textile Workshop as the Nucleus of the Economy of Migration

The textile workshop concentrates modes of labor that exploit "Bolivian nationality"—which is a convenient way of naming nonnational variables linked to a (not only!) Quechua or Aymara communitarian belonging—as a resource of valorization. In this respect, what is exploited is simultaneously a triple differential: of wages, of legal status, and, primarily, of communitarian wealth.

Workshop managers are responsible for contacting and moving workers, often taking on responsibilities in the recruited worker's community of origin. They organize food (what is eaten, how much, when, and where), make documents available to ensure that workers stay in place, and manage pay following ad hoc criteria (family ties, personal preferences, obedience, completion, thankfulness, etc.), according to calculations of qualities that cannot be measured. They organize the system of indebtedness for the advance on the cost of the trip, housing, and food, and they regulate contact with the world outside the workshop, leisure time and activities, contact with the home country, and the conditions and modalities of shared living (warm beds and overcrowding).

How is that community belonging translated into a job qualification? Bolivians are proposed and advertised as a nationality that is especially submissive and hard-working owing to their *archaic* customs and uses. These are specific attributes that, as stereotypes, operate by qualifying and differentiating the labor force, that is, producing ethnic-national difference and giving it value in the market.

How is that specific qualification sustained and strengthened? In the first place, migrant working men and women are alone and do not know the city or their rights. This clearly characterizes the migrant condition. They have arrived because of family and/or neighborhood connections, which function as specific contacts through which they migrate and arrive directly at the workshop. Those modes of kinship and/or community relations obligate migrants to innumerable concessions toward their employers and reinforce the workers' commitment to the workshop. The workshop then becomes an apparatus of reterritorialization; it builds a new type of community in an unknown city.

> She worked in the kitchen for a few months, and then she started working with the machines and earned as much as the rest us. Since I managed all the machines and was the "niece," after four or five months they increased my pay by one hundred pesos. I earned four hundred instead of three hundred pesos. And they would say to me: "We are doing you a favor, because you are our niece, because you learned to manage all the machines, and because you are sort of in charge." And, as the person in charge, I also had to help prepare the fabric before production, stretch it, make it "sleep" so that it would be ready for sewing. I had to distribute the cuts, organize the girls, help my cousin with his tasks, go the market. . . . For all that work they gave me a one hundred peso raise. But we didn't get any breaks. (Colectivo Simbiosis and Colectivo Situaciones 2011, 64)

The work seems endless and borderless owing to a *differential of exploitation* that is maintained through uprooting and through the type of communitarian reterritorialization that is exploited. But it is also supported, as I will discuss below, by a strong will to progress. *There is a double calculation. The first is made before migrating. The second is made when the workers discover that working conditions are worse than they had imagined.*

The workshop economy is not confined to the workshop alone. It includes a constellation of institutions: radio stations, nightclubs, transportation and remittance companies, clinics, certain neighborhoods, and (implicit and clandestine, and explicit and legal) arrangements with authorities (police, city and provincial governments). It is also replicated (although in different ways) in other jobs: among farmhands, fish cleaners, greengrocers, construction workers, and rural workers. Similar working conditions are reproduced in those fields, making the organizational form of the workshop a sort of *prototype*: expansive yet maintaining its relative *invisibility.*[7]

A Transnational Dimension

The type of heterogeneous articulation woven around the workshop demonstrates a transnational assemblage that accounts for a diffused and confusing status of work: it connects the microenterprise to self-employment, family work with waged relations supported by kinship ties, and the workshop using underdeveloped technology to the commercialization of major brands that even export their products.

The textile workshop articulates distinct productive sequences and levels. Migrant workers cut, sew, and go to the market; they also live in the workshops, care for their children and those of others, clean, and cook. The workshop owners controlling that production, who are also migrants but with successful business trajectories, work to order as manufacturers for diverse brands, but they also make a profit producing garments to sell in the megamarket La Salada, sometimes even creating their own brands.[8]

There is another figure: the intermediary who tends to operate as the nexus between the workshop owner and the brand. Sometimes the intermediaries are phantom manufacturers who play a role in laundering money for the brands or serve as a liable figure in tax terms. They locate the top brands sold in the market's most expensive businesses, with some allocating part of their production for export.[9]

At first reading, one could argue that this is the extrapolation of an already existing productive reality from Bolivia to Argentina, that it is a form of integration from below through flexible modes of employment, in a sort of postneoliberal regional homogenization capable of including a variety of increasingly broad labor forms, which are recombined in each territory. This suggests that migration also causes labor forms to migrate, multiplying and transnationalizing the informal status of labor. As Álvaro García Linera notes, referring to Bolivia after the neoliberal reforms of the 1990s, a "dualized" productive system was organized between companies with foreign capital and households and small workshops. He states, "Abandoning the ideal of 'modernisation,' the new business-order has consciously and strategically subordinated the informal shop, home-based work and the kinship-networks of the subaltern classes to numerically controlled systems of production (industry and mining) and the monetary flows of foreign stock-markets (banking). The model of accumulation has thus become a hybrid one that unites, in a tiered and hierarchical manner, the production-structures of the fifteenth, eighteenth and twentieth centuries, with circuitous mechanisms of exaction and the colonial extortion of domestic, communal artisan, *campesino* and small-business productive forces in Bolivian society" (2014, 212). García Linera refers to this mixed mode as *baroque "modernity."*

However, there is a *surplus* in the work carried out by the migrant workforce. Their uprooting, their lack of knowledge of the city and their rights, and their forced seclusion in spaces like the workshop produce a *differential of exploitation* that is essential to productive organization: "As immigrants, the exploitation that we suffer is much worse than the normal exploitation, in our own country. For many reasons: because we don't have papers, because we don't know the place, we don't know the laws that apply to us nor what our rights actually are. Furthermore, not knowing anyone nor how to move around in the city forces you to enclose yourself and ultimately accept everything your bosses tell you" (Colectivo Simbiosis and Colectivo Situaciones 2011, 10–11).

My hypothesis is that the *differential of exploitation* provides the migrant workforce with a complex training built on the calculation that regulates aspirations for progress and obedience. They obey because they calculate that obedience will lead to incalculable sums. In this juncture, the situation of the migrant workers oscillates between being investors in themselves (as in the Foucauldian definition) and being victims who are compelled by conditions of extreme loneliness and personal dependence.

A New Entrepreneurship

A specific form of entrepreneurship emerges from the informalization exploited by the textile workshops, which valorizes domestic-communitarian elements, brings dynamics of self-organization into play, and nourishes concrete political networks. If Saskia Sassen notes that the growing polarization of the economy between the home and the company makes increasingly more sectors of the urban economy informal (2007, 149), I instead propose to think about the home-company mixture and the way it functions in the urban economy.

The ethnic-communitarian component of this entrepreneurship plays a fundamental role in valorizing that difference in terms of flexibilization within the market. It appeals to that difference to build trust and turns family traditionalism into a code of operation for the labor market.

One map is traced onto another: the family onto labor, towns of the Bolivian countryside onto Buenos Aires. However, in this superimposition, everything changes: the value of community becomes flexible until it is turned into a way of extracting surplus value in the workshop, and territorial belonging becomes a form of transnational grouping.[10]

Let me continue exploring the communitarian character of this entrepreneurship. Such entrepreneurship combines competition and cooperation, making its operative modes fundamentally ambivalent. Competition is intrinsic to the logic of proliferation and fragmentation of the workshops that supply garments, through intermediaries, to major brands. Yet there is also cooperation because of the unified representation of the "Bolivian economy" standing against accusations (in the media or from organizations against slave labor), defending the entities that bring together workshop owners. These entities, however, are presented not as labor or business entities but as community representatives. Owing to the same communitarian formulation of their associative structure, they form a political-social business class that assumes responsibility for the quasi-integral management of the workforce: its movement, housing, food, health, employment, leisure, and so on.

The figure of the free wage laborer is called into question by the same logic of operation—meaning profitability—in favor of a mode that has been described as slave labor in the media.

The type of entrepreneur described above assists recent arrivals, finds housing for them, shares contacts, acts as a job board and funeral agency, and intervenes in making complaints to the local government. They constitute themselves corporatively against Argentine business, media, and political organizations. They are effective because of a sort of power of the ghetto: to the extent that they confine the network in which the textile workshop functions to the "Bolivian economy," they establish themselves as the defenders and guarantors of this economy. However, at the same time as that economy is presented as inseparable from a cultural ethos, the employers also validate their representativeness as legitimate interpreters of those cultures and traditions. It is not by chance that a majority of the workshop owners' organizations have names that sound more like a cultural association than a business one.

This entrepreneurship exploits communitarian belonging in two ways. The first is literal: the workshop owners go directly to communities in Bolivia to recruit workers. The second is broader: once in the workshop, the job qualifications reference a communitarian know-how. The entire family's involvement, the relationship with employers (which is often also based on relations of family trust—employers are usually called "uncle," not "boss," whether or not a family bond exists), and the incorporation of ancestral modes of collective labor and knowledge result in a flexible qualification, capable of enormous sacrifices and hardships, which functions as the material and spiritual support for the exploitation of the labor force, which becomes extremely profitable as the first link in the textile production chain.

In this regard, the language of community and the constitution of *the community as capital* are particular to this economy. The language of community is also what allows this economy to be read in culturalist terms, not recognizing the materiality of its constitution as labor power and its productive relations (see also Hall and Mellino 2011).

The emphasis on the nationalization of difference ("Bolivianness") is turned on its head and becomes the *ethnicization of difference*: the native or communitarian way of being as a specific quality in the valorization process. In turn, both mechanisms are reinforced and interpellated by various forms of politics. That identity is simultaneously invoked and defined by the corporativist representation performed by workshop owners. There are two strategic goals for this. First, it is a way of having privileged access to the "communitarian labor force."[11] Second, it is a way of enclosing the migrant economy in itself and reinforcing the segmentation of the labor force.

As Yann Moulier Boutang (2006) notes, if foreign communities faced with conditions of institutional inequality responded by defensively regrouping and generating their own forms of organizations, they themselves, as communities, would be translated into "economic advantage," by minimizing transaction costs, as well as enabling the exploitation of stereotypes as a way of hierarchizing the labor market. Moulier Boutang indicates that they manage to exploit a "rent of position" (13).

This use of community is radically different from that of *ethnicity as strategy* (Baud et al. 1996)—or "strategic ethnicity," to paraphrase feminism's use of the term *essentialism*—deployed as a skill of mobilization, the construction of a political agenda, and a repertoire of demands.[12] At the same time, it signals clear opposition to experiences of constructing the community as an eminently antagonistic resource. It is in this sense that *community can also be used as an organizational image for urban workers from another point of view.*

In this respect, discussing reforms in favor of union and labor flexibilization in Bolivia, Oscar Olivera, a Cochabamba factory representative and leader of the Water War of 2000, says, "The community and the union. Now, we have ancestral roots that refer to the concept of community. The community's way of feeling and acting is being lost and we want to recover it. From our perspective, *the union can be an urban replica of the community*; that is, *nobody can fragment or divide us, decisions are made collectively and by consensus, and there must be a rotation of responsibilities, leadership positions must be revokable,* in short, as it operates in Andean communities."[13] As I will show in what follows, the communitarian features that Olivera points to do not have anything in common with the communitarian tradition that is invoked as a culturalist argument in the exploitation of textile workers.

An Assemblage Economy

Workshop and market, as well as workshop and brand, are inseparable. Therefore, the same can be said about the brand-market relationship. The segmentation of the value chain enables intermediaries, workshop owners, brands, and workers to complement one another, operating in a limited physical space.[14] What is important is the connection between these links: receiving the delivery order, meeting deadlines, moving merchandise, transporting workers. In turn, this allows some brands to also carry out part of their production "over the table," legally, whose invoices and receipts can be presented in case of an inspection, mixing that with another part that is under the table, or clandestine, and remains hidden.

The reality of the workshops can be used to describe a mode of accumulation linked to the microscale, since these are relatively small workshops that do not seek to grow but to multiply through kinship relationships. Is it possible to conceptualize a new popular entrepreneurship of informal economies (market vendors, workshop owners, etc.) by their capacity for "fractal accumulation" (Gutiérrez Aguilar 2011a), in other words, not aiming to change scales?

It is precisely on this scale that what I call "fractal accumulation" is inscribed in the market space. The workshop, as part of the same machinery, functions as an assemblage.

The textile workshops are preferably small. They usually include between ten and twenty people. However, it is difficult to categorize them as small or family based if we assume that this is an interim stage and that they seek to expand or grow. In fact, the largest ones are the least common. It is precisely that small and family scale that makes them productive and profitable, that makes them flexible enough to cope with the rhythm and variation of orders and makes it possible for them to alternate with producing to sell directly at their own stall in the market. This makes the distinction between family businesses and small- or medium-size businesses obsolete.

That microscale, on one hand, generates a profit margin that enables enterprises to multiply, progressing toward the sale of their own clothing in La Salada, or toward opening a bar or restaurant or some other little business. On the other hand, it accelerates competition between workshops.[15]

The workshop, then, functions in a network: it supposes another quantity of small workshops that make the sector competitive. The workshop has been one of the fundamental pieces of the textile industry since the industry was restructured following the end of peso-dollar convertibility and massive importation. Its mostly small scale is not a condition of widespread exception but rather a feature of the textile industry's new mode of functioning.

Its small scale drives the possibility of diversification for small entrepreneurs. The workshop enables the expansion of other economic networks, in which it also finds its reason for being. Apparel sellers in markets and the radio stations that are listened to in the workshop, as well as the doctors' offices and dance clubs where workers go, form a constellation of enterprises that owe their position and initial capital to the textile workshops.

There are real estate agencies that specialize in renting to clandestine entrepreneurs: houses with multiple units that are almost always old and in poor condition but that have various rooms and/or two floors. These real estate agencies know that the properties are intended for unlicensed workshops and therefore do not demand contracts and guarantees as they would for a normal location. Additionally, these properties are not suitable for other uses because of their poor condition.

The workshop then functions as a dormitory, kitchen, play space for children, and work space. There tends to be a cook or someone in charge of the food. There is only one bathroom. Conditions of overcrowding, lack of privacy or individual space, and issues with security and hygiene have been reported by various former workers and collected in different chronicles. They are highlighted, furthermore, as proof that they are working in conditions of slavery.

The workshop is easily assembled. The equipment that it requires is cheap and simple, which enables its eventual removal, or the workshop's complete dismantling. Thus, starting a workshop only requires a house, some not very expensive capital goods, and an electrical connection. Overcrowding and poor nutrition result in anemia, and the dust that accumulates in the environment leads to frequent cases of tuberculosis and other lung diseases. In spite of the high turnover, the supply of workers is maintained by the continuous flow of migrants who follow one another as "apprentices." The technical skills of sewing are widespread among Bolivian men and women, thus fitting the workshop's requirements.

The workshop organizes an entire economy of settling the recently arrived migrant workers. It mixes mobility and immobility: while it fixes shifts in a warm bed, it is powered by a workforce with high turnover, a turnover driven by the extreme working conditions that workers tend to put up with for at most a few years (a rhythm that accelerates with generational change). Meanwhile, there are attempts to flee, requests for leniency in order to return to the home country, arrangements and agreements, layoffs, promotions, and independence.

In turn, the economic importance of the clandestine workshop as the nucleus of the migrant economy is—directly or indirectly—interwoven with the migratory, informal, spatial housing economy that has been established in the *villas de emergencia* in Buenos Aires and its suburbs.

The Textile Workshop as Exception: Three Arguments for Its (In)Visibility

The clandestine presents itself as a condition that is simultaneously exceptional and proliferating. The textile workshop in Argentina is not a *normal* workplace: it is both a workshop-dormitory and a community space, a space of a labor intensity extended in workdays of more than twelve hours, with rotating shifts, and combined with a highly risky migratory wager. For many recently arrived migrants from different parts of Bolivia, their entire life takes place within those few meters, as the workshop solves both the question of living space and that of work in the same space-time. There, people not only work but cook, raise children, and sleep. At first, it is a way of protecting themselves from an unknown city.

A sequence of events led to the textile workshop's visibility as an *anomalous* space. As an enclave of a specific economy, it became known for two issues: the fire in a workshop located on Luis Viale Street in March 2006, in which six people died, and that workshop's subsequent characterization in the media as slave labor. A legal-anthropological polemic later intervened in that definition of labor and was fundamental in the creation of a genealogy of the relations of force at stake in how this type of work is defined. A third moment, after the media coverage of the case and the legal prosecution of similar situations, originates with its incorporation into the global agenda owing to the connection between the new Pope Francis and one of the Argentinean organizations behind the condemnation of these work-shops as neo-slave labor.

Can this sequence be linked in order to understand the operation of strategies of victimization, moralization, and legal prosecution that organize a certain field of visibility of migrant labor in Argentina? Speaking even more broadly, could this suggest a type of connection between the norm and the popular economy that leads to the moralization (and condemnation) of the world of the poor?

Visibilization Strategies

The production of jurisprudence in respect to certain *anomalous* labor situations particularly reveals how the law is confronted with normative production in situations of exception (exceptions that become permanent in the "tradition of the oppressed" that Walter Benjamin (1969) develops in his thesis about history). In the case that I am analyzing here, the exception occurs in two ways: the historically *exceptional* character of the migratory status in respect to the norm of labor law (Moulier Boutang 2006) and, what is more decisive for my analysis, the efficacy of the community as an exceptional dimension in the face of a modern norm of the organization of labor (Chatterjee 2004).

I propose to go beyond this doubly exceptional status to think concretely about a *specifically postmodern articulation of the communitarian*: its capacity for becoming a labor attribute, in the specific qualifications of the migrant workforce of the Bolivian highlands in Buenos Aires, and also being a repertoire of practices mixing life and work, family and commercial ties, relationships of trust and of exploitation. This mixture challenges the exceptional while also exacerbating it.

This communitarian surplus (or community value) is invoked and utilized in conflicting and heterogeneous ways (without ignoring its ambivalence), placing its multiple uses and the pluralization of its combinations as part of an economy of migration in Argentina into tension. However, this perspective— which is not only fairer from the cognitive point of view but also, most important, more active from the point of view of micropolitical strategies— is undermined by a series of arguments that seek to reduce it through what I will identify here as three procedures: culturalization, juridicalization, and moralization. I will examine them one by one.

The Culturalist Argument

The culturalist perspective is summarized in a controversial landmark court ruling in relation to the textile workshops. In 2008 the federal judge Norberto Oyarbide acquitted three executives of an apparel company, who had been accused of "contracting sewing workshops where undocumented immigrants were employed in conditions of extreme labor precarity." In the ruling, the judge argued that this mode of exploitation functioned as the legacy of "cultural patterns and customs of the indigenous peoples of the Bolivian highlands, from whence came the majority" of the workshop owners and workers, and that the people living in the workshop were "a human group that coexists as an ayllu or extended family group native to that region, that functions as a sort of cooperative." This resolution was appealed by both the district attorney and the prosecuting attorney. Bolivian authorities in Argentina, through their general consul, also rejected the ruling, saying that the judge "should have learned about the nature of ancestral customs that do not have anything to do with the sad systems of slavery" of the clandestine workshops.[16]

The ruling aims to make explicit a direct and understandable continuity between the form of the *ayllu* or *family community* and the requirements of new modes of exploitation. Thus, *the ayllu is translated into a productive unit for the textile workshop, but, at the same time, because it is categorized as an ancestral-cultural structure, it is denied as a form of labor organization and therefore left outside the reach of the law.* The paradox is exposed: the ruling speaks of ancestral traditions to situate in a distant *cultural origin* what functions as a form of exploitation here and now. That origin operates as an argument that exonerates the workshops' current mode of organization. This culturalist justification, under the guise of recognizing a tradition, defends and protects the exceptional nature of the textile workshop's labor forms precisely by not considering them labor. If the *communal logic* was created outside of the parameters of capitalist production, this same *reference to origin* would exempt it from being judged according to the *logic of exploitation* in the present, while completely incorporating it into the textile industry's use of outsourcing as a key component of its new flexible structure. The same argument had already been used by the Tribunal II of the Buenos Aires Federal Chamber:

> On that occasion, judges Martín Irurzun and Horacio Cattani dismissed the cases against the workshop owners who had been indicted by the federal judge Ariel Lijo. In their ruling, they made an allusion to the supposed

cultural tradition of indigenous peoples and to the ayllu, a community organization of the Aymara people. According to academic definitions, the ayllu was a form of extended family community that collectively worked on a common property, in the highlands, where they received the same benefit and paid at most part of their production to the Inca state as tributary. Tradition says that discriminatory practices and the possibility of individual accumulation did not exist there, the opposite of the precapitalist systems of exploitation that are practiced in the clandestine workshops operating in Buenos Aires.

How exactly does the discourse of community unity function as a syntax of exploitation? It does so by the *transposition in time* of completely different productive forms, now unified in the space-time unit of the textile workshop composed by migrants. It also engages in *territorial transposition*: it flattens the difference between a common property territory (and its relationship with a form of prenational state authority) and the workshop as a private enclave that the state's judicial power, in this ruling, *exempts* from national labor regulation. In acquitting the defendants, Oyarbide also argued that it had not been proved that the goal of the accused was to "directly or indirectly make a profit," which is punishable by Article 117 of Immigration Law 25,871 ("promoting or facilitating the illegal permanence of foreigners in the national territory with the aim of directly or indirectly making a profit will be punishable by prison or confinement of one to six years").[17]

Oyarbide dictated the acquittal based on the previously mentioned arguments and further inspections in which it was discovered that the migratory situation of people in the place was "regularized," while "not a single person carrying out tasks of the textile industry nor the machinery for developing that labor were found."[18] The ruling was appealed by the district attorney, Luis Comparatore, and the prosecuting attorney, Rodolfo Yanzón. "It is clear that after the first proceedings, the workshop owners stopped producing, moved the workshops to other sites, and regularized the immigration status of the people living there," Yanzón said to the newspaper *Página/12*.[19] He also rejected arguments based on "ancient customs of indigenous peoples, which are totally irrelevant to the case and could even be labeled as discriminatory." The article states, "The lawyer requested the intervention of Tribunal I of the Chamber, which has an opposite approach to that of Cattani and Irurzun: on November 30 of last year, judges Eduardo Freiler, Gabriel Cavallo, and Eduardo Farah requested that Oyarbide not limit the investigation to the workshop owners and that he inquire into the companies 'that could have taken advantage of this activity through commissioning work under these conditions.'"

In response to this argument, the College of Anthropology Graduates published a statement (June 24, 2008) opposing Oyarbide's ruling:

> Although the ayllu and the current system of labor exploitation in the textile industry are fundamentally different and belong to contexts that make them incomparable, the two are conflated in the ruling. The ruling ignores the very organization of the ayllu, which, founded on values such as reciprocity and horizontality, stands in contrast to the asymmetry of the boss-employee relationship. . . . The fact that workers do not agree to these working conditions in situations of equality, but rather in a relationship of unequal power intensified by the irregular condition that employers encourage, should have been taken into account.[20]

The Federal Chamber of the city of Buenos Aires revoked Oyarbide's decision in September 2008. The argument was considered "misguided for attempting to extrapolate structures belonging to cultural patterns of the highlands to explain the functioning of the textile workshops."[21]

There are two sides to the culturalist argument (a ploy of the spiritualization of the economy). In the case of Oyarbide's ruling, it is exculpatory; by restricting the issue of the workshops to a matter of archaic cultural practices, it avoids thinking about a situation that challenges national labor regulations. However, the anthropological-expert statement, which takes responsibility for differentiating the two situations (the ayllu and the textile workshop), fails to consider how certain communitarian elements are assembled with the textile economy led by Bolivian migrants. Both arguments seek to classify and frame the situation of the textile workshop in relation to a definition of the ayllu that it does not fit with. Are there elements of a communitarian practice organizing the space-time of the textile workshop (and the whole economy with which it is amalgamated) that require thinking about the communitarian as an ambiguous labor attribute in an urban and postmodern setting? The contemporaneity of noncontemporaneous elements (to use Ernst Bloch's [1995] expression again) requires a different way of analyzing the assemblage of dissimilar elements and logics in a conjunction (the textile workshop) that ties them together in a new and problematic way.

The communitarian modes—of organization, authority, labor, and so on— find a new compatibility with the post-Fordist world of the partial denationalization of segments of the national state and the weakening of the large centers of work (García Linera 2001; Ong 2006; Sassen 2008).

The Judicial Argument

If, as Marcel Mauss (2002) advised, the colonial problem is the problem of the labor force, the colonial dimension—a determined relation of exploitation and domination—is inseparable from the issue of migrant labor. The question of heteronomy is decisive on this point. Why did the term *slave labor* spread so quickly? Why did it fit so readily into the media narrative as well as with the representations of certain *Argentinean* organizations, spectators, and pundits in general?

This term was adopted owing to its dissemination by the organization La Alameda and the mainstream media, for whom it served as a representation of that situation. In turn, it allowed for two registers: scandal and condemnation. The term was used to categorize conditions of confinement, the fusion of workplace and housing, and relationships mixing labor and kinship, which do not respect any legal convention, but, above all, the term signals that it is *foreign labor. Slave labor is foreign, almost by definition.* The conception that comes through in media descriptions primarily emphasizes the otherness and foreignness of that labor form, thus making it attributable only to a condition of being foreign. There is not a strict legal definition of slave labor in Argentina, although there is a definition of "reduction to servitude" that functions in the legal framing of some cases.[22] This immediately leads to a more general perspective: the debate about human trafficking and the recent passage of a law on the matter (Law 26,364, approved in 2008) that is frequently invoked as a possible legal framework for regulating what happens in the clandestine workshops, associating them with—or even making them equivalent to—brothels. *Thus, prostitution and slave labor share a vague common statute, relating internal and external migration, understood solely from the perspective of trafficking, and viewing foreigners and women, in their own way, as two figures of the helpless other.* The inclusion of minors as workers and cohabitants in the clandestine workshops reinforces this analogy.

The argument for legally prosecuting the textile workshops, then, relies on understanding them within the broader perspective of human trafficking. Thus, this expands the idea of a submission of will, the workers' total deception, and the complete impossibility of leaving the textile workshop, which would be an entirely forced state. This legal framework enables the condemnation of these situations and is inexorably linked to the moralist argument. *Through the figure of trafficking, the judicialization of the textile workshop manages to remove the issue of migrant labor from the debate and reduce it to the figure of the victim.* It was the organizations of workshop managers that first opposed this moniker. They brandished placards saying, "We are not slaves, we are workers." The word *worker* reclaims autonomy, that of free wage labor, as an image that is contrasted to the slave's subjugation. This counterpoint will be a constant part of the debate, which is precisely about the conditions that define a labor or life situation, but also about the national limits corresponding to the status of being a worker.

There is often an oral contract between the workshop owner and the worker. It almost always begins with a family-type contact who makes the connection in Bolivia and organizes the worker's move to Buenos Aires and arranges a place for them to stay upon arriving. Sometimes workshop owners travel to Bolivia themselves to search for future employees. They start recruiting within their own families, later opening up the offer to rings of proximity: more distant relatives, friends, people from the same community. There is also a more independent network, superimposed onto the previous one: announcements and calls for workers that are circulated in Bolivia on the radio and by signs in public places and even in churches. An entire transportation system operates in relation to this movement, and once the migrants arrive, there are key corners (specifically in the neighborhoods of Liniers and Flores) where workshop owners go to look for and "hire" recently arrived migrants.

The oral contract holds a promise that allows it to function: that the workers will be able to save all their earnings since they will not have to pay for housing or food. However, housing and food are deducted from or indirectly included in the wage.[23] What the promise more concretely entails is that the migrant will not have to obtain housing and food after having recently arrived in an unknown place, usually without contacts or only with contact with those who are already in the workshop. However, the agreed-upon wage tends to be a price per garment, which makes the obligation of productivity fall onto the workers.

Is there or is there not a contract? Would this be the blurry boundary between worker and slave? Under the title "Human Trafficking through Employment Agencies in El Alto," the Bolivian magazine *Cambio* quotes the director of employment in the Labor Ministry, César Siles, as saying that the only official entity that can open a job board is the government, through the Employment Promoter Unit (Unidad Promotora de Empleos): "This body fulfills the role of intermediary between the labor market's supply and demand, in accordance with Article 31 of the General Labor Law." However, faced with the high quantity of commercial agencies that are also employment agencies, the government sought to legislate by decree: "This is a stronger legal framework for sanctioning commercial agencies that are also private employment agencies. With the decree we will have a specific legal framework to proceed with closing these businesses," Siles said. "Despite the regulation, agencies sell the addresses of potential jobs and offer job postings on boards, but without giving the employer's contact information because those interested must pay the intermediary between three and five bolivianos for the address or telephone number."[24]

The mixture of contractual forms and trafficking makes this labor difficult to classify and challenges the classification of slavery. It also makes ad hoc regulation necessary for matters of a transnational nature. The chronicle of a workshop owner's detention in northern Argentina, while transporting workers for his textile workshops in Buenos Aires, reveals *the role of the labor contract in noncontractual conditions, a characterization that complicates the notion of trafficking as well as that of the contract*: "First they said that they were going to visit relatives, but later they admitted that they had signed a contract to work in workshops located in Buenos Aires, with a workday from 7 a.m. to 11 p.m. for 500 pesos a month, with the obligation to live in those same workshops," said the Salta police's head of Prevention and Struggle against Human Trafficking, Chief Reinaldo Choque.[25]

The contract alluded to implied (a) a sixteen-hour workday, without planned vacations, (b) a salary of a little over a hundred dollars per month (from which transportation, housing, and food would be deducted), (c) the obligation to live in the workplace, (d) retention of personal documents, and (e) voluntary recruitment by employment agencies and the cross-border move. Are these contracts of servitude? Are they forms of voluntary servitude?

It seems that reducing the migrant's situation to trafficking erases a decisive differential element: a map of deterritorializations and reterritorializations of entire working populations, from the displacement of mining communities in Bolivia in the 1980s to their relocation in the urban peripheries (mainly El Alto), and later through migratory routes toward Argentina, Brazil, and Spain. Repositioning this series of displacements and movements, which are caused by unemployment but are also the effect of vital strategies and decisions, allows for reframing the migratory impulse beyond the issue of slavery, a narrative that completely infantilizes and subjugates migrants. The power differential involved in these movements in respect to a network of human trafficking is incomparable. Instead, it is useful to frame it in terms of what the Mujeres Creando collective calls *exiles of neoliberalism*, extending the term *exile* beyond its meaning in reference to political exiles during the dictatorship and thus reframing the continuity of effects between dictatorship and neoliberalism in Latin America. In turn, this makes it necessary to elaborate an analysis of these migrations as the increasing transnationalization of the workforce, related to the requirements of the global market (Mezzadra and Neilson 2013), but in this case emphasizing the particularity of a South-South movement. This requires recognizing migration as a new family strategy of transnational social reproduction, one that disassembles and reassembles homes and calculates its forms of obedience in relation to longer-term projects of progress.

This idea situates the communitarian issue beyond its culturalist connotation, while still recognizing its *renewal* under new, ambiguous, variable modes that are in constant tension. That flexibility challenges the stereotype of the community as a homogeneous, stable figure, rooted to a fixed and delimited territory. Connecting the communitarian issue to migration requires understanding the community in movement, with all of the ambivalence that this raises. More than anything, it demonstrates a vigorous popular activity that is capable of updating its uses and customs and connecting with a transnational economy. The migratory dynamic then appears in another way: as a complex and strategic force that is ambivalent with regard to the ways in which the communitarian becomes an element of valorization that expresses the variegated character of the circuits of value traversing our cities.

The Moralizing Argument

La Alameda association, which arose out of the neighborhood assemblies following the crisis of 2001, was important in visibilizing the issue of textile workshops and propagating their categorization as slavery. Recuperating the method of the *escrache*, La Alameda receives complaints from former workers and other types of informants and organizes public acts of denunciation in front of the buildings where clandestine workshops are located.[26] Along with No Chains, La Alameda coordinates an international network in opposition to slave labor, which seeks to promote responsible consumption. Its leader, Gustavo Vera, has named and denounced the main clothing brands that contract with clandestine workshops. Furthermore, Vera has become a character with a large media presence, both because of the threats and attacks he has received from representatives of the workshop owners and because of his alliance with Cardinal Bergoglio, who is now the pope and obviously an important global figure. Together they produced high-impact images: "Surrounded by *cartoneros* [waste pickers] and prostitutes, Bergoglio condemned 'slavery.' The cardinal harshly denounced that there are people who are 'left over' in the City."[27] At the request of the cooperative La Alameda and the Movement of Excluded Workers, Bergoglio dedicated Mass to "the cartoneros and the victims of human trafficking, exploited in the clandestine textile workshops and in the brothels. The first was July 1, 2008, in the Emigrants' Church of La Boca. The Archbishop of Buenos Aires reiterated that yesterday, as today, 'there are slaves' in the city."[28]

Vera argues that the only voice of the Bolivian community that is listened to is the bosses' voice; therefore, the owners' perspective is hegemonic. La Alameda's strategy is to give a *voice* to the victims, to those making complaints and those being "rescued." Thus, La Alameda constructs the Bolivian worker as needing to be rescued, as subject to deception, abuse, and confinement. It is no coincidence that this savior business has contact and a growing alliance with the Catholic Church, through the figure of Cardinal Bergoglio, which was consolidated in 2013 with Bergoglio's elevation to become Pope Francis.

The moralization jointly practiced by La Alameda and the Catholic Church is based on the belief that migrant workers do not have their own rationality, that their actions are to be condemned, and that they do what they do precisely because they are subjugated and forced. The savior organizations' colonial imprint organizes an entire discourse of rescue and tutelage that sees itself as betrayed when those who have supposedly been saved return to the textile workshop or defend their bosses, or, even more so, when they reject and/or critique the mission of founding cooperatives in accordance with the organizations' rules.

There are three common features of the procedures of culturalization, juridicalization, and moralization. First, they all come from Argentinean organizations (the judicial system, expert knowledge, social organizations, and the Catholic Church). They all, in different ways, characterize the workshop as an issue of foreignness: in other words, they consider the operation of migrant labor as something strictly distant and foreign. The legal framework of trafficking and its corresponding organizations (La Alameda and the Catholic Church) propose the victimization and infantilization of workers in order to remove migrant labor from its status as *incomprehensible.* This perspective goes hand in hand with moralization that includes condemning those economies, as well as denouncing their operation. The *exteriority* of these perspectives in respect to the logic of the textile workshop is never questioned.

Where Is the Voice of the Textile Workers?

In an interview in Buenos Aires, Silvia Rivera Cusicanqui (Colectivo Simbiosis and Colectivo Situaciones 2011) argues that the voice of the textile workers exhibits a calculation that nobody wants to hear, a rationality of progress that includes and justifies that which is considered slave labor from another perspective. She returns to Gayatri Chakravorty Spivak's (1988) question about the subaltern's power to speak, to observe what no one wants to or is able to see or hear. The tenacity of the migrant who encloses himself or herself in the workshop is like the joy of the widow immolating herself (the celebrated case of Chandra recounted by Spivak). Rivera Cusicanqui's perspective can be compared to the perspective of the former textile workers of Colectivo Simbiosis (Colectivo Simbiosis and Colectivo Situaciones 2011), whose voice does not deny the existence of that calculation but complicates it with an experience, a trajectory that adds levels of meaning, memory, and discomfort to the world of the textile workshop. This dialogue allows us to think about two issues that are radically opposed to the procedures that I described above: on one hand, migrant calculation and its derivations and, on the other hand, the production of an understanding of the injustice and exploitation of the workshop from within the textile workshop itself.

Let me return to Rivera Cusicanqui's explanation of why the workshop's dynamic cannot be encapsulated by the notion of slave labor. Instead, she proposes using the categories of *legitimate domination, paying dues,* and *deferred reciprocity* as alternative ways of understanding a generational, economic, and progressive dynamic of migrant microenterprise.

SILVIA RIVERA CUSICANQUI (SRC): While they are being exploited, they are also building their microenterprise. The idea that there is a dynamic of slavery in play in these places seems totally mistaken to me.
COLECTIVO SITUACIONES (CS): What would you call it?
SRC: Subordination, exploitation, a workforce paying migratory dues as a first step toward receiving what is called deferred reciprocity. This is what your parents do for you and you have the obligation to do for your children. Your mother cared for your daughter, you have to care for

your daughter's daughter, as a repayment to your mother. It is a circuit of repayment, deferred in time: he was exploited, now it is his turn to exploit. It seems to be very cruelly colonialist, but this rule is not colonial. In any case, it would be a class relation. They do not consider the exploited to be savages. They consider them apprentices but not savages. Therefore, the word *slave*, which always comes from a cultural heteronomy, is mistaken. Although it is true that the knowledge acquired in colonial exploitation becomes an input for all forms of exploitation. For example, it is common in contexts of extremely intense exploitation that an othering of workers is deployed, up to considering them savages. For this reason Peronist citizenship is so strong here, because if something has broken, it is that premise, that of the worker as a savage-other, a resource inherited from colonial exploitation, because the repertoire of domination also has its own baggage of acquired knowledges. And they are cultures of servitude, as the anthropophagists say. (Rivera Cusicanqui and Colectivo Situaciones in Colectivo Simbiosis and Colectivo Situaciones 2011, 20–22)

What would actually challenge this type of work's classification as slavery, according to Rivera Cusicanqui, would be the existence of clear rules of manumission. What can perhaps be seen in several accounts is the type of *urban calculation* carried out by the person who migrates, a certain relationship between sacrifice and vital cycle. The nomadism of the migrant workers, especially the youth, is a know-how that combines short-term tactics ("for a short time, no more," as Colectivo Simbiosis says) tied to concrete objectives with a flexibility that enables combining piecework, small contraband enterprises, semirural work (as farmhands), domestic work, self-employment as a vendor, and/or work as a traveling vendor (markets, reselling, etc.).

In *deferred reciprocity* the temporal nucleus is also central. There is also a contentious dimension to the double-sidedness or circularity of this economy of deferred repayment: "In modern Quechua the temporally deferred exchange of equal work is known as *ayni*. But in ancient Quechua, this expression also means vengeance" (Abduca 2011).[29] In the postponed repayment or reciprocity, then, there would be a sort of system of justice and/or revenge, of the inversion of places, of the exchange of roles (as José María Arguedas narrates in "El sueño del pongo" [1965]). *The one who was exploited later exploits: reciprocity-revenge.*

The following image can be interpreted within that circuit: the Alasitas market is held every year in Bolivia and in Buenos Aires in January. In this market, people buy and sell miniature replicas of what they wish to accomplish during the year: bricks portend securing housing, babies invoke fertility, or cash and cars represent such valuables. In Buenos Aires, one of the most widely sold replicas is a model of a textile workshop that holds the promise of having one's own workshop.[30]

The majority of textile workers aim to become owners, to become independent from the workshop's owner and open their own workshop. It is a sort of natural evolution for the workers: they know how the workshop operates from within, they have the contacts, and they understand the dynamic of the work. Clearly, this logic of proliferation "from within" the workshops stresses and problematizes the notion of slave labor used to characterize those workshops. To return to Rivera Cusicanqui: "It seems to be very cruelly colonialist, but this rule is not colonial. In any case, it would be a class relation. They do not consider the exploited to be savages. They consider them apprentices but not savages. Therefore, the word *slave*, which always comes from a cultural heteronomy, is mistaken. Although it is true that the knowledge acquired in colonial exploitation becomes an input for all forms of exploitation" (in Colectivo Simbiosis and Colectivo Situaciones 2011, 22).

Rivera Cusicanqui's proposal emphasizes, then, an *autonomy* in this economy that makes it impossible to conceive it as a system of slavery. The textile economy's dynamism is driven by that calculation of progress, the textile worker's conversion into a workshop owner, even when, as many sewing workers indicate, anyone can make the calculation but not everyone will succeed. Rivera Cusicanqui finds a phrase that sums up the situation: "While they are being exploited, they are also building their own microenterprise."

Dues, Deferred Reciprocity, and Legitimate Domination

These three notions that Rivera Cusicanqui utilizes can be corroborated, or tested, in the context of the textile workshop. In other words, their use originates from labor situations in Bolivia; however, we can ask whether their transposition to the migrant labor reality in Argentina, taking into account the *differential of exploitation* that I indicated above, allows them to continue operating in the same way.

Legitimate domination, based on *dues*, according to the Bolivian sociologist, supposes an economy of generational sacrifice: "The young person is always poor. Except if they are heir to a fortune or have access to an income that does not come from their labor" (Rivera Cusicanqui in Colectivo Simbiosis and Colectivo Situaciones 2011, 19). In this line of reasoning, domination is considered *legitimate because it is temporary.* That temporary nature is, in turn, the core of *paying dues*; it refers to a sort of initiation fee, a status as apprentice, that has its cost, that is presented as a conquest.

Such legitimacy then underlines a *progressive gradation* of labor and remuneration, of abnegation and rewards. It is a logic of apprenticeship and a system of payment, a logic that does not distinguish between the dynamic of the family and the dynamic of work. "In Bolivia, you work with your family your whole life, but this is rarely considered labor. As a child you help your mom, or as an adolescent, you help your aunt, and it continues this way, but this can only be called labor in certain moments." In the textile workshop, a large number of domestic activities, of cleaning and caring, are incorporated into waged "labor" without extra remuneration, as an obligation imposed by the owner, who seeks to replicate the division of family and communal labor. Paradoxically, when family relationships exist, they reinforce that obligation and that conversion of domestic tasks into labor obligations.

How is this concept of *ayni* inflected in the workshop economy? When workshop owners go to towns or communities to recruit workers, the agreement is the following: "I am going to pay everything for you, and later you are going to return what I am investing in you." This is done in the name of ayni. *In part, this use of the term comes from workshop owners from the communities who are familiar with this type of relationship of reciprocity.* A former sewing worker, explaining the ayni, states, "Those using this to manipulate know what they are doing, those who are within the manipulation are convinced that they have to repay the workshop owners. In other words, they feel an obligation to those who brought them from Bolivia. The workshop owners appropriate the trust in a reciprocity economy in order to use it in a perverse way for exploitation."

Colectivo Simbiosis, commenting on the calculation involved in the microenterprise, recognizes the calculation as such, its mobilization of expectations, and also the disappointments and deceptions that occur. Based on their migrant trajectory, they add another fundamental element. If the *differential of exploitation* that is experienced and suffered on arriving at the workshop ruins the first calculation that motivated the migration, this does not impede a *recalculation that takes the new situation into account.* In that recalculation the question of time is once again essential.

The Baroque

Rivera Cusicanqui (2010b) recounts the case of two textile businessmen who host lavish parties for their communities. The first is Edgar Limachi, a workshop owner and a resident of the Charrúa neighborhood, adjacent to Villa 1-11-14. The other smuggles fabrics from a workshop in Beijing into Argentina. They are the forces behind the Morenada dance: they pay for costumes, book the bands, provide beverages, and light the room. The Morenada is a dance where "brown people dress in gold." With lavish costumes, gold jewelry, large bands, and varieties of color, the Morenada is an exhibition of power, a deployment of luxury, an annual occasion of excess.

> The festivity's main sponsor, Edgar Limachi, arrived in the Buenos Aires neighborhood of Charrúa with his wife, where he directs a successful textile company that provides contracts to many subsidiary workshops. His factory, along with the network of microenterprises connected to it, contracts hundreds of Bolivians in the province as piece-rate day laborers. Additionally, it provides work for many of his godchildren and piece-rate workers from other localities and provinces. . . .
>
> The sponsor of the second troupe is also an entrepreneur in the textile sector, but he is engaged in the large-scale smuggling of fabrics produced in one of the thousands of workshops in an industrial neighborhood of Beijing. The Central Morenada adopted a *matraca* [large rattle] with the stereotypical figure of the "Chinaman" as its emblem in homage to its successful "Oriental connection" that has allowed it to spend more than thirty thousand dollars in celebrating Tata Santiago. It contracted a famous *cumbia villera* band, which has been successful with lyrics that speak of the pain and suffering, but also the agency and success, of emigration. (Rivera Cusicanqui 2010b, 4)

Rivera Cusicanqui's questions about these festivities financed by the workshop owners attempt to detect the indiscernible zone where these expenses are used to avoid stereotypical representations: "Can we be satisfied with the dualist and Manichean images that oppose a commercial and capitalist West to a South-East of backwards—or rebellious—Indians, resisting by inertia based on their 'natural' economy or sporadically erupting in shrieks of pain and vengeful violence? Or along the opposite line of reasoning: can we say that we are witnessing the formation of a new, globalized, homogeneous citizenry, a sort of transnational mestizaje that would make 'hybridity' and indeterminacy its principal force?" (Rivera Cusicanqui 2010b, 5). Dismissing both possibilities, the localist-victimist one and the deproblematized cosmopolitan one, the *ch'ixi* (the motley, variegated), in opposition to the more common notion of the hybrid, accounts precisely for a complex recombinatorial form, which does not expel the contradictory or the antagonistic from its interior: "The vitality of this process of recombination broadens this border; it converts it into an intermediary fabric and weaving, *taypi*: an arena of antagonisms and seductions. These are the border spaces where the *ch'ixi* performativity of the festival flourishes" (Rivera Cusicanqui 2010b, 6). That mode of mottling is a form of the baroque, the "*ch'ixi* baroque." The baroque takes on a new inflection, becomes an extremely contemporary expression, when it is connected to the ch'ixi.

The Festival and the Economy of Travel: Saving and Planning

My uncle had come to Bolivia for a festival. He always travels for the festivals, because they dance in fraternities. Later, they arrived for the celebration of Carnival in the premises of Alasita. I was having problems at home that year and was in the process of deciding to quit school and start working. I was studying social communication. When my uncle arrived, I commented that I had decided to start working, and that was when my uncle's wife said to me, "Why don't you come work in Argentina? It'll be easier for you, you'll get paid in dollars, you won't spend money on anything, not on food, not on trips. I'll give you everything, and you'll get your little salary." When she told me that I would get paid in dollars, I was encouraged because I thought I could save up, come back to study, and help my family. Then I was a little more sure about coming. Some time passed after that offer. I thought I was no longer going to come, until they called me and asked if I was still interested. My uncle told me that he would give me three hundred dollars. And since I wasn't studying anymore, I decided to do it. (Colectivo Simbiosis and Colectivo Situaciones 2011, 57–58)

In the economy organized around the textile workshops, festivals are also an excuse for traveling, a way of returning to Bolivia, an excuse for permanent returns and seductive recruitment. They also function as an explanation at border crossings: people are being moved, and it is justified by saying they are coming or going to a festival; it's a way of saying that it is "for a short time, no more." Later, the festival is also a way of continuing and increasing the prestige of those who migrated in search of better horizons. Thus, the trips to Bolivia become an exhibition of wealth, an occasion for displaying what one has obtained: carnival or the Festival of the Gran Poder organizes those movements and also punctuates the calendar.

From the perspective of two former textile workers who later became neighborhood leaders, the relationships among the decision to migrate, the workshop, and the religious festival are threaded together in their trajectory as part of the same interweaving of routes. They recount:

I came to Buenos Aires to work as a *rectista* in a sewing workshop. I worked eighteen hours a day, I barely slept two or four hours, they gave me a bed. . . . I remember that I had just arrived when I first walked to Luján, the youth pilgrimage . . . in 1990. It was the first Sunday, I remember that a compatriot said to me, "It's here nearby." I took my sister because I didn't know it was fifty kilometers away. I had to take her on a stretcher! We arrived at midnight, for the fourth mass. I arrived exhausted. As soon as the mass ended we came back on the bus. And just as I was entering the villa, I was assaulted. Back then I liked to dress in Puma clothing, those flowery shirts, I was being fancy. They pointed a revolver at me, they took my camera, they took everything. From then on, I never wore fancy clothes. Days before I had bought a house. . . . It was a *casilla*, third hand. Later, in 1994, there was a fire, and that is where the Virgin of Luján, or rather the image, was born in the neighborhood. There was a collection where nine hundred dollars was raised to buy sheet metal. Juanito, a deacon who was practicing to become a priest, also showed up and brought the image of Copacabana. And Father Juancho brought the image of Luján. There was a mass, and nearly fifteen priests came. Since then we commemorate it every year. Every year in a different house. The first time was in the house of Nancy, a single mom with three children, who was very enthusiastic. Often the sponsors of the Virgin of Copacabana are Bolivian, as well as the sponsors of the Virgin of Luján. The fire brought a custom from there, from Bolivia, to the neighborhood. We celebrate it just as we did there, with the rituals, the customs, the festivity, drinks, music, dancing. It lasts until six in the morning. It takes place in the street, there on Bonorino. Before, the space was much larger, but over time it became smaller. They are taking land away from the poor virgin! She used to have all of that in front, but people have been usurping it (laughter).

Bolivia as Sponsor

Evo Morales recently proposed the model of the festival and the commitment by the people to the festival's "sponsors" as a mode of regional political integration when Bolivia hosted the ALBA (Alianza Bolivariana para los Pueblos de Nuestra América) Summit. "Sisters and brothers, we are 'sponsors' of the [ALBA] Summit, and when there are 'sponsors,' they must be accompanied by a festival, a democratic, revolutionary, anti-imperialist festival," Morales said in a meeting with campesinos and indigenous people of the sub-Andean state of Chuquisaca, whom he invited to join the international event. "The festival depends on that in order to be successful," he added.[31] Turning the vocabulary of the festival into an anti-imperialist speech, Morales proposes a popular-community figure as a diplomatic resource.

Thus, according to the Bolivian newspaper, Morales locates his country in the "tradition of social prestige surrounding the Andean festivities, financed by one person or a small group of people, to highlight the role that Bolivia will play in the organization of the ALBA Summit and the parallel summits of social and business organizations, which will take place simultaneously in that city of central Bolivia. . . . 'I would like you to accompany us in this event. We would like you to come in your ponchos, with your skirts, with your signs,' Morales insisted. . . . Indigenous people and campesino organizations also declared that they would wear their traditional costumes for the 'festival of reencounter between brothers.'"

The festival, along with the figures responsible for it, is projected to become part of the state's international policies and a formula for interpellating local communities. In some of these festivities, China was turned into an emblem and now remains tightly linked to Bolivia: it slipped into its parties, was imprinted on its images. This dynamic of contamination participates in and, at the same time, reinterprets that space of global production.

Speaking with one of the dancers of the Morenada, I asked her why her troupe's sponsor had chosen the image of the "Chinaman" as the emblem for his *matraca*. She responded, in Aymara, "It's that the Chinese are very smart," because "they know how to do everything, they manufacture everything." The manufacturing power of China is embodied in the matraca as a fertilizing *illa*. It is not only a metaphor. Organizers of Andean festivals directly intervene in the productive process of the textile industry in Chinese cities. The women of the winning troupe of the Tata Gran Poder festival in 2009 were dressed in attire designed by the artist Mamani. A Tiwanaku-style design with cougars could be seen on the bottom of the skirts; a stylized sun god in orange and yellow could be seen on the blankets. This sumptuous outfit, which nearly a thousand dancers wore, could be seen as a logo of these new aesthetics and productive forms. The sponsor brings the fabrics to Bolivia through smuggling routes that involve dozens of affective relationships and ties. In La Paz and El Alto, the garment manufacturers and skirt makers produce the outfits; they braid the tassels or sew the tucks, being very careful about the quality and the proper measurement according to the sizes. Thus, the completed apparel turns into an emblem, a prodigious product of a sort of globalization from below, marked by informality and illegality but endowed with a force that is both symbolic and material, capable of inverting the very direction of the domination of transnational capital (Rivera Cusicanqui 2010a).

Calculation as Conatus

Calculation is always a mode of doing. This is not to imply reductionism to the principle of utility or profit as the only logic of action. Rather, it involves broadening the idea of utility as a tactical sense, as a principle of perseverance, similar to how Laurent Bové (2009) understands the Spinozist conatus in terms of strategy: as a set of modes of doing composed to construct and defend the space-time of their affirmation. In this way, the trajectories are better understood based on a vitalist pragmatic. I use this idea to distance myself from two perspectives: certain functionalist arguments of the "moral economy" that displace class identities and conflicts (Spivak 2013) but also the argument of prepolitical victimizing that neutralizes migrant workers (and popular economies in general) as subjects of decision, calculation, and strategy.

A perspective from within the textile workshop, one that is capable of creating justice and confronting modes of exploitation but also, most important, of thinking of alternatives that do not delegate labor and existential problems to savior organizations, requires that the dense and complex web of that calculation be taken seriously. There is a larger political problem here, and an unanswered question arises about the rationality deployed in these popular economies and the struggles taking place within them.

Where does the initiative originate for another type of activity that questions the rules of exploitation structuring the textile workshop? Leaving the "bed inside" is a decisive step. This implies no longer depending on the workshop owner for housing and food, not allowing life and work to merge completely and thus be comprehensively regulated by the production schedules governing the workshop. According to several former workers, the essential thing is to create an outside: with contacts, information, imagination of other activities and possibilities. This outside implies the need to liberate time, to make it available. But making time available is a way of reorganizing the calculation that regulates the desire for progress and obedience. They obey because, at the same time, they calculate that obedience will bring incalculable sums. In that crossroads, migrant workers move between an "investor in himself or herself" (Foucault 2007) and a person who is compelled to resist and overcome conditions of personal dependency now woven into new communitarian uses.

There is no simple legal formula capable of resolving this situation. If, as John and Jean Comaroff (2009) argue, the modern nation is experimenting with a historical departure from the ideal of social, political, and cultural homogeneity, which "has pushed nation-states, often apprehensively, toward more heterodox self-imaginings" and "a reactive xenophobia" (2009, 47), it is because it is translated into a heterogeneity that challenges the traditional governmentality in cities. I want to emphasize the relationship between heterogeneity and normative production: "And difference also begets more law. Why? Because, with growing heterodoxy, legal instruments appear to offer a ready means of commensuration. . . . Hence the global flight into constitutionalism that explicitly embraces heterogeneity in greatly individualist and universalist declarations of rights, even in cases where states pay increasingly less attention to those declarations. Hence also the effort for making the discourse about human rights an increasingly global and serious discourse" (Comaroff and Comaroff 2009, 48–49). However, difference, to be understood as a material, productive, and dynamic source of heterogeneity in our cities, has to create its own (institutional and constitutional) norms and measures to be recognized based on its production of value, beyond an abstract and moral declaration of the human.

The Ethereal Voice: Radio

Where the voice of the Bolivian workers and workshop owners can be heard is in the community's radio stations. The functioning of the community radio stations is organic to the workshop economy. There are more than twenty of these radio stations in Buenos Aires alone. They are the main means of communication, since there are significantly more of them in comparison to print and television media linked to the Bolivian community. Long working hours distributed in rotating shifts throughout the day and night, the monotony of working with the machines, and, above all, life spent in an enclosed space, away from home, and often away from family and friends, make the sound space strategic.

The sound space is simultaneously converted into a means of communication and a way of sharing information about the new country: it provides basic references to places, contacts, possibilities for leisure and consumption, and job offers. Yet it also provides information on the place that has been left behind: the radio stations circulate news of a country that is missed. However, the radio stations construct a certain Bolivia in Argentina: they delimit a circuit of Bolivian women and men who move and travel through particular zones, who are offered particular jobs and places of entertainment, and thus organize certain networks of resources, solidarity, and opportunities.

The radio stations replace conversations inside the workshop. They are the hum competing with the noise of the machines, while also accompanying daydreams. Thus, the radio stations form the soundtrack of the textile workshops. They are owned by the same people who own the workshops. In this sense, it is a conglomerate that cannot be separated. For this reason, work is a taboo topic for broadcasters. The sound continues in the nightclubs promoted by these stations, which are owned by other workshop owners, who open these clubs instead of creating their own apparel brand. In fact, there are club-workshops: they function as workshops during the week and turn into clubs on the weekends.

The Communitarian as a Condition

How does that communitarian character reappear in the textile workshops? Clandestine workshops appropriate communitarian conquests for their own benefit. The electricity and sewage services that the body of delegates of Villa 1-11-14 obtained through struggle function as free infrastructure for the workshop owners. In the same way, owners also take advantage of the services of community soup kitchens, often sending their employees to eat lunch for free in those soup kitchens, which are largely maintained by women working as activists or in a mostly unpaid role; the food is subsidized by the municipal and/or national government. This creates very entangled and politically complex moments of fusion between the economy of the workshop and the economy of the villa, as the workshop exploits communitarian resources and is supported by a series of political conquests, which, paradoxically, start operating as an inverted communitarian web, that is, one that favors the exploitation of workers.

The electrical overuse generated by establishing workshops is a major problem in the villa, because it causes accidents (fires) and repeated power outages. The workshop-*slum* economy dramatically aggravated the gap between the increase in consumption and the precarity of the space, as well as that between communal efforts and speculation. Further, the communitarian is also expressed as a flexible and cheap way of obtaining resources. However, it is two-sided: it is also a space of a dynamic informality that innovates forms of progress.

What type of political representation does community value demand? A series of organizational leaders are fighting among themselves for this representation, supported by a booming economy, which aspires to be translated into possible representation in Bolivia. The framework for voting abroad and the arrival of Bolivian political forces in Argentina rely on the potential support of the nearly three million Bolivians living outside their home country.

The fact that the workers in the workshops are migrants allows them to be excluded from the category of citizens in the host country; therefore, the solidarity between worker and citizen ceases to apply, and the features of their productive insertion become extremely precarious. However, an effort is under way to value and translate their economic force into citizenship rights, starting in the home country. Alfredo Ayala, leader of the ACIFEBOL (Bolivian Federative Civil Association), is the organizer with the most coverage in the media. He appears at all the Bolivian community's events as a defender and representative of that community in its totality. His relationship with the workshop owners is constantly ignored in comparison to his management of the multiple dimensions of the problematic of Bolivian migrants.

Ayala's discourse, which epitomizes that of the workshop owners in general, is considered as representing not the workshop owners as a body but *an economy*. On one hand, Ayala accuses Argentine organizations (especially La Alameda) of "exaggerating and generalizing" the cases of abuse, and, on the other, he also rehearses a justification: "What happens is that many people, Bolivians, for example, come from marginal neighborhoods. And on getting a job here, they aren't going to go around worrying about their living conditions" (Colectivo Simbiosis and Colectivo Situaciones 2011, 53). Another of his arguments in defense of the workshop economy reverses the accusation by blaming the Argentine authorities for monitoring only the small workshops, that is, those not capable of paying sufficient bribes. He argues that the authorities give preferential treatment to the large workshops, important contributors to the police's illegal collection, to the detriment of the smallest workshops. Ayala's leadership is constructed through the type of communitarian institution that he has been able to maintain and that, in reality, occasionally replaces the consulate since it takes care of all the migrants' contingencies, thereby obtaining legitimacy and winning their support:

> What we do is defend people's rights: whether a bricklayer, greengrocer, shoemaker, workshop owner or not. They come to our offices. When something happens to someone, they come to our radio stations and we offer them help. Suddenly, they don't have money to pay for a funeral or a birth or an operation, and we help them. . . . Each time that something happens, we go and protest. And today we have a fairly strong structure. There are many brothers who support us. If the consulate were to exist and take responsibility for all of this, we would not exist. (Colectivo Simbiosis and Colectivo Situaciones 2011, 53)

Working Inside

"My hips and thighs and upper back hurt, when I leave work I can't go on anymore, it would be impossible to continue for another hour; my vision would cloud, and I could no longer see the threads or the stitching," said one seamstress whose testimony was collected by Bialet Massé in 1904, when he traveled the country to depict the situation of the Argentine working class (Massé 2010). Indeed, the first textile workers in Argentina were also migrants, just as they are today, only at that time they came from Europe. The majority were women. They won the regulation of their activity with the Home Work Act, which emerged precisely because of the textile sector's needs. Championed by the socialist senator Alfredo Palacios and gathering conservative support, it was approved in 1941. Even today—more than seventy years later—it regulates the activity that gave rise to it, and even today it incites resistance from some players in the textile industry; complaints against brands are still based on this law.

The Home Work Act recognizes the figure of the workshop owner under a twofold status: as an employee to whom work is entrusted and as an employer in respect to sewing workers.[32] In 2008 the national government presented a bill bringing together some of the main business demands. According to Lieutier (2010, 121), those include eliminating the criminal articles, modifying solidarity as a co-responsibility between brands and intermediaries, and eliminating the figure of the *tallerista* (workshop owner).[33]

This last demand suppresses the labor relationship between the manufacturer and the workshop owners. According to Lieutier, "this is, undoubtedly, the business sector's most important demand; it is the nodal point of their claims. The manufacturers want their workshops to be recognized as suppliers and not as workers that are dependent on them. Thus, on one hand, they are released, in part, from the responsibility for what happens in those workshops, and, on the other hand, their pricing is deregulated" (2010, 123).

The figure of the workshop owner became visible with the tragedy of the fire in the workshop on Luis Viale on March 30, 2006, which killed six people. It was then that the workshop owners organized a discourse to counter the accusations being made against them, leading several marches and making their own demands. This was especially necessary since the national media labeled the workers in the textile workshops as slaves and characterized their activity as slave labor. The recently inaugurated government of Evo Morales expressed its discomfort with such a label and officially requested that it be replaced with the term *servitude*, and also requested that "raids" on the workshops not be spoken about, because in Bolivia that term was translated as detention and deportation (Estrada Vázquez 2010). In turn, Bolivian authorities made it understood that the massive return of Bolivian women and men should be avoided because it would create a social problem that would be difficult to manage. This reinforces the argument that migration as neoliberal exile (Mujeres Creando 2007) operates as the solution to internal social problems. Following the same line of reasoning, the possibility of return would correspond to the overcoming of those neoliberal conditions; however, the postneoliberal era of South American countries has not reversed the migratory flow.[34]

The articulation between the consulate and the workshop economy had previously functioned in a closely connected way: Álvaro González Quint, the deputy consul at the time, acted as the mediator in labor conflicts between workshop owners and workers.[35] Despite complaints in the media, his consulate functioned as a de facto management body for the foreign workforce in Argentina.[36] The book *No olvidamos* (We do not forget) by Juan Carlos Estrada Vázquez (2010), an activist in Colectivo Simbiosis and a former sewing worker, is the first to draw a map of the workshops based on a perspective from below, that is, from the experience of the workshop workers. He reveals the complexity of the actors involved, the web of silence promoted by workshop owners, and the complete chain, from the brands to the recently arrived migrants, involved in the textile economy. In this regard, he raises, in a precursory way, the issue of how community organizations function to discipline conflict, serving as points of pacification in the workshop economy. He also inaugurates a political perspective, pointing to the dilemma that young workers face in deciding to leave and find an alternative to the totalizing economy of the workshop.

From the Regulation of Work to the Regulation of Life

The temporality used to think about the labor season can be summarized in one phrase: "for a short time, no more." The original idea tends to be precisely that: one comes with a limited objective, seeking to save a determined sum, with the idea of returning as soon as possible with a small amount of capital. That contraction of time motivates enormous sacrifices. Intensifying work simultaneously allows for bearing the costs of almost interminable workdays to shorten the length of the stay. However, this short time is expanded. First, the expenses of the trip and also food and housing costs must be paid. Everything is deducted from the salary, since the employer-owner, who is also responsible for daily maintenance along with housing, tends to *advance* the salary to cover the costs of the trip. Therefore, there is a time of deduction. Then, the boss often does not distribute wages regularly but "guards" them, as a way of forcing workers to save. The assumption is that workers do not need cash to move about or to cover daily expenses, other than to use a phone booth to communicate with relatives. Workers are given a specific minimal amount of cash for calls when they are authorized to go out. Many testimonies reveal that when workers decide to return to their country and ask for the total amount of what has been saved for them, the amount is always disconcertingly low. Then explanations ensue about all types of deductions, and/or the owners accuse the workers of theft to justify the meager figure.

The money-labor transaction, as Moulier Boutang (2006) indicates, is determined by political, civil, demographic, and property rights that expand or restrict the efficacy of that transaction. When we speak of a *differential of exploitation*, then, we must take into account that the effective limitation of rights has a negative effect on this differential. The situation of enclosure—the production of the clandestine condition implied in the workshop—creates such a restriction of rights, even as legislation regarding the migrant population becomes progressively more inclusive.

This modality of contractual temporality requires us to stop talking about the regulation of labor in order to unravel, more broadly, forms of governance concerning life as a whole. From the regulation of labor, in determined conditions of production, to governance of the sphere of life (Samaddar 2009), there is a substantial change, a decisive passage in terms of *biopolitics*. The Foucauldian perspective that describes neoliberalism as the liberation of modes of doing, as well as a form of promoting innovation, also explicitly specifies the qualitative change between *regulating* and *governing*.

The networks of jobs and businesses formed by workshop owners, who manage the sewing workers' labor—from their recruitment in Bolivia to their conditions of living, socializing, and working in Argentina—provide us with another image of labor, one that comes into conflict with attempts at regulation (especially by the state) since the government manages budgets that do not correspond to the complexity of management implied by this workforce. The profitability of that complete management of the life of the migrant workforce results from vital variables (from the migratory impulse to the will to progress) that become factors enabling a specific mode of exploitation, a certain way of producing value.

Beyond Slavery

From Spinoza's perspective, the persevering *potencia* of being is the sign of men and women's capacity for autonomy. As Bové (2009) recounts, that power is infinitely surpassed by the power of external causes that situate how we associate images and constitute habits in a heteronomic regime. That *negotiation* between the power of autonomy as a feature of perseverance and the multiplicity of external forces accounts for the variable and complex composition of the very thing that we call perseverance, not as an uncontaminated force of autonomy but rather as a way of dealing with a complexity that aims to function as a mode of insisting on autonomous life.

The body of the child is that which, according to Bové, most often finds itself infinitely surpassed by external forces, putting it, in existential terms, "under a regime of near total heteronomy" (2009, 119). I want to make two points. First, the almost complete state of heteronomy corresponds with the existential state of childhood. Hence, the conditions of servitude or slavery are the extreme realization of heteronomy, whether as forms of infantilization or, as Paolo Virno (2008) would say, of the childishness of experience.

Second, the lack that is installed then opens the way for an impotent body, understood as a body that is not aware of its own power to act.

Understanding migrant labor situations from the optic of slavery reinforces, in the national perspective, an idea of a difference of natures between nationalities. In the case of migrants coming from Bolivia, there is a diffuse zone: nationality colored by the indigenous issue; that is, certain attributes are tied to ancestral customs and uses and are doubly foreign. What is clear is that if workers are categorized as slaves there cannot be reciprocity or a measure of equality, because "at the core of the political there is a mechanism of discrimination on the basis of anthropological difference: gender difference, age difference, the difference between manual and intellectual capacities, specifically insofar as it justifies the institution of slavery" (Balibar 2015, 15).

Therefore, as I stated earlier, migrants and sex workers are understood as and made into minorities through human trafficking legislation, and they are considered as victims in public opinion. Thus, the difference of nature is sexualized and ethnicized and, simultaneously, confined to two specific economies, which border the clandestine and whose protagonists need to be rescued and saved, according to the rhetoric of guardianship.[37] Jacques Rancière also emphasizes the question of the body in regard to the consecration of all types of hierarchies that distribute functions and capacities: "a difference of bodies must be produced that cannot be reduced by any moral medicine" (2004, 51), he says to explain the division of labor between philosophers and artisans.

Anthropologized difference, as the key to the *naturalized* justification of slavery (or manual or servile, ultimately feminine, work), becomes essential to the political order. Migrants are capable of doing what they do (and incapable of what is considered morally correct) precisely because of a particular nature that, in the most politically correct versions, will be called culture, tradition, habits, and customs. Is it possible to think about difference in another way?

Multinaturalism

Eduardo Viveiros de Castro (2014a) proposes a radical inversion. From the very title of his book, *Cannibal Metaphysics*, this movement is made clear. It is not about tolerating difference, nor culturalizing it, and even less about spiritualizing it. Difference is given by bodies, Viveiros de Castro says. Indeed, the issues, like the modes used to justify the hierarchical order, go through the body. However, this does not become an excuse for that order nor for that which would have to be domesticated, catechized, or educated to hide its *difference*. For Viveiros de Castro, the body is the heart of a *perspectivism* that shows that *the point of view is in the body.* All difference or disjunction starts from the body, and each body (whether individual or collective) is a singularity. The singularization of the body is produced by its strengths and weaknesses, by the way it lives and eats, by its ways of moving and communicating, and so on. Yet this singularity is not an argument for servitude or lordships, for intellectual or manual inclinations, nor is it a portrayal of differences as cultural relativism.

In opposition to abstract spiritualism, the body is a set of ways of being. This gives rise to a *multinaturalism*, a term that means "variation as nature" rather than "many natures." A generalized difference as nature ("to exist is to differ") inverts the Western tolerant formulation of multiculturalism, which, under the idea of "one" nature, admits and administers diverse cultures (in a watered-down version of differences as if they were exoticizing idioms). Ultimately, the Amerindian perspective and the multinaturalism that Viveiros de Castro proposes both become unexpected allies of certain contemporary philosophies, the basis of a method that the author calls "generalized chromaticism." It is a formulation of opposition: between the antinarcissism of continuous variation and the narcissism of small differences. Contemporary philosophies of difference can be assumed as versions of indigenous knowledge practices, tracing a strict continuity between such anthropological and philosophical theories and the intellectual praxis of indigenous peoples.

This proposal argues against a common position of intellectual narcissism: that indigenous peoples are the object of study for those who contribute the language and theory. Rather, on the contrary, the variations and innovations that are produced in theory are owed to the imagination—"the imaginative ability"—of the people or collectives being studied, not to the discipline's internal progress. Anthropology's narcissism is repeatedly wounded each time it thinks it is naming something from scratch that the collectives it proposes to study have already thought. When anthropology is placed in continuity with (or becomes immanent in) those collectives, it undertakes its most important task: decolonizing thinking. Rather than explaining the world of the others, thought attempts to take up contact with different others as part of an experience that implies, above all, a "putting in variation" of the imagination itself.

What political philosophy emerges from this indigenous perspectivism? A cannibalism that involves devouring the enemy, that is, incorporating its attributes, capturing "names and souls, persons and trophies, words and memories" that make alterity, the enemy, a point of view over one's self (Viveiros de Castro 2014a, 144).

This cannibalism (or *antropofagia*—a concept taken up again by Oswald de Andrade's famous manifesto [(1928) 1997]—is inseparable from another key element of that political philosophy: the alliance (which includes forms of theft, gift, contagion, spending, and becoming). The alliance as putting affinities into practice is the flip side to kinship. Or, in other words, the alliance among the affines is an elemental theory of antikinship or a way of understanding the family differently. Cannibalism—and the political mode of alliance that it involves—implies a concrete form of the connection of heterogeneous elements that constructs a baroque complexity, Viveiros de Castro (2014a, 111) says. Contrasting it with romantic organic totalities, that baroque complexity projects a fractal ontology that ignores the distinction between the part and the whole.

CHAPTER 4

Between the Workshop and the Villa

A Discussion about Neoliberalism

Postneoliberalism?

If neoliberalism, unlike its predecessor, depends on an innumerable quantity of institutions and regulations—such that Michel Foucault (2008) defines it as an active politics without *dirigisme* and therefore the object of direct interventions—the crisis of neoliberalism in Argentina did not signify the crisis of the free market but rather the crisis of the legitimacy of its *policies*. Thus, what must be illuminated is the terrain of resistant subjectivities that led to the crisis of that system of regulations on the continent and opened up a new series of rhythms and scales for thinking about and practicing collective life. The key issue is emphasizing the *variations in meaning* that are produced in struggles in recursive, nonlinear rhythms, which are always disruptions propelled from below, as Raquel Gutiérrez Aguilar (2014) proposes.

Neoliberalism is not the reign of the economy, subordinating the political, but the creation of a political world (the regime of *governmentality*) that arises as the projection of the rules and requirements of market competition. Denying this premise, by defending the dichotomy of the state versus the market, allows for a new autonomy of the political to arise from postneoliberalism in Latin America.

Appealing to the recovery of the state aims to abstractly separate the sequence "liberalism-market-economy" from "developmentalism-state-politics," and to assume that the latter on its own can correct and replace the former. However, this expression already risks an immediate and comprehensive relegitimation of political neoliberalism, owing to the lack of critical reflection about the modes of articulation between institutions and competition (between liberalism and neoliberalism). Renouncing singularity in the diagnostic corresponds to policies without any singularity in regard to current challenges.

In a certain sense, the whole continent is experiencing the same problem: can the repositioning of the state and new antiliberal leadership overcome neoliberalism? My argument is that, in recent decades on the continent, only the movements and revolts have been able to anticipate new subjects and rationalities, which are constantly challenged by the reintroduction of a properly liberal rationality based on the "recovery of the state."[1]

Based on these premises, the following questions can be formulated: How can we conceptualize the collective affection and rationality that, rather than pure and strict neoliberalism, is being deployed here? This affection-rationality led to neoliberalism's political crisis and, *at the same time*, incorporated much of the neoliberal calculation, while also disputing and using its idea of freedom and subverting and encompassing certain contemporary modes of obedience. Where do we see that affection-rationality act? What type of politics does it lead to? What economies does it sustain? How does it use urban space? What types of conflicts does it develop? What type of institutionality can it build? How does it negotiate with different scales of public-state authority? What social composition does it exhibit?

Neoliberalism: Foucault's Reading

Foucault argues that starting in the eighteenth century, physiocrat economists, theorizing the concept of economic government, developed the notion of government as a "letting things take their course" (laissez-faire). For these philosophers and men of business, this freedom was both "ideology and technique of government" (2007, 48). This "freedom" (letting things run their course) was one of the conditions for the development of capitalist forms of the economy (2007, 48) and should be understood within transformations of the technologies of power.

I want to highlight that it is not only an ideology but also a technology of power, power that is understood as physical action in nature and as regulation only through each individual's freedom and supported by that freedom. The concept of government becomes "economic government" in the sense of the physiocrat concept of specific techniques of managing populations. Governing becomes the "art of exercising power in the form of economy" (Foucault 2007, 95). This allows Foucault to define economic liberalism as an art of governing. Undoubtedly, this is a paradox for the political and economic theories that, until then, had theorized the capacity of government as a virtue based on the negative: in other words, the possibility of restricting conducts based on a certain order and obtaining more or less continuous obedience.

The art of government is radically transformed: now it is about the proliferation of initiatives, not limiting them. Ultimately, governing is "knowing how to say yes to that desire" (Foucault 2007, 73), *desire* as synonymous with *free enterprise*, as the very driver of capitalist development.[2] There is a blunt contrast with the Hobbesian sovereign, which is formed when people are capable of renouncing their desires to give rise to a unified political authority. However, in a government that arouses and promotes desire, it is no longer the totalization carried out from the perspective of the sovereign that ensures order. On the contrary, the efficacy of governing consists of liberating the interaction of a plurality of specific and diverse aims.

Desire is governed at the same time as it is fostered. Therefore, at first glance, it is a paradoxical mode of governing, through *freeing and not restricting* action. The economy becomes a way of managing the unexpected—through techniques of security—that takes each event "as a *natural* phenomenon" and, therefore, as something that is neither good nor bad, but rather that "is what it is" (Foucault 2007, 36). The event is *naturalized*.

This implies a key moment: the passage from a technology of sovereign power to a postsovereign art of government. Foucault summarizes this passage: "thanks to the perception of the specific problems of the population, and thanks to the isolation of the level of reality that we call the economy, . . . it was possible to think, reflect, and calculate the problem of government outside the juridical framework of sovereignty" (2007, 104). In that sense, it is an art that deterritorializes: it relinquishes control of the territory as the fundamental axis (or, in other words, territory is now considered from a deterritorialized perspective), marking the decline of sovereignty and grounding its effectiveness in that multiplicity of specific aims that become the productive force. We can see that these characteristics cover an unprecedented efficacy of intervention expressed in a *new realism*: it starts from things as is and the effective relationships between them, and attempts a mode of regulation on that same plane. According to Foucault, that postulate, of the political technique as following the fluctuations of reality in respect to itself, is what should be called liberalism (48).

However, it is an anti-Machiavellian realism. Foucault specifies that the physiocrat turn is a type of realism in which government is no longer based on the prince's skill and pedagogy in respect to his subjects but rather on an economy that concerns itself with problems of the population and things. Here a fundamental political problem takes shape: accepting things as is assumes that there is a principle of adequacy of things belonging to liberal naturalism. However, there is a process of modulation that operates on the same level as the formation of reality. This operation is the *immanentization of a transcendent logic of capital as this new realism is identified with liberal naturalism.*

Here a dispute over realism should be noted. The economy, as well as politics—in the midst of a process of fusion or reabsorption—is treated as *physics*: abandoning the moralist exhortation or the threat of repression and opening the way for a sort of *radical empiricism* that can be characterized based on some fundamental and interlinked features: (1) the indistinction between nature and artifice, (2) an amoral or realist logic, and (3) a strategic understanding of forces.

The Role of the State

It was the economists, then, who invented a new art of governing, heretical— Foucault would say—in respect to the thinking of raison d'état and the police state (from the sixteenth century to the first half of the eighteenth century): "Economic reason does not replace raison d'État, but it gives it a new content and so *gives new forms to state rationality*" (2007, 348; italics added). The counterconducts that were opposed to the previous hegemony of raison d'état *anticipate* some features of the new governmentality, starting with the conducts through which society is opposed to the state (355).

The salient features of those counterconducts were focused on positing the end of state hegemony, which claimed to be indefinite. What could stop it? "The emergence of something that would be society itself," Foucault says (356). The rupture with the very idea of obedience allows "civil society" to impose itself on the state in the name of a right to revolution, so that, ultimately, the state ceases to be perceived as the possessor of the truth of society (356–57).

Foucault, however, marks an important distinction between the liberalism of the eighteenth century and the neoliberalism that begins following Nazism in Germany: the former was about introducing freedom of the market, confronted with the existence of a raison d'état and police state that originated in the previous century. In postwar Germany—where Foucault situates the development of neoliberalism under the ordoliberal school—it was instead about founding and legitimating a "nonexistent" state.[3] Freedom is still in the center of the question of government, but now it is invoked for another task: "How can economic freedom be the state's foundation and limitation at the same time, its guarantee and security?" (2008, 102). According to Foucault, this change of planes—the radical transformation of the starting conditions, from the limitation of an existing state to the simultaneous invention and limitation of a nonexisting state—imposes a "reelaboration" of the liberal doctrine of government.

The German ordoliberals carry out a series of inversions of the physiocrats' liberalism. These are radicalizing operations: (1) there is a shift from a market supervised by the state to a state supervised by the market (Foucault 2008, 116); and (2) it is no longer about liberating the economy but rather verifying up to what point the economy functions as a formal principle for organizing the social, the political, and the state. The principle of competition as a supreme maxim no longer requires only the free play of behaviors and individuals but also an active governmentality that produces it. There is a new passage: from laissez-faire to permanent activism. However, this passage that Foucault poses as going from a natural principle to a formal one can be understood in terms of a radicalization of the paradox between subjection and subjectivation. This paradox, in turn, accounts for another radicalization: the relationship between freedom and security becomes increasingly more extreme as each term's dependence on the other is highlighted and remains exposed, without the state in the background to buffer it. Its maximum radicalization is how society as a whole becomes a business, as a dynamic of management of a growing necessity of freedom-security.

It is also the decentralization of the state on behalf of a directly managerial dynamic that ends up diluting any mediation of the individual with himself or herself, with the management of one's self: one's freedoms and (in)securities. In fact, the reconceptualization of social policy in neoliberal terms demonstrates this shift: it goes from being a more or less paternal form of state protection to becoming a mode of "according everyone a sort of economic space within which they can take on and confront risks" (Foucault 2008, 144).

If the neoliberal moment, then, is about a postsovereign moment from a certain point of view, it can be said that sovereignty appears, however, to be reterritorialized in the body of each individual. Sovereignty is redefined as a relationship to one's self, as control, organization, and production of a territory that is the body itself, as a set of norms for its defense and enrichment. Each body is thus produced as a finite segment in a network of variable relations. The paradoxical relationship between freedom and security that Foucault points to is duplicated in another nonantagonistic pair: singularization and universalization. There is a parallel interweaving between an increasingly complex notion of the individual (as singularity, autonomy, and continual self-investigation) and a standardized mode of collective functioning, which operates on the level of the population, simultaneously demanding and reducing the continuous singularization of each person.

Neoliberalism from Below and Baroque Economies

When I argue that the crisis of neoliberalism that Argentina experienced did not signify the crisis of the free market but rather a crisis of legitimacy of its *policies,* there are two points to take into account. First, we need to focus on the terrain of resistant subjectivities that, not only in Argentina but across the continent, led to the crisis of this system of neoliberal regulations. Second, we must think about neoliberalism's persistence beyond the crisis of its political legitimacy from the point of view of how it becomes rooted in popular subjectivities, resulting in what I call neoliberalism from below.

After two years of critical destabilization (successive changes of government and the repression and murder of activists), in May 2003, with the call for early elections and Néstor Kirchner's inauguration as president, a process of normalization began in Argentina, partly based on a strong economic recomposition. In the wake of the region's so-called progressive governments, the new form of state intervention led to the simplification of political rhetoric and diagnoses related to neoliberalism, understood simply as the absence of the state and, thus, of political regulation. But if neoliberalism is not the economy's rule, subordinating the political, but rather the creation of a political world (the regime of *governmentality*) that arises as the projection of the rules and requirements of market competition, the very notion of the overcoming of neoliberalism needs to be complicated. Negating this premise, limiting the discussion to the assertion of the dichotomy of the state versus the market, confines the intense debate around the possible significance of postneoliberalism in Latin America to a new autonomy of the political. This is what I am interested in debating.

It is possible to think of the sequence of neoliberal governmentality in Argentina based on four central concepts, projecting some features for Latin America as a whole. The first is to highlight the relation between *money* and *labor power*, beyond the tradition of their economistic readings, in order to understand them as "the two fundamental modalities—let me say it in Marx's own terms: *power* and *potency*—of subjectivation resulting from capital's encounter with its multiple constitutive outsides" (Mezzadra 2011, 160). This can be done by analyzing the role played by migrant informal economies and social benefit packages for the unemployed during the height of the crisis of 2001 from the perspective of the financialization of popular life today. The second key element in this schema is the massification of consumption, fueled by government benefits, economic growth, and large-scale indebtedness. Looking at these issues, I propose a discussion of the notion of "citizenship through consumption," which would situate consumption as the pressure for new forms of value creation, in opposition to an argument that posits it as the path to democratization for Latin American societies.

This trajectory allows me to argue for the need to expand the concept of extractivism toward the idea of it operating as a prototype for finance's action in the region, so as to take it beyond the critique of the reprimarization of Latin American economies and their dependence on commodities. For this, it is essential to think about Argentina's insertion into the global market, highlighting its connection to modes of financial penetration into popular sectors. I am interested in the extractive dynamic, linked to mechanisms of consumption and debt that promote new forms of value creation in the urban peripheries through a variety of informal economies, with blurred boundaries between the legal and the illegal, which can be read as the prototype of financialization's arrival in the territories. There, capital's frontiers are expanded, exhibiting the need for specific logistics to connect high finances with low finances and make neoliberalism operational as simultaneous dynamics of territorialization and deterritorialization from above and from below.

In this vein, I should note at least one decisive sequence of the "violence of money," to use Michel Aglietta's (2001) phrase, in Argentina since the crisis in 2001–2: the end of peso-dollar convertibility, the banking system's collapse and confiscation of savings, the attempt and failure to dollarize the economy, the multiple currencies that coexisted in the national territory during the crisis (formal and informal but recognized by different levels of provincial and municipal state authority), and experiences of alternative economies that emerged in the heat of the crisis of money as a sovereign authority. Later, this was followed by the dynamic of economic recovery and growth, the promotion of credit for low-income sectors, and the progressive financialization of popular economies (2003–13), ending with the current acceleration of inflation corresponding to the duplication of the dollar's exchange rate (the legal exchange rate and the nonlegal rate, referred to as the "blue" rate) and recent looting (2013–14). Such a saga, merely listed above, aims to signal a relationship: from the crisis of 2001, a moment when money is revealed as a social relation subject to a field of forces expressing a synthesis of social value (Aglietta 2001), to a new moment of looting and inflationary tension, where the conditions under which capital's operations are given in this moment of neoextractivism are once again openly disputed, with money as one of its most sensitive and expressive variables.

Redefining Neoliberalism from Latin America

In proposing the idea of neoliberalism from below, I want to emphasize that neoliberalism's complexity makes it impossible to define it in a homogeneous way, since it depends on its landings and connections with concrete situations. These situations require us to pluralize neoliberalism beyond its definition as a set of policies emanating from above, as structural planning. The Foucauldian point is precisely that neoliberalism's strength as governmentality lies in including freedom, which in modernity threatened all order, in the very heart of a new apparatus of *free order.*

Neoliberalism, whose foundation is the expansion of *homo œconomicus* as a rationality of political order (as Albert O. Hirschman [2013] indicates in the genealogy of political arguments in favor of capitalism before its triumph), supposes a particular idea of calculation. I want to propose a shift.

That calculation forms the basis of a vitalist pragmatic means that it can be understood strategically as a way of affirming precisely those sectors that remain outside of both economic and political calculation, either as the assisted or surplus population or as those who are déclassé. In any event, that which Jacques Rancière calls "the part of those who have no part" (1999, 9) is usually exposed only as calculations of survival that, statistically, organize these populations' management as victims of the calculations of others.

Thinking of calculation as a vital condition in a context in which the state does not guarantee the conditions of neoliberal competition (prescribed by the ordoliberal model) implies that calculation adopts a certain *monstrosity,* as popular entrepreneurship is obligated to assume responsibility for conditions that are not guaranteed. At the same time, this imperfection is given as indeterminacy and organizes a certain idea of freedom, which, in its own way, challenges some of the most traditional forms of obedience.

There is a significant *utilitarian* sense of the vitalist pragmatic that emerges. First, we must move beyond the moralizing understanding of the useful as stingy calculation, oblivious to the metaphysics of the incalculable. As Spinoza states, all people seek what is useful to them, and "those things are most useful which can so feed and nourish the body" (2005, 27).

Calculation as a Vitalist Pragmatic

Antiutilitarian philosophies point to calculation as the commercial model of relating to the world, hence their defense of the antiutilitarian—of waste, purposelessness spending, and the useless—as a moment of acceptance of the incalculable. From Georges Bataille to Jacques Derrida, it is about giving without return, suspending the logic of benefit and remuneration, of expectation and equivalence.

However, it is possible to shift this mode of reasoning. When calculation is a mode of doing driven by a vital strategy, it cannot be reduced to the liberal idea of benefit. In this regard, calculation is a way of reading a vitalist pragmatic where calculation is conatus, where calculation functions as conatus.

I will develop the formula: *calculation is conatus*. It is not a simple issue. I'll explore two strategies of elucidation. The first is purely philosophical-conceptual, and the second is political.

First, conatus is perseverance in being. For Thomas Hobbes, it is fixed and corresponds to the force of being of each individual who pursues freedom or, conceived negatively, the nonblocking of their movements. As we know, this conatus is defined by a "cold" passion called fear that facilitates calculation as the fundamental reason of the person who decides to obey by making a pact. In Spinoza's philosophy, in contrast, the conatus is much more variable, and its development is plural: it is developed and enriched by being, rather than merely preserving and conserving being. In this sense, a conatus can be understood as a life's vitalism. The conatus involves affective constellations: infancy, resistance, habit, sadness, memory, desire, deployment, common notions, the organizing *potencia* of the encounter, the measure of the encounter and melding of bodies, the discovery of one's own singular being in the world. It is singular, simultaneously personal and collective. At the extreme, there is a conatus-nature that holds the unconscious (to us) reasons—the human body that is extended into the body of nature—of our subjectivity.

Calculation arises from a very different history of signification. According to Martin Heidegger (1982), for example, it is inseparably linked to a way of being in which the world is presented as reduced to the present; it is the in-front-of-the-eyes, the objective and representable. In the world, that which we can calculate (that we can have expectations about, that we can count on) stands out. For the German philosopher, this mode of being is essential in itself and as such must be accepted, but, at the same time, this truth, of the world as a technical world, tends to absorb other worlds of being in its dominating and exclusionary requirement of accuracy. Faced with this situation, Heidegger does not fall into skepticism but rather calls for dwelling on the fact, which is also essential, that, like all truth, the modes of being human are, above all, "modes of being" and not the true disposition of the world. When understanding about a mode of being, a destiny of being, is reached, we access being as a destination with other possible destinies.

A large part of the Marxist tradition denounced this as a force of domination over human activity. Let us recall one of Antonio Gramsci's important texts: "Americanism and Fordism." There he states, "The history of industrialism has always been a continuing struggle (which today takes an even more marked and vigorous form) against the element of 'animality' in man. It has been an uninterrupted, often painful and bloody process of subjugating natural (e.g., animal and primitive) instincts to new, more complex and rigid norms and habits of order, exactitude and precision" (1971, 298). It is this violent process, Gramsci adds, "which can make possible the increasingly complex forms of collective life which are the necessary consequence of industrial development." In the sphere of knowledge, this process of subjugation is translated into the struggle to establish an increasingly complex measure that allows for segmenting, extracting, and privately appropriating value that is collectively produced, in other words, engaging in exploitation.

In this perspective, calculation is also—as Heidegger says—a "negative piece" that may well recuse itself (anti-instrumentalism) or be confronted by a calculation of another order, a properly "worker" calculation, that the party and later the socialist economy would rationalize and institute.

Antonio Negri's (1997) own path includes thinking about the potential of excess, the crisis of measure and of calculation. He does so based on feminist theorizing that raised the issue of the impossibility of measuring affective-domestic labor, in a pioneering way that challenged the very measure of the wage as quantitative remuneration for a quantity of hours of labor. Hence, affect becomes a potencia that destabilizes the measure and is the origin of the excess (Marazzi 2011).

If we look at a certain phenomenology, such as that deployed by León Rozitchner (1996, 2001), calculation speaks of the empire of abstract rationality, the mutation of the Christian spirit that preserves and radicalizes a deadly system of hierarchies. (Thus, the exit is seen as a condition without condition.)

More ambiguously on this point, Foucault's analysis of neoliberalism supposes the convergence between individual freedoms and mercantilist normative truth; that is, the market provides calculable freedom. Neoliberalism is presented as the effort to read people's freedom and incorporate even the incalculable element of their motives and actions into calculation. The incalculable does not seek to be restricted but rather aims to be stimulated through the presence of a medium and the interactions that are given there. This perspective (while retaining all of the above) leads to the context where the formula becomes clearer: *calculation is conatus*. Calculation appears as the mode of the maximum immanentization of transcendence, as freedom and human singularity are recognized as never before, but that recognition also positions it as the object of a complex calculation of each of its actions and motivations.

Neoliberal rationality recognizes freedom as the basis of its calculation. Let me clarify: freedom is not neoliberal; what is neoliberal is the positioning of this freedom as the basis of the calculable—or, in other words, the inclusion of the incalculable as the stimulus for a calculating rationality. From then on, not only do markets conquer their place, but something more complex emerges: new modes of government (governmentality) that preserve and defend the properly capitalist productivity of this freedom, to the point that—also following Gilles Deleuze in "Postscript on the Societies of Control" (1992)—people make calculation immanent as the reason that organizes life and that now motivates the conatus. But, in this schema, it is about a historical conatus, a conatus promoted by a certain unprecedentedly skilled and permeable social order.

The formula that I am trying to open up (*calculation is conatus*) falls at the exact moment when the ambiguity of the present is shown in its most exasperating and active form: calculation can be taken at its essentially neoliberal face value (in other words, the recognition of the tentative freedom expanded in calculation, the exhibition of the subjective-collective operation from the view of exploitation and government as governmentality) and, at the same time, as a moment of conatus ("vitalism of life," "health," "wanting to live") that produces a reality that was not previously calculated, opening space for new modes of organization, sociability, exchange, the creation of language, points of view, and, ultimately, of value in a broad sense.

It is important to indicate that this vitalism of life is not merely coterminous with the field of neoliberal calculation but rather is recognized in the signs of its rejection. If conatus is the variable term and subject of new compositions, calculation appears to be simultaneously divided into two (promiscuity): adaptation to the rule of control (or to normalization, the logic of security) but also production beyond measure, surplus, excess. This excess, however, is not pure waste. *It is a relation of promiscuity and not exclusively of antagonism to measure.*

Second, let's turn to the political grammar of this formula. *Calculation is conatus* means stealing, working, making neighborly bonds, and migrating to live. It does not accept dying, or seeing life reduced to a minimum of possibilities. The acceptance of the rules of calculation is intimately paired with a movement of the production of subjectivity, of "wanting." These are verbs: "undertaking," "getting by," "saving yourself." Perhaps at this point the conatus would have to be opened up, divided.

In Spinoza, the conatus is linked to the experience and production of knowledge about itself and the world. The conatus is subjected to the passions, and in that subjection points of the development of desiring-knowing-creating are found (or not). The fundamental question, the political question, would be, how is the conatus's variable experience translated and expressed in the modes of calculation? Along this line, another essential hypothesis would be that the variations of the conatus give rise to a new reality, a new world (networks, institutions, territories). How does calculation vary in the conquest of these territories? Finally, how do modes of power, government, and knowledge occur in these new territories (which redefine the communitarian without losing it or recuperating it as a primary essence)?

Ultimately, the conatus that seizes hold of calculation inverts the neoliberal motive (with the neoliberal considered as the political mode of domination for exploitation founded on a calculating mode of being in the Heideggerian sense) and leads calculation toward operations whose basis is no longer the measure but rather the self-deployment of collective conatus. But it is a deployment that a Marxist rationalism does not manage to foresee, to accept, or to value.

The Financialization of Popular Life

Finance can be thought of as an opportunist system of understanding those exchanges produced from below. What finance reads or attempts to capture is the dynamic of subjects linked to the structuring of new entrepreneurial, self-managed labor forms arising from the poor sectors in parallel with their condemnation as excess or surplus populations. Finance also descends.

If the proliferation of neoliberalism from below is strengthened by money flows that organize an entire system of popular finance, then certain distinctions within those flows must also be recognized: on the one hand, finance that circulates from below and fuels a monetary system capable of funding business initiatives for the popular or lower classes and, on the other, financialization driven from the top down through particular state, banking, and nonbanking financial institutions. I am interested in the conflicting logic of assemblage deployed by both dynamics, because this is where the question of the production of subjectivity, which capital attempts to impose as a social relation, emerges as a terrain of dispute (Mezzadra and Neilson 2013b).

First, let's look at finance circulating from below. Maintaining the thesis that financialization driven from above operates as a way of reading, appropriating, and reinterpreting popular forms linked to certain practices of productive and reproductive autonomy, I can hypothesize that its current penetration of and boom in popular life in Argentina should be understood in relation to two key precedents related to the crisis of 2001: economic practices closely connected to a certain migrant economy of the past long decade and self-management initiatives generated by the organized movement of the unemployed in the midst of an employment crisis at the beginning of this century.

Thus, these conditions allow us to point to the *anteriority* of those money flows circulating from below, by positioning as a precedent those economic institutions and interventions that, before and after the crisis, constructed a concrete network of immediately productive forms of cooperation and mutual aid and were able to canalize flows of money (scarce at that time), loans, favors, and solidarity, articulated with a multiplicity of transactions in the informal economy, channeling an entire circuit of credit and investment, goods, services, and enterprises, without needing formal-legal requirements or banking-financial mediation.

Those practices were (and are) part of a material fabric that, in the case of the migrant economy, made it possible for people arriving in a foreign country to obtain resources to settle, invest, and produce, functioning as a material resource and social guarantee of a popular productive rationality. Years later, the state itself and a series of banking and nonbanking financial institutions would recognize and reinterpret this migrant economy. Similarly, I can point to the resolution from below of the employment crisis (in the sense of its management, not its disappearance), thanks to the capacity of movements of the unemployed to organize to seize resources from the state and promote a series of productive activities with important social value in the moment of crisis, which would later be recognized by the state as well as by the financial markets descending into the neighborhoods. *Emphasizing their anteriority has a double objective: signaling that these initiatives produced jurisprudence, in the sense that they enabled the creation of rights and reopened the discussion about the scope of inclusion through citizenship, and showing that during the crisis this social productivity was unrecognized, feared, and/or repressed* by state as well as banking institutions (although they awoke to an early desire for connection).

Financial penetration of the villas, informal settlements, and many peripheral neighborhoods occurs in a postindustrial landscape marked by the rhythm of plebeian consumption, sustained by a multiplicity of incomes that bring together in the same economy state benefits, odd jobs, and diverse and intermittent jobs combined with income from informal economic practices (with a broad zone of diffused illegal activity). The year 2003 marked the end of five consecutive years of a falling gross domestic product in Argentina; since then, there have been increases in income for the middle class, in employment rates, and in redistributive policies for the popular sectors, concentrated on the transfer of money through benefit packages. These factors enabled a generalized increase in consumption and opened the possibility of credit for low-income sectors. Being a recipient of a benefit package (from the national or provincial government) turned into a guarantee of debt, as these benefits, through being implemented by means of banking, "replace or complement the traditional accreditation of the roles of the formal worker" and allow "financial and nonfinancial institutions to directly accrue their quota, whether through a discount from the Uniform Bank Code (CBU) or by obtaining a card" (Feldman 2013, 19).

The compulsive bankarization of unemployment benefits individualized a relation that originally implied strong collective coordination of how money was received and distributed (which, in fact, was one of the primary tasks of the unemployed workers' organizations and an intense field of dispute with political party territorial leaders and governors). Banking and financial instruments take advantage of that mutation to convert the subsidized population into subjects of credit. However, those same tools catch and capture the migrant discipline of industriousness, saving, and investment in the sectors experiencing growth in recent years: the textile and market economies.[4]

Thus, the articulation occurred as follows: the system of microfinance from below, which functioned as a resource originating in the migrant economy during the crisis, and the network of microenterprises organized by movements of the unemployed during the same period constructed, in a parallel but confluent way, a nonwaged productive branch, which included various forms of contracting, such as the informal wage. However, in Argentina's case, those complex systems of microfinance from below did not decrease with the end of the crisis but, on the contrary, expanded. There are two reasons for this expansion. As mentioned above, the government sought to link its benefit programs with these economies in order to incorporate them into the general growth in consumption. Yet they also drove the reactivation of certain traditional sectors, such as the textile industry, which had been dismantled in the 1990s by the opening to imports.

In this dynamic, the social-benefit packages stopped being conceived and promoted as a temporary palliative for unemployment and were converted into subsidies for new forms of employment, on the assumption that the cooperative and self-managed forms created at the height of the crisis held the knowledge and ingenuity of productive processes interwoven into the territories where waged formality had disappeared some time ago. At the same time, they were a way of imposing compulsive banking as a way of controlling the money coming from the state, which had been a key point of dispute for social movements organized in the era of the crisis. That control is principally a form of extracting rent from the beneficiaries of those subsidies, since banking already constitutes an indispensable technical condition of indebtedness, the heart of financial exploitation.

However, the consolidation of diverse modalities of the informal economy, with a strong migrant-market component, expanded to Argentina's enormous lower-middle-income sector and encouraged some large banks and different banking and nonbanking financial institutions to focus on a specific segment of the population—the migrant, informal, productive, and decapitalized sector—after the state progressively decided to fund the social economy.

Therefore, there was a multiplication of forms of income, beyond the popular sector's growth through the formal wage, which explains the growth of the consumption capacity of sectors that up until a few years ago were seen only as "excluded" (from formal wages and, as a consequence, from any other social inscription). That multiplicity of incomes is reconstructing the map of labor beyond the waged-unionized world and can no longer be conceived in transitory terms or as belonging exclusively to moments of crisis. The dispute raises new issues in respect to old forms of understanding the relation between inclusion, money, and peripheral neighborhoods. It should be emphasized that this form of finance dedicated to exploiting the popular sector's productivity appeared in Argentina at the moment when neoliberalism (that is, its policies of structural adjustment) was experiencing a crisis of legitimacy and the state was becoming increasingly involved in financing that segment of the popular sector, using a rhetoric of opposition to austerity.

It is clear that these economies, previously considered insignificant and merely subsidiary, become dynamic and attractive territories for capital, expanding the frontiers of its valorization, now uniting things that seem incompatible from capital's point of view, although, from the popular sectors' viewpoint, they are already connected: finances, peripheral neighborhoods, and sectors that do not receive formal wages.

Citizenship through Consumption: A New Relationship between the State and Capital?

As opposed to the twentieth-century debate over social citizenship linked to the type of Fordist inclusion defined by Thomas H. Marshall (1950) in the postwar context, here I propose to revisit the question of citizenship, thinking about its current "material constitution," to use Étienne Balibar's (2015) formulation, starting from the financialization of the popular sectors.

Between 2003 and 2012, the evolution of financing for consumption in Argentina increased in absolute terms: from 4.5 billion pesos in January 2003 to 106.3 billion pesos in April 2013, a twenty-three-fold increase over nine years (Wilkis 2013). Financing was also diversified in the hands of banking and nonbanking credit cards, financial agencies, mutual societies and cooperatives, retail stores, household electronic appliance and clothing chains, and superstores. The multiplication of instruments drove the acquisition of domestic appliances and, especially, motorcycles and cell phones, by this segment of the population.

A report by the Attorney's Office for Economic Crimes and Laundering of Assets (Procuraduría de Criminalidad Económica y Lavado de Activos) leaves no doubt in respect to the financial system's penetration of the popular sector's economy through the issuing of credit and cash loans. The report also makes it clear that "the generalization of these financial instruments, far from having an integrating or democratizing character, reproduced the social differences that operate in other areas of society" (Feldman 2013, 9). According to the report, the popular sectors' indebtedness makes them "vulnerable" because it complicates their subsistence. Thus, "a paradoxical system operates that is known to not take away inequality: people with low incomes pay more to purchase the same products. Popular sectors, then, are subjected to a level of economic violence unparalleled in other sectors of the population, which generates a social harm whose consequences have repercussions for specific families and potentially for the national economy as a whole" (40).

The government carries out a double operation by encouraging mass consumption. On one hand, it recognizes the impossibility of full employment (the persistent image in the national imaginary); on the other, it attempts to link democratization with access to consumption. Citizenship, as the exercise of rights, is no longer linked, as Balibar says, to "the universalization of the anthropological category of 'labor' as the uniquely human trait" (2015, 49) but is displaced onto consumption as the form of guaranteeing social inclusion. However, this consumption is no longer solely the product of incomes from wages but also results from money that the state transfers to peripheral neighborhoods through benefit packages, and principally, as already mentioned, from the multiple modes of income gained through an industriousness that is also multiple. Therefore, consumption is a mediation and an incentive that, along with the debt mechanism, promotes new forms of value creation. What anthropological category would be the basis for this generalization of consumption? In post-Fordism, there was a mutation of the anthropological connotations of productive forces, which can be seen in the accented mediation of consumption, as well as in the constitution and development of financial capital's abstract apparatuses of command. It is a dynamism of demultiplication in respect to the anthropological universality postulated by Balibar: the heterogenization of the homogeneous and universalist figures of labor in favor of those characterized by Paolo Virno (2004) as the Universal Exposition of dissimilar historical forms of labor requiring increasingly complex articulations and assemblages.

Eduardo Viveiros de Castro (2014b), speaking about Brazil, points to two key issues for criticizing the idea of democratization through consumption on which the legitimacy of the region's so-called progressive governments is based. First, because it relies on access to credit, the consumption engaged in by the popular sectors implies a displacement of the state's obligation to provide public and free services, favoring indebtedness, and, second, class difference is renewed through the popular sector's conversion into creditors who are always disadvantaged in respect to other segments of the population.[5]

The popular sectors' informal economies call into question the new forms of inclusion and construction of citizenship, challenging the liberal republicanist schema because participation is no longer expected to come via the formal-institutional path or via the Fordist wage labor path since the contractual wage does not constitute a sufficient universal mediation. What is most interesting, however, is how popular sectors' informal economies defy the parameters of populism—and here I differ from Balibar (2015)—which deposits the full capacity to decode demands and promote rights in the agency of the state. Identifying populism as state reason ignores popular forms of doing even as it encloses them in terms of demands, wagering that they will coagulate into a unitary identity and endorse a sovereign authority, locked within the parameters of the nation-state. The state proposes citizenship through consumption as a *palliative* or *reparation* that is provided against neoliberalism, endorsing the idea of a non-neoliberal state to the extent that it subsidizes the poor.[6] In this sense, populism as state reason attempts to monopolize "democratic invention," situating itself as the privileged actor in terms of conquering rights. Here, as Balibar argues, we "have to replace the idea of inventing democracy with the idea of preserving it" (2015, 37), identified as the political regime of the state.[7]

From another point of view—one that emphasizes the radical nature of autonomous popular practices without ignoring their radical ambivalence—citizenship through consumption can be projected as a pragmatic ambivalence of conquests and not a simple case of victims receiving compensation. In terms of the political philosophy at work, it could be said that this perspective places its trust in the plane of immanence where the popular sectors—or the governed, to use Partha Chatterjee's (2004) language—do politics, beyond the state, which implies pragmatically taking advantage of the state's resources without being enrolled in the symbolic scene that accompanies these resources from above. Above all, it implies trusting in the nontraditional political modes through which they defy their status as governed. Thus, neoliberal governmentality acquires an *irreversible* aspect at the same time as it is submitted to the *variation* imposed on it by struggles and territorial dynamics that do not necessarily lend themselves to being read from the opposition of republicanism versus populism.

Toward an Expanded Concept of Extractivism in Latin America

It is necessary to broaden the concept of extractivism beyond its reference to the reprimarization of Latin American economies as exporters of raw materials in order to understand the particular role played by territories in the urban peripheries in this new moment of accumulation. These territories remain marginalized in the productive framework when the economy is thought of only in terms of primary materials and the countryside.

Additionally, the region's progressive governments propose a politically complex relation between those populations and natural resources: primary-material commodities function as the funding source for social benefits. Exploitation by transnational agribusiness corporations is thus legitimated by the state's discursive mediation that emphasizes the function of social integration achieved through the capture of a portion of this extraordinary profit. Confronted by this situation, attempts at politicization from below by resistance to those companies are constantly infantilized or treated as irrelevant by those outside of them, who seek to disqualify their forceful critique of the region's neodevelopmentalist discourse. What can be observed is the mechanism of interrupting fluid communication between social antagonism and governmentality. In effect, the state's denial of the legitimacy of the demands arising from the mode of accumulation blocks precisely that dynamic of democratizing recognition characteristic of a democracy that maps its constituent practices based on points of antagonism.

Also, according to this perspective, anyone who opposes the extractive model is opposed to a form of financing *poor* populations. It is essential to note to what extent these urban populations are part of an extractive and not merely a subsidized dynamic, in other words, how these dynamics are articulated with one another and what role the state plays in this articulation.

The dominant form of extraction of value is neoextractive insofar as it configures the relationship between territory and the global market. The internal circulation of goods and products depends on the success of the country's insertion into the global market. Thus, the capacity of state mediation (rent extraction to finance social programs and subsidize production) is inserted into the broader set of institutional assemblages. The mechanisms of insertion, mediation, and legitimation through which the governmentalization of the state takes hold produce the current political process's interventionist and non-neoliberal effects.

From this perspective—that of the governmentalization of the state—it is possible to detect at least two wheels rotating around the same axis: one powers the businesses linked to natural resources (*commodities*), and around the other unfold myriad businesses based on the internal circulation of capital, money, and goods. Any narrative that attempts to separate and oppose these dynamics hinders an understanding of the levels of internal articulation and the way each influences the production of modes of life in the territories.

This governmentalization overflows any theory focused on the state's sovereign attributes (correlating with the strong denationalization of key segments of the state, as Saskia Sassen [2008] notes), as the power of public-state intervention depends on dynamics that are presented as contingent or purely exterior, such as the effect of financial speculation in determining international commodity prices or economic actors' capacity of articulation to create businesses with global reach involving all or part of the national territory. It is those businesses (the first wheel) that drive and offer a prototype for an infinity of businesses on different scales spreading throughout the territory.

The interesting thing is that the problem of generating financial logistics capable of creating an effective dynamics of valorization arises in both spheres, problematizing the image of a radical separation between finance from above and finance from below (and of financial flows as purely abstract). The logistics of finance are permanently reinvented, as an internally conflicted system, seeking to capture assets produced in high as well as low finance.

The articulation of both spheres supposes, then, the establishment of communication pathways between global logistics—which a territory's insertion into the global market depends on—and a plurality of ad hoc infrastructure, which translates and multiplies territories' dynamics of valorization, again on diverse scales.

If global financial business takes the form of extractivism (territory value for money value), especially in Latin America, its success causes the mode of accumulation to take financial rent as its prototype. However, this system of exchange is not developed without the simultaneous production of a state form that is capable of partially determining these processes. At the level of microprocesses, this dynamic is translated into proliferating prototypes around which the very fabric of society is reorganized.

There is a simultaneous triple component that combines state neointerventionism, a relaunching of accumulation through extractive operations, and the penetration of this modality from above and from below, linking diverse scales and territories. This triple component requires inflating the concept of extractivism. Furthermore, the extractive operation, to use Sandro Mez-zadra and Brett Neilson's (2013b) term, is differentiated from exploitation in the factory by the fact that it does not unfold based on the organizational capacity of value production from within the process itself. Rather than the (phenomenologically true) appearance, in which the exportation of commodities is less determinant for the production of modes of life than these microprocesses—which replicate the prototype in a contingent, variable, and generalized way—I think that precisely the opposite can be affirmed. It is the essential global connection (aided by state management) that determines the possibility and intensity of the "opportunist" and "cynical" (Virno 2004) reorganization of modes of life. This occurs without the emergence of another social class that is capable of organizing production apart from the architects of global connection (modes of know-how). Thus, an appropriating, versatile, and conflicting translation of social activity feeds back into a financial code, at the same time as the financial code is developed and deployed thanks to that social activity.

However, state rhetoric expresses a much more restricted (and simple) consideration of the mechanisms of capital reproduction, based on parameters linked to the supposedly traditional labor contractualism of traditional definitions of national citizenship. Thus, the state works—narratively—to ignore a part of popular doing that takes place outside this relation of valorization, even if it reproduces the state's prototype of global insertion into the world market. But while it seems not to recognize those other forms, it is increasingly obligated to engage in transactions with them, producing a sort of "second reality" of the state itself, increasingly necessary for its own financing through means that are not strictly formal and legal (Segato 2013).

Thus, we see a displacement of the concept of extractivism in the process of its expansion: first, in extensive terms, from the countryside and commodities to the city and peripheral populations, and then, in an intensive turn, as the insertion of territories into the global market disseminates a prototype that functions at different scales and territories.

The compulsion to valorize (to create a "little business" [bisnesito]) expands as a mode of relation and makes logistics imperative. Developing logistics implies making the rhizome of finances grow. Debt is one of the internal mechanisms of this process but not the only one.

Consumption as mediation and the financial as the figure of command put all the world to work without replacing the homogeneous figure of labor. This diffusion of the imperative to self-entrepreneurship is exploited, promoting the invention of new forms of value production beyond the confines of wage labor and the parameters of its legality. The extractive form is exterior to this schema because it prescribes the valorization but not the mode (as occurs with industrial control). From there comes its amplitude.

Looting: The Exasperation of Consumption

In the political system's discourses, the expansion of credit is presented as the counterimage to recurrent episodes of looting in the face of inflationary crises in Argentina, enabling a sort of developmental evolution: from condemning looting to defending the fulfillment of debt by those who have the least.

However, the wave of looting that spread across Argentina in December 2013 makes it necessary to rethink the opposition that poses the constitution of the lower classes as subjects of credit as an antidote to the unregulated appropriation of looting. In other words, there is a continuity between the two phenomena. The looting was centered on domestic appliances, as well as food, but not necessarily basic necessities. This image doubled the moralistic onslaught. Media and public opinion concentrated on one point: the poor loot but not for necessity or for hunger; instead, they appropriate electronic, almost luxury goods, considered superfluous by the standard of necessity. Price inflation appears to be preceded by another kind of inflation: the inflation of the necessities of the poor accustomed to consumption, thanks to state subsidies and easy and expensive credit.

The internal relation between looting and consumption is that of exasperation, of border crossing: mass consumption outside the Fordist paradigm is fueled by incomes with broad and diffused borders with illegality. Therefore, there is an informal or illegal access to consumption that simultaneously involves laundering incomes on a small and medium scale. For the poor, consumption is supported from above by the idea of a palliative and driven from below by an informal dynamism capable of brokering heterogeneous forms of labor (composed of sidewalk piracy and drug dealing, flea market enterprises and street vendors, informal self-employment and clandestine workshops). The border between the formal and the informal is regulated by the police forces, who led the strikes that preceded the December looting and symbolically made the looting possible.[8]

Looting foregrounds the problem of consumption as well as the threat of its restriction owing to inflation. It also sets the urban scene for a certain impossibility of adjustment or austerity measures. And, most important, it enables of a form of "street negotiations" for those without the institutional possibility to conduct such negotiations precisely because they engage in under-the-table jobs.[9]

The context and the Argentinean inflationary tradition turned debt into a mode of hoarding the currency's value, as the currency is being devalued at an accelerated pace. The inflationary experience has an effect on the demystification of money. Talking about Bolivia, Silvia Rivera Cusicanqui (2010a) says, "We play with money. At one point, we sold money (in the Alasitas market). We know that it is a convention agreed upon by society. And this has to do with the fact that in Bolivia we have experienced the most inflation since the pre-Hitler inflation." Argentina is also rich in inflationary experiences and the multiplication of currencies, two indexes of the experience of the crisis and the upheaval of the measure of value.

The subjectivity of indebted women and men could be thought of as subjective figures in variation. In a situation of relatively abundant money, they construct themselves as microentrepreneurs; in a situation of limited money, they are capable of political destabilization. This variation of figures also allows for detecting the tactical action and not only the passivity involved in debt. This is what Silvia Federici is arguing when she says, "The financialization of everyday reproduction through the use of credit cards, loans, indebtedness, especially in the United States, should be also seen in this perspective, as a response to the decline in wages and a refusal of the austerity imposed by it, rather than simply a product of financial manipulation" (2012, 106).

This uncontrolled form of consumption invokes, returning to Foucault (2007), a remaking of pastoral power in the dispute over the orientation and conduct of the multitudes, especially of youth. Religious spirituality both complements and competes with the promise of finance from below. The disciplining of the population is linked to what I posited as the monstrosity of calculation, owing to how the notion of calculation relates to conatus. The monstrosity of calculation also lies in fully carrying out the massification of consumption, which, during looting, becomes completely detached from its dependence on (and balance with) incomes, but also from a supposed rationality of necessities and their classist segmentation. The state's pretense that mass consumption is opposed to looting is revealed to be precisely the opposite: looting is the continuation of consumption by other means.

Mapping Neoliberalism

Mapping popular economies is a way of mapping neoliberalism as a battle-field. Popular economies are the space-time of situated economies, which are key for thinking about how capital, through the diversification of financial forms, attempts to incorporate new territories. These territories are what allow us to understand how neoliberalism is simultaneously delegitimized as macrostructural policies of adjustment and at the same time incorporated in forms of popular know-how for dealing with the consequences of those struc-tural reforms.

Thus, it is not about choosing between localist ethnographies or struc-tural statements. As Jamie Peck notes, the question of "how neoliberalism is specified in a variegated landscape of institutional, economic and political forms" emphasizes its "polymorphic" features and the "mutual and multiscalar interdependence of local formations profoundly articulated in a 'horizontal' and hierarchical mode" (2013, 149). Neoliberalism is thereby made to vary, in recognition of the simultaneously structural and situated character of the differential dynamic that characterizes it.

The perspective I raise with the idea of neoliberalism from below, however, aims to highlight the dispute over the idea of calculation practiced by the popular economies. I anchor the proliferation of financial operations in the popular sectors on this terrain because that is also where the "operations of capital" are anchored in the phase of new conquests. If "logistics, finances and extraction are not only economic activities" (Mezzadra and Neilson 2013b, 13) but also forms of capturing labor, which produce concrete policies and spaces, I can argue that the populations of peripheral neighborhoods become key subjects of that new exploitation and are not simply marginalized as subsi-dized populations but rather are the targets of new modes of (neoextractive) exploitation.

In this sense, neoliberalism from below is a field of ambiguity that does not assume that neoliberalism's hegemony is complete, in the sense that it does not accept its full hegemony, nor does it grant neodevelopmentalist and stat-ist policies the capacity to replace it. Instead, it is a perspective that looks to "below" to find something that antagonizes and ruins, spoils, and/or confronts that supposed hegemony.

When I refer to the ambiguity of neoliberalism from below, I am think-ing of a "mass opportunism" in line with Virno's (2004) reflection, for whom "opportunism and cynicism" constitute the "emotional tonalities of the multitude," in other words, an ambivalent mode of being corresponding with the socialization processes of labor power that involves not only the classic work places, but the entire metropolis as a productive space. Colectivo Situaciones (2009) talks about a "promiscuous" fabric, in which elements of a heterogeneous nature coexist—in a nondifferentiated way—beyond the logics that those elements belonged to in the past. My hypothesis is that neoliberalism from below consists of the convergence of the action and rationality of the popular conatus and finance's ability to operate on concrete mediations on this fabric.

My aim is not only about understanding or describing the mutations in South American popular life and the innovations of capitalist subsumption but taking on key political questions that emerge from the current conjuncture's tense scene, where praxis deployed outside the state faces the dilemma of converging in a new presentation of the neoliberal politics of the capitalist elites or, instead, creating institutional and political elements capable of reforming the theory of the state.

CHAPTER 5

Between Postnational Citizenship and the Ghetto

The Motley City

The Coming City

Villa 1-11-14 seems to drag a piece of Bolivia to Buenos Aires, or, more precisely, a piece of El Alto—the multitudinous city that surrounds, like a ring, the hollowed-out urban center of La Paz. Villa 1-11-14 replicates the constructions of El Alto in height and the use of unplastered brick that tints the landscape with a red-orange color. This material—unplastered brick—has changed the villa's appearance in the last ten years. In Argentina the villas were traditionally settlements built out of sheet metal and cardboard. However, Bolivian and Paraguayan migrants (mostly workers in the construction sector) have recently transformed the techniques and materials with which the villas are built. Now housing is made out of brick, enabling a new possibility: vertical growth. Thus, the villa of Bajo Flores rises; it develops in height, defying the lowlands—ancient wetlands—for which the neighborhood is defined as *low*.[1] With limited possibilities for horizontal expansion (the villa is surrounded by property belonging to the Argentinean Federal Police), dwellings proliferate upward and overlap, one floor above another. Today there are buildings with up to five floors.

Beatriz Sarlo (2009), in her book *La ciudad vista* (The seen city), issues an urban-aesthetic judgment on this issue: "Everything harshly exhibits, with a confident air of the natural under expansion, a sort of precarious monstrosity destined to remain, since the buildings are made from real materials that are there to stay." Sarlo speaks of the villa as a neighborhood that exudes a "definitive incompleteness," now compounded by the contrast between old and new construction materials: "precarious constructions, made up of sheet metal, wood, cardboard, plastic, are impressive. But when the incomplete is made of brick, the quality of being unfinished contradicts the properties of the solid materials that go into their composition" (73). Thus, she confirms that the brick construction belies the illusion that can still be maintained when precarious dwellings are made of less definitive materials: brick confirms that these constructions are there to stay. They are a part of the city that is not momentary or transient. There is something that Sarlo judges as "precarious monstrosity" that is *already* constitutive of the city and not fleeting, not subject to being disassembled according to the fluctuations of public policies and labor requirements. Even if the villas were never so volatile, her analysis is mostly appreciative: those constructions, "monstrous architecture," according to her *are* the city of the present, its most striking part.[2] Even if they are included as its low part, they are there to stay, which signifies that they definitively reshape urban space and permanently subsume Buenos Aires in this logic of the unfinished. Additionally, this monstrosity does not have fixed boundaries; it is not limited to the villa: it spreads beyond the villa's borders through street vendors (who usually live in neighborhoods built this way). The monstrous constructs the city, "the city of the poor."

In this city, for Sarlo, two traditional binaries are debated: the distinctions between the public and the intimate, and between human and nature. She explains, "The suburb passes over intimate intimacy to bring public intimacy onto the scene. There is a different notion of what can be seen, of what is allowed to be seen. Human bodies and materials from nature enter into a peculiar symbiosis in the suburb: between vitality and deterioration, as if the processes were always uncontrollable" (79).

The contemporary city therefore challenges these two distinctions, which have already collapsed, according to her analysis. The intimate versus the public and nature versus the human enter completely different formations here. There are two rules of distinction. The first is that of the *polis*, that is, the rules of the city styled after the illustrious Athenians, where the public and the private define the spheres of the political and the domestic in an exclusive and hierarchical way. The second is the very norm of *civilization*, understood in terms of a modern classicism capable of discerning the natural and discriminating it from the human. The city as seen by Sarlo, against the light, reveals how the border between the human (civility) and the nonhuman (nature), between the public (civility) and the domestic (nature), materializes as a civilizing course.[3] Such a perspective shows, above all, everything that a city no longer is nor declares itself to be, a certain clo-sure of what some intellectuals, in the midst of a democratic transition and of modernizing expectations, thought of as the *future city*.

The Villa as Intensive Space

If the villa is not thought of as a nonmodern remainder or as a monstrous enclave in the fully derogatory sense of the word "monstrous," another visual economy emerges: one that makes the villa visible as a productive space for small businesses, family enterprises, and informal economies through which, as Saskia Sassen says, "ancient material economies can prosper." However, even if those economies initially appear to be anachronistic (in their technology and labor forms), Sassen clarifies that their articulation with advanced economic sectors is what gives the villa its global character: "The increasingly homo-geneous landscapes and built environments of the glamorous zones tend to obscure the fact that the current urban blossoming of advanced economies is frequently nourished by an earlier urban economic history that provides them with particular specialized advantages."[4]

The economic, social, and physical architecture of the villa thus becomes a comparative advantage for certain economies. The economy of the textile workshop and the market is one of those. A sequence is constructed from the market La Salada to the textile workshop that includes the villa as the third space completing the assemblage: the clandestine textile workshop is submerged in the villa to take advantage of it as a space with communitarian resources, labor, protections, and favors. The migrant population in the villa is constantly being renewed, and it is the site of the production of a multi-plicity of labor situations ranging from self-employment to small enterprises, including domestic and communitarian labor, and work in relationships of dependency. It involves, then, a genealogy going from the villa to the textile workshop, and from the workshop to the market La Salada, that reveals a complementary and contradictory logic of mutual contamination and per-manent returns. The trajectories and temporalities that are woven among the villa, the textile workshop, and the market demonstrate a complex articula-tion, as each intrudes into the other. At the same time, they provide a glimpse of that corridor in its multiple connections to other transnational temporali-ties and zones.

Dispersion and Agglomeration

Is the villa a city-within-a-city? The villa is a constitutive part of the city at the same time as it is positioned as its radical outside. Located literally in the center of the map of Buenos Aires, Villa 1-11-14 has developed its own economy, while it is also assembled as part of a broader economy, not only the surrounding metropolis but also a more extensive and dense set of cross-border transactions. Its rhythm of growth has to do with that economic vitality. The enterprises, businesses, and traffic grow within the villa and from the inside out.

On one hand, it is constituted as the place where a certain invisibilized service infrastructure for the city is settled: especially domestic cleaning and care services, construction labor, and maintenance personnel. On the other hand, it produces a visible infrastructure of services for the service providers who live within it: breakfasts eaten on the highway or sidewalk while going to work, lunches and dinners for when they return (many residents are renters and therefore do not have space to cook or simply don't make the time), childcare services for women who have outside employment, popular soup kitchens, and medical, communication, and financial services.

A perspective taking into account the ecology (Davis 2007) of this city-within-a-city could project it simultaneously as an agglomerated city and as a dispersed city: concentrated by overlapping levels of construction, services, generations, and experiences of self-managed services, while also dispersed throughout the rest of the city via its mobile components, especially those related to the production of circulation, since that social composition of the city-within-the-city spreads and multiplies through the proliferation of markets and street vendors.

Up until now we have seen two compositions: on one hand, the migrant majority populating the villas of Buenos Aires and, on the other, the multiple economies with which they are connected, not only as a workforce but also as microentrepreneurs, businesspeople, retailers, and social workers. There is a double scale to this economy: it operates "both at the macro level of global labor markets and at the micro level of translocal household survival strategies" (Sassen 2005, 460). These two levels should in turn be analyzed by taking into account their intimate relation. The villa becomes the space of a new transnational political economy.

Villa 1-11-14

According to official information, approximately 200,000 people live in villas and informal settlements in Buenos Aires.[5] Villa 1-11-14 of Bajo Flores is one of the most populous. These government figures are refuted by neighborhood organizers, who have their own ways of measuring and accounting for the dynamic of velocity and population growth that official inquiries cannot register. They speak of 80,000 people currently living in that villa alone, doubling the official number.

As the arrival point for migrants from the Argentine countryside and bordering countries since the middle of the twentieth century, Villa 1-11-14 was occupied, evicted, and repopulated various times before conquering the thirty-one blocks that it takes up today. During the last military dictatorship, it suffered the most ferocious onslaught attempting to eradicate it.[6] Bulldozers destroyed homes and flattened part of the land, while hundreds of Bolivian women and men were compulsorily repatriated through an agreement with the Bolivian dictator Hugo Banzer, as part of the regional coordination of forced expatriation that took place alongside the also-regional repressive operation of Plan Condor. Activists were shot on some of the villa's streets, and various neighborhood residents have remained among the disappeared ever since. In that era, barely twenty-five residents remained, but after 1983, with the return to democracy, the villa began to grow again. Since then, numbers have been added to its name, compiling the history and the denominations of different eras. Today it is known by that numeric sequence: 1-11-14.

Starting in the early 1990s, with exchange-rate parity between the Argentine peso and the dollar, Argentina became a massive destination for migrants from neighboring countries, and the villa received thousands of new residents, who came in order to be able to send substantial remittances in dollars to their home countries. The crisis of 2001–2 also entailed the end of the peso-dollar convertibility (Matellanes 2003). However, the majority of migrants did not return to their countries as had been expected; instead, the villa of Bajo Flores continues to be a place of arrival for those searching for a better life and job opportunities. Since 2005, with Argentina's economic recovery, more young people began arriving, driving a generational renewal of migration.[7]

The Villa as the Sphere of a Forced Internationalism

With respect to their origins, the majority of the villa's residents are foreigners. The local government confirms this for the largest villas (31, 31 bis, and 1-11-14) of the city of Buenos Aires. Furthermore, the majority of the population is thought to be receiving social subsidies.[8] The mostly migrant social composition—Peruvians, Bolivians, Paraguayans, and, to a lesser extent, Chileans—has marked one of the most novel and least known political experiences of Villa 1-11-14's recent history: the constitution of a plurinational body of delegates that won important victories for the territory and its inhabitants and that consolidated a form of neighborhood self-management. This body of delegates was recognized by the city legislature as a legitimate mechanism of authority. Through Law 403, sanctioned by the Legislature of the City of Buenos Aires on June 8, 2000, Villa 1-11-14 obtained its own regulations for implementing the Program for Participatory Planning and Management, which dictates that the executive board of that program must include "five representatives from the current Commission of Neighborhood Delegates of Villa 1-11-14." Thus, *only for Villa 1-11-14* does it set aside the previous regulation, Law 148, that called for "one representative from each villa" to participate in discussions about interventions in the neighborhood. Villa 1-11-14's body of delegates is an anomaly in respect to the organizational forms of the rest of the villas because of the representational pluralization that it implements, as well as its capacity to pressure and negotiate for the recognition of this new mechanism of neighborhood authority.

Additionally, there is a space that goes beyond the regulation: not only is the quota of five delegates exceeded, in practice, having been expanded to thirty-one (one for each block), but, further, the explicit exclusion of political parties from the collective body also marks a substantial difference from the previous one-person mechanism, which was much more prone to being appropriated by parties and their patronage systems of territorial insertion.

Law 403 expresses a moment of victory for an experience of popular self-management, with its daring organizational dimension and decisive and innovative plurinational character. However, the force of the law is not immutable, which signals an interesting relationship between the creation of law and the capacity for social innovation.[9] In other words, the social capacity of innovation forces the creation of new rights, the expansion of their frontier, and, therefore, the deepening of democracy. In this regard, the jurisprudence that social innovations formulate is immediately political: effecting law and the repertoire of legitimate popular struggles. In any case, even when the legal plane seems to crystallize a set of conquests in time, it is liable to setbacks when the social capacity that keeps them effective decomposes.

A Common Body: The Emergence of the Body of Delegates

The emergence of a new political form is also the emergence of a new people, of collective forms of doing led by people who become something different through their combination with others. In this sense, analyzing the social infrastructures and practices of managing a space allows for signaling the material dimension of that collective constitution. From that perspective, we can speak of a composition and recomposition of a common body in the villa, a concept that—originating in Karl Marx's work (1993) and later taken up again by the Italian *operaismo* tradition—allows for thinking about the ontological status of social forms (Karakayali and Yaka 2014).

In this way, the villa as a sphere of forced internationalism became the possibility for popular political innovation, a challenge to existing organizational forms, and for several years (1999–2004) created modes of participation, dispute, and negotiation, mixing strategies, discourses, traditions, and trajectories from different origins. In practice, this innovation operates in at least two senses: it promotes a reconfiguration of national political culture and the tradition of struggle in the Argentine villa, and it also deploys a reinvention of the political culture of the migrants' countries of origin. This means that it creates something new in terms of a repertoire of organizational resources that lead to fuller deployment of the social capacity for self-government.

This territory's transnational character turns it into a laboratory for new organizational forms seeking to transform living conditions, through demands and conquests, usually related to place.[10] At the same time, they redefine the notion of citizenship to the extent that they require the formation of new rights or, at least, the pressure for existing rights.

Initially, when the delegates carried out a hunger strike to demand recognition in the legislature, the legislators were heard saying among themselves, "Those damn Bolivians are coming here to shake things up!" A former delegate recounts:

> We wanted transparency and wanted to be respected as an organization. Despite being foreigners, we wanted them to recognize us. We were not only Bolivians. There were Argentines. Panchito Aragón, an Argentine,

was one of those who stood up, who faced them. Since he was Argentine, we pushed him forward and we stayed behind him. Yet despite this, on seeing the multitude full of black heads, brown faces, there was very open discrimination. And we said out loud, "Why do they have to discriminate against us?" Our children are Argentine. You and your parents were also immigrants once. We also want them to recognize us as equals.[11]

Through the experience of its body of delegates, the villa creates a space from which to extract new forces to redefine that territory and shelter a growing heterogeneity of trajectories, histories, and relationships. They started blocking streets, the socially established way of drawing attention: Perito Moreno, Cruz Avenue, Varela. They demanded recognition of the new formation of authorities and also the handover of the previously promised and already constructed housing. "Those were our demands, simple and easy. But it was not so. Neither simple nor easy," one of the protagonists recalls. The creation of a new mechanism of authority—a single collective body, consecrated by direct election—appealed to street action as the way of establishing an institutional dialogue. It proposed combining representative pluralization with the form of a single collective body to manage what seemed to be the most urgent problem: the housing, the spatial issue of the villa's inhabitants. It is a question that never was and still is not either simple or easy to answer.

The Right to Be a User

By definition, the villa is a set of properties where a series of land takeovers, sales, and resales occurred in a way that was parallel to the formal legal system; it is established as a space without basic services. Therefore, obtaining each of those services was a political victory. The body of delegates managed to make the villa's population visible as a single collective and negotiate their right to services with both state (municipal) authorities and private enterprises (companies providing services).

Based on this practical resolution and direct negotiation, the delegates began disputing representation in the villa and expanding their conquests to all thirty-one blocks. Thus, they challenged the existing authority, the authority that was currently in power but was not the true authority. They went directly to the private electric companies (Edesur and Edenor) to berate the managers. They threatened to set up roadblocks, organize protests, and call the media, which led to results. They successfully negotiated to have the company provide the cables but had to raise money to pay for the posts to support them. Those cables and posts still light Villa 1-11-14.

The privatized service companies face a nontraditional resistance from the body of delegates to the very idea of their privatization. The delegates do not ask for the services to be renationalized (as a way of recuperating a benefit that was once appropriated and linked to state ownership of the service) but call for services to not be provided exclusively to some neighborhoods. It is about demanding a use right, the right to be users, beyond the status of the services' ownership. This is not incompatible with the proliferation of clandestine connections, which coexist with demands for legal installations from the companies and the discussion about what type of social tariff is appropriate and possible for the villa. As the villa grows, there is a limit to the precarious connections: for security reasons (fires become more frequent), because of the increase in consumption (in quantity and intensity), and owing to the necessities of social inscription (for example, having a landline phone number to use as a reference at work or at school). Yet they continue to exist because it is a way of having free services, that is, a minimum infrastructure, for many recent arrivals.

The delegates' negotiation challenged the implicit assumption that the mode of life in the villa is not in a condition to receive the services enjoyed by the rest of the city. Thus, the delegates rejected Telefónica's classification of the villa as a "red zone" and therefore not fit for service.[12]

The companies and the government deal with this situation. The companies and government negotiate rates and forms of cofinancing of the installation, but they also manage to ignore maintenance while the government avoids undertaking inspections. This *exceptionalism* for the inhabitants of the villa is experienced as injustice by the citizen-neighbors in Buenos Aires, who argue that the inhabitants of the villa in general and migrants in particular continue coming to the country, and especially to the villa, because "they live for free."

The fact that the villa's exceptionalism is perceived as both an advantage and a disadvantage at the same time is covered up. The villa is preserved since cheap resources are extracted from it, and therefore its geographic confinement is maintained, while it is simultaneously denounced because that exceptionalism would suppose comparative advantages for its inhabitants: a place of a parallel law where the same urban and contractual regulations—of services, of security, of costs—do not apply.

In turn, the local (and national) governments must justify that exceptional treatment to the villa's residents themselves as well as to the neighbors in the rest of the city. But this distinction is also reproduced among the inhabitants within the villa: between Argentines and foreigners, between those who have lived there for years and recent arrivals, between those who have Argentine children and those who do not, between those who work and those who do not, between those living in the immediately adjacent neighborhood (Rivadavia and Illia) and those living in the villa proper. One delegate's analysis warns that the logic of internal discrimination that marked the intense conflicts over autonomy in the Bolivian region the Media Luna in 2008 is being replicated in Buenos Aires:

> But what is striking is that the Rivadavia neighborhood is also basically made up of Bolivians, perhaps second- or third-generation migrants, where the children come from these roots. And what is also striking is the racism of those families, coming from these roots. It is as if we were experiencing the moment when there was migration in Bolivia to Santa Cruz de la Sierra, of los Coyas, as it is called, and the second and third generations have been born racists to an alarming degree. It is something similar.

The importance of the territorial space promotes and articulates demands and is translated into an organizational dynamic. A *politics of place* (Harcourt and Escobar 2005) recognizes the strength of a concrete position when projecting discourses, gathering forces, and composing political collectives. In this regard, the material space of the villa is at the same time a site of enunciation, a way of marking or outlining a territory, but also its projection onto the city as a form of resisting confinement. "It annoys many people that you, a foreigner, are fighting for things. They [the politicians and officials] think that we are fighting only for our countrymen and women, but that is not so. We are fighting 'in general'; the struggle is general."

The Villa: A City of Businesses

One of the delegates challenges the idea that the villa does not pay for basic services like the rest of the city. In his argument, it becomes clear that paying for services is proof of the condition of citizenship (for themselves and, above all, for other residents of the city), while the condition of being subsidized reaffirms the exceptional status of the villa's population. It is about making "the citizens"—in other words, the rest of the city—stop seeing them as a subsidized population.[13] That negative differential is inverted by paying for services "like the rest do." At the same time, what is confirmed here is that the villa's population is not exactly poor but, rather, deploys an economy that is mostly capable of paying for services like any other neighborhood.

An article in *La Nación* states, "The villas of Buenos Aires, with more than 163,000 inhabitants, are lit clandestinely: with precarious and risky connections, electricity reaches each dwelling of the marginal neighborhoods, paid for by the city government that, in 2010, spent some 23 million pesos on that project. There is more: according to official sources, the consumption of a household in the villa is up to four times greater than that of an average property in an urbanized neighborhood such as Palermo, Villa del Parque, or Belgrano."[14] The use of metaphor is revealing: the clandestine, traditionally associated with the dark and hidden, is now a form of life that consumes more electricity than the homes of white, urbanized neighborhoods like Palermo, Villa del Parque, and Belgrano. Taken to the extreme, the counterpoint states, "There is more: authorities assure that they can verify that a house in Villa 31 consumed 196 percent more than an apartment in the traditional Kavanagh building, both in Retiro. Sources from Edenor confirmed this with *La Nación*."

The article's story line is equal and opposite to the one posited by the delegates a few years earlier. The segregation of the villa's population as a subsidized population is translated into the confinement of a space of exception given by an equation that is irrational according to the logic of citizenship: overuse coupled with the lack of private fees that would limit consumption. The article adds, "There is an absence of rationalization of consumption, precisely because its inhabitants know that they are exempt from paying for that type of service." The idea of imbalance between parts of the city exhibits an image that reveals a prejudice about a situation that seems absurd: *how can those who have the least consume the most?* It is precisely their status as noncitizens that allows this type of irrationality, which the government—according to the allegations in this article—favors with subsidies. The article continues, "Today the villas of Buenos Aires have transformers with communitarian meters. However, within them the cables continue as the neighbors want, without control from the state or the companies that guarantee a secure connectivity. Currently, the city assumes the complete cost that this consumption implies."

The *communitarian formula* (of the meters, for example) is the flip side of citizen individualization. Or, in other words, the possessive individualism that citizenship guarantees is sabotaged by communitarian forms of unmeasured spending, the irrationality of consumption. According to the data revealed in this article, residents of Villa 1-11-14 consume twice as much as those in the Caballito neighborhood, a middle-class neighborhood in the center of the city. However, for the electric companies, the villa is equivalent to a *baldío* (wasteland). That is, one of the most densely populated urban spaces is called a wasteland. The Royal Academy dictionary defines *baldío* as follows: "Said of a particular area that is on strike, that is not tilled. Futile, lacking a motive or foundation. Vagabond, lost, without occupation or profession."[15] *The villa, in the city's imagination, appears as a space of vagabonds, of leisure, of free life.*

Its inhabitants have the opposite perception: "Villa 1-11-14 is a small city, where money is generated twenty-four hours a day, not only through drug trafficking, but also people going out to work. And those people who go out to work take their family with them. Things, such as food, are sold starting at six in the morning. Later, when people leave work, there are also businesses selling food, all of that. It is like that twenty-four hours a day, every day. It is a small city that works day and night. Along with the workshops, each shop begins growing overnight. And the workshops, for example, there are more than a hundred textile workshops on each block," another former delegate says.

The Monstrous as the Nonmodern

Why would the government not want titling (that is, the normalized provision) of services in the villa? Where do the difficulties in recognizing the tax-bearing capacity of its inhabitants come from? Why does the state allow parallel tax regulation, a parallel property regime, and, related to that, a parallel system of security in the territory? It would seem that an underlying consideration of the villa is in operation, one that classifies and preserves it as a *monstrous* space. What does it mean to describe the villa as a monstrosity? How is this done?

There are three ways. First, the increasing proliferation of economies sustained by the labor power of the villa's population is characterized as *monstrous* in the national (neodevelopmentalist) ideology. Second, these activities are believed to imprint *monstrosity* onto the city, through what are considered anomalous spatializations: markets, villas, and any architecture that, because of an expanding and long-standing precarity, becomes the symptom of urban depreciation and deformation. Last, the villa is characterized as monstrous by referring to the *monstrosity* of speech of those who inhabit these spaces and participate in these economies. The mixture of nonnational languages and the slang of informal and illegal activities brings to the forefront a politics of language that defies the norm.

Attributing a monstrous character to the villa—to its economies, its forms of speech, and its architecture—is a way of depoliticizing and invisibilizing its population and, at the same time, of recognizing and framing it as the monstrous other of the city, its dark part. The question of how to characterize the villa is decisive in an internal debate among the villa's inhabitants: is it better to demand state institutions (schools, day-care centers, medical clinics) within the villa or to call for its inhabitants to be provided with services outside of the villa? For some, requesting the state's presence within the villa would mean enhancing their confinement and accepting a degraded level of services precisely because they are for the villa. Thus, they would basically receive the services of a ghetto: the teachers who worked there would be activists or those who were being punished, and the same would be true for health care professionals. Those who make this argument prefer to interact with the city and traverse it, and, if anything, they demand that the state guarantee the means of transportation to ensure the mobility of the villa's inhabitants. Those who believe and propose this argue for a right to the city, to cite Henri Lefebvre's (1996) celebrated idea, opposed to policies of ghettoization. "If they make schools, soup kitchens, gardens, services, everything here inside, our children won't have a relationship to the outside, it is a way of enclosing us. The reason for going out is precisely so that our children relate to and interact with the outside, so that they can develop other skills, learn and teach other things. We have often discussed the issue of soup kitchens and accepting state assistance. We are constantly debating whether or not we want schools and soup kitchens inside the villa because this makes it so that our children do not see other things." Another delegate explicitly states that the spatial issue is under dispute: "If they make a little plaza or soccer field for us within the villa, they leave us enclosed, while they [those from outside the villa] are able to leave and they have a different vision of space. Therefore, I don't want them to do these things inside, because our children are part of society, and sometime they are going to develop abilities and activities outside of the villa." On the other hand, those who call for institutions for the villa are demanding its recognition as another neighborhood and thus the institutions corresponding to such a status.

The monstrous as a form of exception, with a parallel legal status as a territory of the excluded, is a decisive point when it comes to thinking about community. There is a division between those who eugenically link "origin" and "command" and those who wager on the "monstrous creativity of *living in common*" (Negri 2004, 138). In any case, the monstrous imaginary persists as the unfolding of one city within another. The villa tends to be treated as that urban fold within the city, simultaneously internal and external to it, immediately and radically foreign. In a similar perspective, analyzing the Brazilian favela, Alejandra Mailhe links the territory of the *sertón* (back country), the landscape of the emblematic nineteenth-century revolt of Canudos, to the contemporary favela, as if that rebellious space far from the city would be replicated and translated to the very center of the metropolis through the poor neighborhoods: "In the limit, the favela is 'the sertón away from the city' within the city itself, since there 'one had . . . the impression one would receive before the entrance to the settlement of Canudos, or in the grotesque idea of a vast multiform henhouse'" (2010, 43).

What is the monstrous but something more than that which is referred to purely as the excluded? Is there a political *potencia* in the monstrous capable of reappropriating that which is disparagingly considered a deformation, negative difference, abnormality? In this regard, the monstrous can be thought of beyond the dichotomy between the modern and nonmodern, as being instead that logic that contaminates, expands, and infects features, putting that binary distinction into crisis. In the case of the villa, its declaration as an exceptional or anomalous space in respect to the city ignores how it produces the city and, above all, how it is profoundly imbricated with the postmodern development of an increasingly heterogeneous city.

The Villa Is the Effect of Progress

Contrary to the common image that the villa is a transient place that grows in moments of crisis, the statistics show the opposite: the population of the villas grew approximately 52 percent between 2001 and 2010. According to the census of 2010, "there are 163,000 people living in the villas of Buenos Aires." "The city of Buenos Aires does not grow except for population movements. *The villas are the only things that grow.* We have returned to the volume of 1989" (italics added), declared Victoria Mazzeo, chief of the Department of Demographic Analysis of the city of Buenos Aires.[16]

After several years of economic growth, the villas continue to grow. This disproves the idea that their eradication depends on increasing employment and economic activity, and instead reveals the opposite: *progress produces more villas.* With this finding, an entire modern discourse of progressive inclusion into a model of majority employment, housing, and social services is shown to be, at the very least, insufficient.

The other point that should be emphasized in the census data is the *intensive* growth in the villa, driven by the lack of space: Laura Rocha reports, "Despite the increase in the population of the villas, the surface area they occupy has not grown substantially. In 1962 they occupied 146.5 hectares; in 1980, 246.5; in 2001, 292.7; and in 2010, 259.9. In the last thirty years, they have not increased in surface area but rather grown in height. There is no more land, except when they carry out an illegal occupation next to the train tracks, for example, Nora Zuloaga, deputy general director of sociodemographic statistics, indicated."[17]

Analyzing the same information from the previously cited census, Ismael Bermúdez indicates that the growth in Buenos Aires's villas contrasts with low growth in the city of Buenos Aires in general: "Thus, in these marginalized neighborhoods, the rhythm of population growth is very similar to, and often higher than, in most of Greater Buenos Aires. Therefore, some specialists indicate that there is a 'Buenos Aires peripheralization,' almost establishing a sociogeographic unit since many of those neighborhoods border the counties of Greater Buenos Aires."[18]

A subtle concern for what is implied by the periphery's contamination of the city sphere becomes clear in this remark. The periphery intrudes into, interferes with, and overlaps with "the city," displacing its limits and reproducing itself within the capital city itself. This supposes an image of inverse colonization: the peripheral neighborhoods are taking parts of the center itself—and coloring it with their logic of growth. In that movement, supposedly peripheral or suburban areas are created in the middle of the city.

Living Well

The Argentine nationality of their offspring is a point of tension in the majority of accounts of the citizenship status of the villas' residents. Argentine nationality is exhibited as a status to ensure the attribution of rights, yet it also fails to ensure such rights. The type of recognition deserved by those who sing the national anthem in school never manages to come into effect, despite the song's sentimental demonstration. Through Argentine nationality, the parents attempt to ensure a mode of citizenship and legal inclusion for their children; this is not realized but rather shows in its impossibility to be an exclusively political problem.

Does these children's presence challenge the national language? Is it an internal sabotage, as in the scene of Latino migrants singing the U.S. national anthem in the street recounted by Judith Butler (in Butler and Spivak 2007, 56–74)? What the children of migrants introduce into Argentina is not strictly a matter of language translation but rather one of tones: of voice and of skin.

These children of migrants carry with them contempt of the institutions that discriminate against them (schools, hospitals, police) and, at the same time, alter the lyrics, the sacred cry, that emblematically organize the nation. When they sing the anthem, what makes one suspect that they are not Argentine? The answer is skin color and certain inflections within the Spanish language that they twist, a pronunciation that slightly modifies it, as well as stereotyped attributes of the "character" of foreigners, corresponding to introspection or shyness (translated in labor terms as docility).

What does it mean to sing the anthem? It is not simply adherence. It is a tone of defiance, a certain way of uncoupling word and image, dismantling the stereotype of who those who emotionally intone that song, who put a voice to that defined territory, *should be*. Traditionally, the national anthem has been the mode trumpeted by the institutions that sustain the nation-state and establish its membership.

Are there are other ways of creating a sonorous territoriality? "Song and path are paired heteronyms in *Quechumara: taki-thaki*. They allude to a sonorous territory, which is displaced in space-time" (Rivera Cusicanqui 2010b, 14). This image, which pairs the voice of the song and the movement of walking, perhaps accounts for a voice that opens the territory by singing, even that most tightly established with regard to national belonging. The song-path could be opposed to the song-state. It is a voice that pierces, with its movement, the language of the homeland.

The Language of the Homeland

Butler values Hannah Arendt as "one of the first twenty-first century political theorists to make a very strong case for performative speech, speech that founds or 'enstates' a new possibility for social and political life" (in Butler and Spivak 2007, 27). The constitution of a "we," Arendt says, is a requirement for a political life. Butler reads this as "a kind of ontological claim at the same time that it constitutes a political aspiration" (57). She relates it to the issue of *song* (although she confesses that she cannot imagine Arendt singing). Butler argues that Latino migrants singing the U.S. national anthem in Spanish disrupt the monolingual requirement of the nation and "install the task of translation in the very heart of the nation" (61). It is worth citing at length:

I want to suggest to you that neither Agamben nor Arendt can quite theorize this particular act of singing, and that we have yet to develop the
language we need to do so. It would also involve rethinking certain ideas
of sensate democracy, of aesthetic articulation within the political sphere,
and the relationship between song and what is called the "public." Surely,
such singing takes place on the street, but the street is also exposed as a
place where those who are not free to amass, freely do so. I want to suggest that this is precisely the kind of performative contradiction that leads
not to impasse but to forms of insurgency. For the point is not simply to
situate the song on the street, but to expose the street as the site for free
assembly. At this point, the song can be understood not only as the expression of freedom or the longing for enfranchisement—though it is, clearly,
both those things—but also as restaging the street, enacting freedom of
assembly precisely when and where it is explicitly prohibited by law. This is
a certain performative politics, to be sure, in which to make the claim to
become illegal is precisely what is illegal, and is made nonetheless and precisely in defiance of the law by which recognition is demanded. (62–64)

She is concerned with the relationship between language, performativity, and
politics. Butler explains why a political position may well be based on a "performative contradiction," to then expose the thesis directly: "there can be no
radical politics of change without performative contradiction" (66). Freedom
and equality, she argues, are affirmed in relation to an authority that seeks to
exclude them, depreciate them. Launching and articulating them beyond a
determined mode of existence requires a political practice of creation. The
relationship between this concern and the classic formulation by Gayatri
Chakravorty Spivak (with whom Butler is in dialogue in this case)—can the
subaltern speak?—takes on a new twist.

Sensible Democracy

"We went singing. It was the famous pilgrimage of the neighbors in Villa 1-11-14.
Perhaps we had no idea that we were carrying out a new form of struggle,"
they recall on one block of the villa. The Virgins of Copacabana and of Luján
accompany those "walking assemblies," as they are now remembered in the
neighborhood.

Thus, they managed to camouflage themselves in the festival and disorient
political repression and, additionally, convert those religious celebrations

into moments of convergence, of the impure montage of traditions, nationalities, calendars, and rituals. The overlapping of festivities causes affinities to emerge between the Virgin of Copacabana and the Paraguayan Virgin of Caacupé, between the Peruvian Señor de los Milagros and the Virgin of Luján. On Perito Moreno Avenue, the image was quite confusing: "it seemed to be religious festival, but with a certain air of movement where the needs of Villa 1-11-14 were clearly felt." The role of the Catholic priests who have passed through the villa was a central element in this religious-political syncretism. The stories refer to the priest Ernesto Narcisi, for example, as one of the instigators of the block-by-block organization. Years later, his figure coexists alongside photographs of Bolivian virgins, such as the Virgin of Copacabana, in some festivals. A similar exercise of mixture occurs with language: a conjunction of new vocabularies invokes a polyphonic rhythm in the Spanish language itself. It incorporates Quechua and Guarani words, mixing them with prison slang, and spreads to the speech of the entire city. It is a language that travels in informal cabs; it swarms in markets; it is consecrated in prayers and pleas; it hovers over recipes and is reinvented in music.

The march-festival. The procession-*piquete* (picket). And, in the middle, the festival again. The festival's migration supposes a capacity of transformation, renovation, and adaptation, which, to a large degree, explains its long duration, its persistence.[19] It is both a mode of fixation in a new space and a replica of a previous one. Then, the landscape is altered; it absorbs new music and movements. But one landscape also opens up within another. Villa Celina is known as Little Cochabamba (as much as Bajo Flores evokes El Alto): the market Sundays with blue tarps and orange brick houses resemble a Buenos Aires copy of different Bolivian cities. The festivals support new forms of appropriating space, and, as such, they fill those spaces with extremely ancient as well as new dynamics.[20] The festival, in these cases, is a cannibalistic feast: it cannot ritualize without devouring novelty; it does not celebrate without inviting everything that surrounds it; it does not persist without becoming increasingly promiscuous. As Eduardo Viveiros de Castro (2014a) indicates, speaking of the predatory logics that Claude Lévi-Strauss (1992) narrates, a society is itself only in moments that are outside of itself. And the festival is one of the most propitious and favored moments for finding that outside.

The festival lives off of a prolific and growing economy: that of the textile workshop. But it is also the occasion for and prolongation of the market. The festival continues to be interwoven with politics since that is where certain appointments and positions of power are at stake—they occur, are legitimated, are preserved—but it is also a form of exposition and opening, of renovation and consolidation. It is a collective way of making transitions, passages, of putting yourself out there and protecting yourself, of reminiscing and waiting, of celebrating the routes and accompanying a calendar that inscribes us in a diagram of larger forces.

The Transnational Villa

The political struggles carried out in Villa 1-11-14 are simultaneously connected to Bolivian and Paraguayan politics; they draw from a certain guerrilla tradition from Peru, restart the urban discussion in Buenos Aires, and inform us of dynamics of labor extending from cities like São Paulo to Beijing. How can we understand that sort of connectivity and resonance that makes this particular and circumscribed space into a complex assemblage of territorialities, times, and problems? Does it constitute the experience of an immediately transnational space-time axis (Sassen 2008)?

The territory, as an assemblage, is also the home and the body. The feminist perspective insists on that overlap when unraveling the positions from which one speaks, acts, lives. Seen in this light, the territory is unfolded, opens up, is multiplied. Along this line, neighborhood politics cannot be disconnected from a politics related to domestic labor, social policies, the way bodies produce the city, and even ways of imagining and projecting a region like South America.

How can we think about a multiscalar concept linked to neighborhood politics that is no longer restricted exclusively to the neighborhood but rather traces lines of transnational convergence and connection? The construction of place as affective-collective materiality implies the concrete space from which enunciations, organizational forms, and moments of community are produced. There it becomes involved with multiple trajectories of movement, discontinuity, and routes that make the temporal (temporalizing) dynamic a fundamental axis of such territorial construction. In this sequence, a politics of place produces combinations that do not respond to the previous maps, nor, therefore, to preestablished scales.

How does a politics like that of the villa's body of delegates allow for analyzing the use of the multiscalar as a tactical moment, as a source of multiple identities and dynamics that are not restricted to an idea of the local as that which is fundamentally limited? The idea, on the contrary, is to verify up to what point localization is the surface of projection and amplification of the capacity for political dialogue and, therefore, the ability to rescale, to jump scales and link them (Swyngedouw 1997) in a way that challenges the globalized partition between the local and the global but also the national geometry.

Mapping the Territory

The first task that the body of delegates took on is that of a demographic and cartographic production of the villa. A delegate describes it: "That was our job: making relief maps, plans, demarcating the street openings, making an infinity of things, taking censuses. Those from block 10 knew us, we were on the rooftops measuring; we were topographers, we were land surveyors, we were engineers, we delegates were everything." In a synthesis of the polypragmatism that Jacques Rancière (2012) claims as the true workers' liberation from their historic enclosure in specialization (unfailingly in manual labor), the delegates experiment with the practice of multiple trades and skills.

The collective confirms that the authorities do not know who the villa residents are, or how many they are, and also do not have a reliable way of finding this out. Therefore, the first thing the delegates did was taking their own census, producing information about themselves with the goal of constructing a realistic, updated image of the unique population of the villa. They know that there will be no basis of support for negotiations without that information. Without that information, merchandise is always calculated insufficiently, the complexity and velocity of the growth resulting from the constant arrival of migrants are not taken into account, nor is there awareness of housing, health and sanitation, educational, and family problems. Additionally, delegates suggest where to construct recreational area and what land can be used to expand the housing supply, detailing the specific composition of the diverse population. The delegates' census is able to map the neighborhood, reaching where the government's census takers do not have access, and planning demands and projects that will later be the subject of negotiations with authorities, which they will attempt to translate into some type of public policy.

The delegates seem to be the only ones capable of measuring and translating that baroque complexity that mixes economic prosperity, population growth, the proliferation of high-rise housing, and new businesses. In that respect, they are the ones with the urban imagination capable of designing, planning, and proposing the deferred urbanization. One of the delegate-cartographers recounts, "To present to the UGIS (Unidad de Gestión de Intervención Social) a request for paving or for a paving block of 8 by 150 meters, of Bolívar Street,

I made the plans, I made a model of how the streets could be, where old covers are, the passageways and the numbers of the houses. As my block's delegate, I know this 1,600 square meters, 58 by 28 meters, perfectly, and I know how the thousands of people living here live."

The Jungle and the Polis

"We believed that there were no laws in the villas, as these are public lands belonging to the government. . . . We thought that it was like a jungle here. From when I entered until the body of delegates was founded, there were fights, and everyone would say, 'Well, this is the villa!' and if there was joy and celebrating in the street, they would also say, 'Well, this is the villa!' That was always the answer, until one day we organized ourselves." The image of the jungle is not just any image. The favorite scene of modern political theory and the synthesis of the precivil state, the jungle supposes a state of nature without rule, mounted on the domain of the strongest. The image is pervasive.

The villa as a space without laws or with parallel laws, a space of non-citizens, is broken only via the communitarian organization that is able to present a common, organized body, the subject of concrete rights. The articulation with the state is not immediate, nor do citizens have such articulation a priori.[21] That self-organized body of delegates needs to invent and impose a form of dialogue and force the state to engage in mechanisms of direct negotiation. The discrimination experienced by the villa's inhabitants, whether for being foreigners or for living there—and their mutual reinforcement in the marginalizing stereotype—requires the invention of a community of action.

However, that communitarian practice is also, especially in the case of Bolivian migration, a know-how, an experiential wealth, that migrants have at hand. Therefore, there are *two aspects of the communitarian figure as an organizational resource.* On one hand, it is a mode of conjunction of that vital, plurinational heterogeneity that populates the villa and compels multiple coexistences. On the other, it is a practical repertoire materialized in the very construction of the villa that overflows its Bolivian origin and spreads through common procedures: from the communitarian form of building houses to solidarity lending and saving institutions, including the economies of care and reciprocity that make up the vital fabric of the production and reproduction of the villa's inhabitants. These communitarian figures are innovated and transformed through their own circulation and reappropriation.

The formation of the body of delegates expresses a moment in which those knowledges achieve a level of articulation of force and, in turn, create a space from which to extract new tools for negotiation. Bringing communitarian knowledges into play here implies and imposes a specific mode of their flexibilization. The body of delegates as an organization exhibits an enormous ability to make communal belonging flexible in the sense that the repertoires of action become resources of social construction and organization outside of their sites of origin and reference. It is a reterritorialization that *makes a new origin out of moving*: the constitution of a territory that is simultaneously the effect of displacement and the evocation of an absent territoriality.

The traditional notion of community as inextricably linked to a territorial space is remade by migrant movement, and it is that movement, which mobilizes its own community belonging and resources, that is capable of constructing a new type of territoriality. Connecting community and migration thus implies opening the problem of community in movement, the community that is displaced from its stability and yet still persists.

The Borders of Politics

Crossing a border, leaving the neighborhood, entering the city legislature and filling it with mud: this is also escaping confinement and foreignness, and it is possible only with a previous accumulation of forces that is tied together block by block, that is sheltered in the collective body.

> In that moment, when I started being a delegate, I didn't feel like a foreign woman. I was simply another resident, with needs like any other, and it was in that moment that I did not feel discriminated against in Argentina. When we entered a large body like the legislature, they opened the doors for us, and we had to go in and walk on the carpets with our muddy shoes. The truth is that I wiped my feet on the carpet several times to make them feel that we had mud on our feet because they weren't doing what they needed to be doing. And, well, . . . it was beautiful.

The state manages the villa based on policies focused on calculating the imminence of overflow. This overflowing is lying in wait and causes many of the policies governed by a sense of order to fail. That sort of pragmatic calculation of the imminence of overflow is appropriated by governors and the governed when negotiating.

In that respect, the body of delegates expresses a broader organizational mode. Insofar as it is founded on an accumulation of social knowledges, neighborhood management, and micropolitical conflict resolution, it is inseparable from a network of organizations with which it is articulated and from which it is nourished: popular soup kitchens and snack providers, training workshops, enterprises, festival organizers, and so on. Its effectiveness and publicity are achieved through a transversal diffusion (gossip, comments, rumors, etc.) that spreads the delegative formula block by block, working on that scale thanks to a network of popular institutions that enabled it and provided the basis for its development. It was the body of delegates' know-how, concrete victories, and capacity for negotiation with authorities that created a capital of trust among neighbors.

Now, how can that know-how be converted into political capital with the authorities? One delegate summarizes it as follows: "The government gives you functions to fulfill but not solutions." Finding solutions falls onto the delegates themselves, onto those who have territorial knowledge and insertion. However, assuming those functions—for example, delivering food boxes from government programs and/or distributing construction materials (sheet metal, bricks, membranes) are among the most urgent needs—also leads to extreme exhaustion when you are not protected by the role of government official, and this exposes and endangers the communitarian figure of the delegate: "They moved the conflict onto each delegate. And those from the secretary of social promotion, from the city government, put down that line in the villa. They would say to the neighbors, 'Why don't you ask your delegates?' And a delegate is not God, they can't make things multiply."

Unloading conflicts onto the delegates places them in a role of mediation that appropriates their popular legitimacy and problem-solving efficiency, while also covering them with suspicion related to the management of policies that are deficient by definition. In this sense, the systematic inadequacy of the government's calculation also fell onto the delegates, from the responsibility of managing scarce resources to the need to demonstrate that construction materials and/or apartments had been distributed or granted based on nonarbitrary criteria, based on the people's confidence in the delegate: "The government, intelligently, has transferred all of that work into mandatory work for the delegate, where the delegate even had to give names, surnames, ID numbers, everyone who gets an apartment or not. . . . This created conflicts on the blocks."

Does the body of delegates function as a type of mediation for the government to reach the territory? "Rather than mediators, I think that the body of delegates was used as personnel of the government of the city of Buenos Aires, without receiving any type of salary or anything, but rather it was an obligatory part or a requirement in order for the government to recognize them as delegates. It started taking shape like that. . . . That was the government's work, and it was the point of division and separation for the body of delegates. That was the vile, punctual work of the government."

The delegates worked in tension with the government: producing information about the villa's population to specify their demands and, at the same time, resisting being instrumentalized as the mediators of a distribution policy that was known to be meager and inefficient. However, in its moments of strength, the body of delegates was able to build its own standards and evaluate state policies without being defined by them nor subordinated as mere executors. The government offered to compensate some delegates, and with that the body of delegates disintegrated from within, as its capital of legitimacy was exploited. On one hand, the trust in a task that is initially done "for honor" is broken, and, on the other, the selection of those who will be offered compensation (and/or a government position) is made unilaterally by the government. "They speculated with the legitimate needs of many *compañeros* who were unemployed," one delegate comments. With the offer of a government position and/or payment for neighborhood activism, the government exploits the problematic knot of that unpaid social work, which is not recognized with a wage but through political subordination. At the same time, the government dismisses collective decision making as a mechanism for designating who would receive some type of economic help for making their time and work available for the neighborhood.[22]

The Economy of Inclusion and Exclusion

Depoliticizing life, Butler argues, implies erasing "matters of gender, menial labor, and reproduction from the field of the political" (in Butler and Spivak 2007, 38). These are modes of exclusion produced as such, politically preserved under that exceptional status. The confinement of a part of the population supposes an economy of its exclusion.

Butler, discussing Arendt again, reframes the stateless—"these spectral humans, deprived of ontological weight and failing the tests of social intelligibility required for minimal recognition include those whose age, gender, race, nationality, and labor status not only disqualify them for citizenship but actively 'qualify' them for statelessness" (15)—as a population category that is not simply made up of the excluded, of those left aside, but rather is *produced* through its exclusion. Butler clarifies that there cannot be dispossession without producing the conditions in which the disenfranchisement—of rights, citizenship, name—unfolds and takes place. Ultimately, it is about a critique of the idea of sovereignty as a limit or boundary, as that which would demarcate an *outside*, "a metaphysical state outside of politics itself" (12).

Again, in opposition to Arendt, how is it possible for her political geometry to leave *outside* precisely that which is a constituent *part*—in spite of, or even because of, its invisibilization, nullification, or dispossession—of the definition of politics itself, understood as the projection of the public sphere become city? If Arendt makes the public the political space par excellence, following the model of the Athenian city, and banishes those who would not belong to the field of politics thus defined—slaves, women, and foreigners—to the "darkness" of the private-domestic sphere, Butler denounces the overly crystalline operation of inside versus outside: "In different ways, they are, significantly, contained within the polis as its interiorized outside. Arendt's description in *The Human Condition* leaves uncriticized *this particular economy in which the public (and the proper sphere of politics) depends essentially upon the non-political or, rather, the explicitly depoliticized*" (16; italics added).

This emphasis on the production of dispossession allows an analysis of its effective, productive side. It also requires seeing it as double-sided: if that dispossession or exclusion needs to be produced, it is because it must oppose and compete with a political productivity belonging to the very sphere that it seeks to exclude.

That political productivity belonging to those who at the same time are produced as dispossessed would be, Butler seems to warn, recognized and negated by derogatory, demeaning, passive characterizations *even and especially when* that productivity enters onto the scene, is activated or mobilized and/or speaks: then it will be spoken of as the prepolitical, protopolitical, apolitical, antipolitical, or, directly, the nonpolitical or depoliticizing.[23] These modes of reactive valorization will be used to disqualify or, better, to "actively qualify" the political action of the "disenfranchised."

Following what I have described as Butler's method, along with the Foucauldian premise of a positive power that is not simply characterized by its repressive and exclusive side, leads to a better understanding of the apparatuses of government.

Butler, on constructing a definition of the state that starts by definitively removing the capital S from the term, allows for displacing and interrogating all of the meanings, even literal ones, of the word itself: "state" as the "conditions in which we find ourselves"—Butler clarifies, almost as a "state of mind"—and "State" as "the legal and institutional structures that delimit a certain territory (although not all of those institutional structures belong to the apparatus of the state)" (3). A tension *connects* them. More precisely, the state will be the connecting and disconnecting ability between the state as *states* of mind (a certain "disposition to life") and the state as "juridical and military complexes that govern how and where we may move, associate, work, and speak." The state, while it unifies in the name of the nation, can also "signify the source of non-belonging, even produce that non-belonging as a quasi-permanent state" (4).

Let's return to the question of the apparatuses of government, starting from one of Butler's questions: "And what does it mean to be uncontained or discontinued from the state but given over to other forms of power that may or may not have state-like features?" (5–6). The condition of being "stateless," in light of this polemic between Arendt and Butler, offers the possibility of transferring the question of statelessness to another image: that of the governed populations. These populations are situated in a state *beyond* citizenship (and not beyond it in the way Arendt claimed, in that metaphysical political outside) that is *internal* to citizenship itself, which is increasingly visible in its divided way of functioning as a synthesis that includes by excluding and excludes by including.[24]

When the question is posited in this way, there is not an outside delimited by sovereignty but rather an expansion of spaces of power not based on sovereignty. A sequence collapses: if the sovereign space is not that which strictly defines the political space as such, it cannot exclude from the political field those without rights and those who carry out unpaid labor. In other words, politics is no longer confined to the sovereign space that, as I said earlier, excludes by including and includes by excluding those who are considered nonpolitical subjects.

Narrowing the political to the state-sovereign requires—and has been the ex post facto basis of—a sort of predominance of the political over the economic. We are confronted with a defense of the autonomy of the political as the properly *active* sphere of the human compared to the automatisms of economic rationality. However, another link in Butler's critique is fundamental for undoing that separation of spheres (the political versus the economic) that organizes Arendtian thought: "the elision or marginalization of the economic or, indeed, its demonization as a threat to politics as such, severely restricts this effort to rethink the terms of concerted action and conditions of stateless-ness alike" (26–27).[25] Why?

The precise demarcation of the political is affirmed through an exclusive logic: that which is signaled as not belonging to that field is defined as the depoliticized. What happens when, as Butler says, life has already been "en-tered into the political field in ways that are clearly irreversible?" (37) Life and politics are interwoven, indiscernible, in relation to power and resistance. In this situation, "any effort to establish such an exclusionary logic depends upon the depoliticization of life and, once again, writes out the matters of *gender, menial labor, and reproduction* from the field of the political" (38; italics added).

The expansion of power as biopower, and the extension of the terrain of the political to life as a whole as biopolitics, exposes the politicization of that which had remained relegated to the nonpolitical in the Arendtian political model and its subsequent politicist conjugations. *In such a perspective, gen-der, menial labor, and reproduction, to return to Butler's enumeration, function as the* internalized *outside of the polis: its* dark *economy.* Ruling this outside as a sovereign act does not recognize—or, rather, recognizes and denies—those whose exclusion the very constitution of the public sphere as a lumi-nous surface of "public action" depends on, in counterpoint to their resources without speech, without state, without retribution. The marginalization of the economy in the Arendtian political analysis can be understood in this way: its invisibility operates as the material basis for the separation of spheres.

It is the importance of this economy that forces us to go beyond the limits of political thought organized by nation-state sovereignty, in order to analyze the apparatuses of governmentality that directly intervene in *gender, menial labor, and reproduction* as politics of life.

Going beyond theories of sovereignty, even the forms that enable it to sur-vive in its exceptional modes, as Giorgio Agamben (1988) shows, supposes the necessity "to find postnational forms of political opposition that might begin to address the problem [of the stateless] with some efficacy" (Butler, in Butler and Spivak 2007, 41).[26] In this regard, privileging the political vocabulary of sovereignty risks making certain lives unthinkable.

Urban Space and Accumulation

The villa is a place that concentrates dynamics that pertain to the city as a whole. Problems related to housing, race, and rights, which cause constant tension in the villas' everyday operation, project a broader conflict: rivalry, cooperation, and competition between techniques of urban governance and the forms of self-government adopted by the city's inhabitants in the framework of neoliberal logic. In this respect, the villa functions as a stage for setting an example of a politics of security (the villa is permanently marked as the space where criminal delinquency resides and is reproduced and sent out to the rest of the city). This turns the villa—for the media and campaigning politicians—into the favored scene of fear and their securitist rhetoric. But the villa is also a space of experimentation with forms of struggle seeking modes of urban justice (Nichols and Beaumont 2004), and it constantly grapples with—negotiates with, combats, resists, and is intervened in by—diverse apparatuses of governmentality.

One way of governing the villa is to declare it an exceptional territory, simultaneously outside of and within the city. Through the concrete struggles of its residents, this category—that of a territory in a state of exception—is permanently questioned, confronted, and shown to be problematic, in the name of a "right to the city" that, paradoxically, becomes stronger as it is claimed by those who, because of their migrant condition, have the fewest rights.[27]

The concept of urbanization is constantly disputed within this web. That is where one of the origins of the body of delegates can be located, as a way of producing a political authority capable of dealing with that problematic of undefined space. A permanent redetermination of the urban is at stake in the villa's housing policy since while the villa is confirmed as a space for confining the poor, it also clearly shows the strength of a growing economy that expands the villa and connects it in different ways to the city and even beyond national borders to migrant, commercial, and labor flows.

The construction of monoblock apartment buildings on the edge of the villa—also as a way of limiting its horizontal expansion—seeks to circumscribe the space and *posits an ideal of conversion: from the villa to the neighborhood.* This is an old ideal that makes use of the ancient image of the "working-class neighborhood," of standardized constructions, regular allowances, family stability. However, if there is one thing the villa has nothing in common with, it is the old working-class neighborhood: these two vital spaces are radically distanced by the composition of their inhabitants, their modes of life, the economies that are articulated within the villa, the dynamics of constructing authority, the villa's velocity of expansion and change, and its parallel legal status. In this regard, the local space of the villa concentrates a broader redefinition of the urban and shelters a housing, family, social, productive, and monetary dynamic that exhibits the features of an intensely heterogeneous territory, located in the center of the city while being managed as a peripheral and marginal zone. In any case, it is a space for thinking about the features of new proletarian economies.

The property logics are neither stable nor stabilizing. Many subsidized houses have been sold by their beneficiaries. They are part of a fast-paced informal housing market. The delegates became conscious of the impossibility of governing a dynamic that surpasses any official calculation: tenement buildings that make construction grow vertically, clandestine textile workshops established in the villas that appropriate the social conquests of services as free infrastructure, the multiplication of commercial microenterprises, fluctuations among the informal, illegal, legal, communitarian, and social economies that consistently sabotage the possibility of neatly classifying the population. All of this puts the delegates—in their simultaneous roles as cartographers, census takers, planners, and surveyors—on the brink of collapse.

This role of the delegates, at the center of the villa's urban politics, allows their figure to be projected as the key to understanding the new reality of the villa, but it is also the nucleus of their problems and the origin of their decline. Being charged with the responsibility for defining criteria for a completely insufficient housing policy makes them responsible for the management of scarcity but, at the same time, demonstrates an abundance. The delegates will be responsible for conflicts in a housing policy that is at the center of the tension in the villa because it is in the housing policy where the dynamic of the velocity of nonstop growth is expressed. More specifically, it is where the tension is played out between urbanization as urban regulation or normalization and the maintenance of the villa as an exceptional space (in which, for example, the police do not enter for control and security) in which certain economies are embedded.

One of the body of delegates' requests was for the government to provide materials to support a policy of self-construction and not the conservation of precarious houses. In practice, this self-construction already existed. What was needed were government resources to be used within an already effective policy of popular construction. (Is it not ironic that there is a constant debate about whether or not the villas are safe or, as is insisted, unsafe constructions, when their builders are the construction workers building the whole city?) The duty of supervising housing policies (blueprints, materials, budgets, modes of construction, etc.) is claimed by the delegates as their own right. In this respect, they are proposed as an apparatus of control against the companies contracted by the government. Thus, they intervene in a policy designed for those who are not passive recipients but rather active and demanding "owners" and experts on the issue. This allows them, for example, to denounce construction companies for gluing baseboards on top of plaster. For skilled plasterers, which is what many of the bricklayer-delegates are, that is an aberration.

Architecture and clothing, according to Spivak (2013), are art forms and privileged spheres for the inscription of nature within culture. Workers from both specialties are among the villa's main sectors. Even so, the villa continues to be perceived as closer to the jungle than the polis, more a space of nature than of culture.

El Alto: The Tenement Buildings

The tenement buildings correspond with the moment of vertical and intensive expansion of the villa, with the acceleration of the "informal real estate market" (Cravino 2006). There is no longer an extensive space to occupy, yet people continue to arrive. Driven by a certain economic recovery in which the textile workshops are a favored sector for migration, an entire new housing economy and new population layer is arising: *the tenement building*. There are already towers of up to five floors driven by the business of renting rooms where land is scarce.

In turn, this generates a completely new sector of owners among the villa's residents (the first occupiers of the land), whose income is swelled by renting rooms and/or beds. The *anticrético* communitarian system (which I will explain below) becomes essential for this real estate expansion, whose construction was also carried out by communitarian initiatives during recent decades. Some delegates decry that the villa has become a "dormitory-city" linked to the industry of the workshops operating both within and outside the villa.

As a dormitory-city, services arise within it for those who rent a room or bed and do not have space to cook, along with clandestine (nonauthorized) childcare facilities. There is an entire system of infrastructure that is simultaneously visible and invisible.

Thus, as migration drives the development of technologies of flows of news, money, and people (telephone and Internet cafés, money wiring and postal agencies, travel agencies), there is also a whole technology of internal domestic and care services (food, nursing and medicine, child care, security, etc.), which are multiplied as more people arrive in the villa. A technology of settlement as the construction of a new place, especially linked to tasks of reproduction, corresponds to those other technologies. A block that in 2000 contained 115 houses and 180 families eight years later is populated by 700 families and the dwellings become impossible to count: the same house, with the same street number, now has three or four floors.

The living space of the villa has been mutating recently. The historical occupants of the blocks are there, but there are also the subsidized apartments and tenements, occupied by renters and owners. How can a delegate represent the different modifications? How has this expansion and diversification of the population influenced representation? One of the delegates situates the possibility of an integrated construction of citizenship and community in a previous era, when the population was different. The tenement complicates the villa's composition, making it even more heterogeneous.

The Tension between Urbanization and Eradication

The villa is being populated at an unstoppable velocity. One delegate who settled in the early 1980s, when the site was still a "jungle" owing to the quantity of vegetation and water and there were barely fifteen houses in her sector, remembers that it was then populated in a few months. But she never imagined the current rhythm. Even today it is surprising to see the taxis, bringing up to twenty people, arriving directly from the Ezeiza's airport at daybreak. Each time she sees them unloading their luggage, as she washes down the sidewalk at the break of dawn, she ask the same question: "Where are they going to go?"

From the perspective of governmental planning, urbanization supposes a layout of streets and a type of regulation of housing that assumes, at least theoretically, the villa's eradication, that is, its replacement by another type of urban layout.[28] The image is that of a passage: from the villa to a neighborhood made up of apartment buildings.

The official logic seeks to empty the houses built by successive occupations—and the entire parallel real estate market that followed them—and relocate their inhabitants to the monoblock apartment buildings. However, the villa's rhythm of growth impedes the relocation. Instead, apartment buildings fill up, and the buildings in the villa are not emptied but rather continue growing. Rather than relocation, what occurs is a dynamic of growth by overlapping.

Beneficiaries sometimes leave their buildings in the villa, sometimes they sell them or exchange them with family members or strangers, and other times they rent them informally, since they would not be authorized to have two houses. The idea that urbanization would imply a progressive "eviction" of the villa is constantly resisted and sabotaged. A powerful real estate dynamic shapes those thirty-one blocks, which become denser and higher and more expensive.

Additionally, there is the looming fear of the *transient nature of what has been won*: delegates know that conquests cannot be taken for granted in the case of a change of government; they could even be at risk with a change in officials within the same government. What has been won never seems irreversible. And this is known, calculated, taken into account. Negotiations can be reopened, closed, stalled, or reversed. This is the source of the delegates' sensation that they have to remain alert and organized. Conquests are temporally unstable, always provisional. Therefore, a certain administrative passion drives the delegates to seek reassurance, to obtain signed papers, to receive legal protections for rights. In turn, the conquests are also always *partial*, because of the reductions necessarily produced by recognition from government entities and because of the perpetual communitarian excess that is unrealizable in terms of demands. The partiality is simultaneously a show of two diverse performative economies and at the same time evidence of the contingent mode in which conquests are won.

Diverse Economic Institutions

A set of communitarian economic practices forms a solid network of mutual aid and forms of cooperating and channeling flows of money, loans, favors, and solidarity. Articulated with the informal economy, these practices enable an entire circuit of credit and investment without formal-legal requirements or purely banking-financial mediation. They are part of a material fabric that makes it possible for those arriving in a foreign country to obtain resources to settle, invest, and produce.

These economic institutions are not legible from a purely contractual logic. Nor can they be described as noncommercial. However, they share some attributes with the gift economy: the relationships that they propose cannot be simply reduced to a rule or law insofar as they involve a more complex system of obligations. If the gift is always within a rhythm, as if it had to do with being incorporated into a cycle or dance, these institutions require something of that *atmosphere* (Karsenti 2009): a climate in which such a temporality of reciprocal obligations is made possible.

I am interested in these economic institutions from a specific perspective: how they were used during the crisis as forms that appeal to a communitarian wealth that sustains the network of movement of diverse communities, as well as how they become a resource in a territory exceeding that which is delimited by the community.

These transactions are performative because language and rituals are inherent to them (Dufy and Weber 2009). *Ayni*, meaning reciprocity, was a concrete mechanism for the material construction of housing in the villa. Spreading beyond Bolivian migrants, the system of reciprocity enabled the collective construction of housing, as in a relay system, using the inhabitants' joint strength, and taking advantage of resources and efforts. "I give something to you, and when you are able to, you give me what you can, it works like that. But it's not that I give you a sack of potatoes and you give me back a sack of potatoes. You are going to give me what I need like I gave you what you needed when you needed it." This is how a former delegate defines it, showing how its logic adjusts to the variation in needs rather than the equivalence of things or quantities. As Raquel Gutiérrez Aguilar (2011a) shows, here reciprocity implies that "the objective of circulating material and symbolic goods is the—individual and collective—expansion of use values" and that, "with guidelines of reciprocity, the circulation of material and symbolic goods constantly oscillates around equilibrium guided by the systematic call toward a limited imbalance. Thus, it generates a dynamic." Another delegate provides more detail: "We shape it when we move, when we change place, we use it differently depending on where we are. In Villa 1-11-14, we helped build a new house for someone. Later he participated in constructing someone else's house and so on. The ayni is giving when someone needs it and receiving when you need it."

The *pasanaku*, which means "it passes between us," also operates in the villa. It is a widely disseminated mode of finance and savings in Bolivia, and particularly in Villa 1-11-14, which enables the development of enterprises for members of a certain group. Based on individual and/or family contributions, a sum of money is raised that is distributed once a month (or according to intervals stipulated by the participants), so that each person receives the complete contributions once per cycle. Receiving all of the money that has been gathered at once allows participants to count on a sum that they pay for in small amounts over a long period of time. Thus, they manage to obtain loans outside of formal banking institutions and, therefore, without any type of interest or requirement of demonstrating the attributes of bankarized subjects.

A fundamental temporal variable influences the pasanaku: those who are favored by the draw will receive the total sum long before they finish paying their contributions. In this sense the pasanaku is "played," since it combines a financial practice with an element of chance that also subjects the benefit to a playful dynamic. The commitment and responsibility of the contributors (or players), especially the first beneficiaries, are fundamental, as they must continue making their contributions until the end, that is, until each of the participants has received the total sum.

The drawing's random criteria can be changed by collective decision. If one of the participants has an emergency or circumstances worthy of being prioritized, it can be collectively decided that they will benefit from one of the first rounds. In Villa 1-11-14 the inhabitants play pasanakus ranging from a hundred to a thousand dollars, every week, every month. It is the favored communitarian form of microfinancing for hundreds of commercial enterprises, the means of acquiring materials to construct or expand houses, to buy domestic appliances and/or machinery, and to fund festivals and family and neighborhood events.

It is an efficient form of savings and loans that eludes any type of formal mediation, that is agreed on—in time and space—according to the needs of the participants and sustained by intracommunity trust in the sense that there is no guarantee of compliance other than the commitment assumed by those who play.

In the type of obligation that is contracted, pressure must be applied by the group itself and requires a discipline of saving that is simultaneously self-imposed and monitored by the group. One has to be invited to participate; therefore, the one who does the inviting deposits their trust in another, betting on their future solvency, in front of the rest of the participants as well. Money and trust circulate within the circle of players, that is, trust in the game and a wager on a form of small-scale savings and mutual aid. This does not exclude situations of noncompliance, fraud, and attempts to take advantage of the game, but each of these irregularities or cases of cheating is also punished according to a collective decision.

The pasanaku is an economic institution but in a way that involves play, obligation, trust, and credit. It is an economic institution that articulates a time of chance with the possibility of implementing projects, combining enterprise and cooperation, and appropriating the temporal difference enabled by credit without the cost of a banking intermediary.

There is also the use of the *anticrético*, a common housing policy in Bolivia that has been expanded to living arrangements in Villa 1-11-14. This consists of advancing a sum of money to the owner of a house or apartment that is calculated at three or four times a year's rent. At the year's end, the contract can be renewed for another year or the owner is obligated to return to the tenant the sum of money that they had initially given.

The person receiving the sum of money in the anticrético benefits from receiving a large sum of money in cash and having it available for other investments over the period of one year, which offers a fairly long period to make the money yield more profit. The person who obtains housing through an anticrético has to make an effort in order to advance an amount of money that is larger than they would spend on a normal rent divided month by month, but with the advantage that at the end of the year the entire sum of money will be returned to them. That is, for the tenant their housing expense is canceled out as they recuperate the money after using the housing. For the owner, it supposes that they will recover the money that they had the benefit of being able to invest and multiply. The system is strengthened by mutual benefit and backed by juridical contracts, although often made informally.

In Bolivia it is a very common practice, but it is adjusted—made flexible, in terms of lengths and circumstances—to the needs of migrants arriving in Buenos Aires from Bolivia. It is a way of ensuring housing for a period that allows one to settle, obtain work, and bring one's family, and it is a sort of first payout, a cost of installation, that is later recuperated. For those who are already in Argentina and have become property owners, it is a way of obtaining large sums of money and expanding their capacity as entrepreneurs and investors, perhaps even building more housing and rooms to offer new anticréticos to those who continue to arrive.

The Spanish Royal Academy defines the figure of the *anticresis* as "a contract in which the debtor consents for their creditor to enjoy the fruits of the farm that they give to them, until the debt is canceled."[29] That is another way of presenting it, but there is a fundamental difference: the anticrético in Villa 1-11-14 is not strictly organized by the notion of the debtor. Rather than a debt, it is a *credit*: someone hands over a sum of money in order to enjoy another person's property, and that sum is returned at the end of the period of using the property. What occurs then is a *return* and not a cancellation of debt.

The change of terms is decisive: it is not a creditor-debtor arrangement but rather a pact between the person making the loan and the person returning it. Rather than debt, the key figure is that of the loan as an advance that benefits both the lender and the borrower in a more or less equal way. We have already seen, however, that this web functions as the basis for a more complex and fast-paced financial deployment.

The Night of the Delegates

The gift can be thought of as a question of time. According to Jacques Derrida, Marcel Mauss's spectacular maneuver is to make the notions of gift and exchange compatible. The gift would no longer be (as Derrida himself originally argues) the interruption of circulation. Rather, there is only a gift in the exchange because the gift is the temporal-temporizing difference that connects them (Derrida 1992, 39).

Derrida synthesizes: where there is a gift, there is time. "Giving time" is at the core of the gift economy, so that it ceases to be an antieconomy to become a more generous and complex economy than that which deploys the rationality of *homo œconomicus*.

The gift is not the gift if it does not give time and if does not also give the time. As Derrida states, "the thing must not be restituted immediately and right away. There must be time, it must last, there must be waiting—without forgetting" (1992, 41). Mauss works with this notion of time, which is nothing other than *time or the term* as a specific feature of the gift. This, in turn, distinguishes it from debt and payment as emblematic forms of the Western economy.

Derrida points out that the objective of Maussian theory is to both safeguard the original specificity of the gift in respect to economic rationality and account for the symbolism that traverses cold economic reason and those other (religious, poetic, discursive, etc.) phenomena that are inseparable from the gift and that organize it within the *total social fact*. In this sense, the time period—or the supplemental *différance*—becomes an interest of the thing itself, of the thing given.

There is no gift without time. And who gives time for political organization? How is that time made? Various accounts describe the function of being a delegate as full time that involves multitasking. Initially, the unemployment of many of those who became delegates played a key role: they were free to give the time.

The body of delegates has, then, a collective power that acquires time from the unemployed. An entire economy of time, of effort, of administration of resources, and of trust sustains the collective body. However, the possibility of broadening participation depended on occupying the night, when more neighbors could participate in meetings. Nocturnal organization was the key to expanding representativeness and to planning and supervising tasks for those who also had several free hours during the day to dedicate to the organization.

Crisis in the Body of Delegates: Natives versus Immigrants

The division emerged, at first, according to nationality, skin color. The natives say that they have more authority because they are from here. That was the southern zone, composed of blocks 1, 3, 5, etc. . . . The majority of them were from here, from the Federal Capital. In the northern zone, where we are now, there are a few Argentines, but the majority are immigrants. They tried to see how they could continue moving forward together, and they were divided. But as the budgets fell, *the natives were grabbing everything.* Later an internal struggle started between them. Since there were two or three delegates on some blocks and only one on others, according to the demand of each block, the groups began regrouping; they began splitting that way. *There was also division within the part with the highest immigrant population owing to the economic power that came down from the government.* They [the government] divided them [the delegates] because it suited the government. For them, the immigrants are not worth anything; that is their position. If you go to the city center they tell you that immigrants don't have any rights. (italics added)

In the interviews, at least three causes of the crisis of the body of delegates can be discerned:

- The emergence of a *tenement economy* dismantled the neighbor-house relationship as the basis of representation and action in the neighbor–body of delegates equation. The tenement buildings are interwoven with a thriving machinery of exploitation. They often house the same people who work in the textile workshops. With exponential and rapid growth, the tenements tend to be superimposed onto the urbanization plans as de facto realities. They are expensive, and their renters live in horrible conditions.
- The tenants form a very important and growing population that remains excluded from participation. The problem of their housing

(its precarity and the relationship of exploitation with the tenements' owners) also remains invisible.

- Another population dynamic is consolidated: on one hand, increasingly high turnover and, on the other, the development of an exponentially and constantly growing new population that distorts the stability that proximity gives to ties between neighbors.
- Therefore, the tenement owners themselves are opposed to urbanization plans and the collective authority of the body of delegates. The tenement is developed as a complement to and as part of the web of illegal economies growing in the villa. It constitutes one of the least visible and most irritating aspects of the exploitation of the labor force, a fundamental issue for the development of collective power in the villa.
- Another cause of this crisis is the *changeover of delegates*: the replacement of a first generation of delegates, who made it into an experience of struggle, and the first phase of construction by the second generation, which assumes the delegate role as a privilege, an element of power, without the same work discipline that the first generation had. There is a difference in experience, on one hand, but also a blurring of a more communitarian dimension of the form of labor and a more instrumental and immediate perception of collective power. All of this should also be seen in light of the divisions within the body of delegates, the IVC's (Instituto de la Vivienda de la Ciudad) maneuvers for those purposes, and the discrediting of delegates in the eyes of many neighborhood residents because of how some of them managed the criteria for allocating apartments and failed to comply with the obligation to leave their homes in the villa when they received subsidized housing.
- The delegates ended up being charged with a properly governmental function tied to distributing food boxes, merchandise, and influence. The delegate who is transformed into someone who possesses and distributes a power linked to the state has established another relationship with the neighbors and among the delegates themselves.

Festival and Enclosure

The "urban island" is how Josefina Ludmer describes the fictionalization of territory as the key to speculation for the public imagination: "If the urban island in Latin America is the fiction of a territory that can be deterritorialized, abandoned, and destroyed, literature is no longer the manifestation of national identity. It is a form of territorialization that is the site and scene of other subjectivities or identities and other politics" (2010, 135).

Representations of the space of the villa fluctuate between, on one hand, characterizing it with a festive vitalism, a disorder of smells, tastes, libations, and colors in which popular solidarity is reinvented or, at least, a form of unexpected pleasure is found, and, on the other hand, projecting it as a small-big inferno, whose narrow streets duplicate prison rooms when their internal bars—which block streets and passageways after a certain time—subsume it in a prison logic. A whole sequence of fiction and nonfiction texts explore that territory: *Si me querés, quereme transa* by Cristian Alarcón (2010) and the novels *La virgen Cabeza* by Gabriela Cabezón Cámara (2009) and *La villa* by César Aira (2006), as well as the saga *Bolivia Construcciones* (2006) and *Grandeza Boliviana* (2014) by Bruno Morales, meticulously narrate the everyday of the villa as a deliberately vital and deadly space at the same time.

The flow between the villa and the prison is also explicit on visiting days, when dozens of informal cabs from the villa bring families (mostly women and children), supplies, money, and messages back and forth between the neighborhood and jails. There are many sides to the villa-enclosure continuum. One of those is the villa-workshop.

The Festival Traverses the Neighborhood: From the Organizational Moment of the Body of Delegates to the Change in Authorities

In the villa, the festival is the religious festival. Virgin figures are put in their best dresses, spend the night in the houses of a select group of caregivers, and live among all the believers, opening both a physical path and a movement, sustained by the faithful who move them down the narrow passageways, so that they bless with their gaze that which each person dedicates to them. The traveling chapel of that sanctified and generous woman radiates confidence and sows a community of committed walkers in its path, even if only temporarily.

For the body of delegates of Villa 1-11-14, the festivals, as religious processions, were shields for the body's emergence at the end of the 1990s. It was the first way of making themselves visible and publicizing themselves, of convoking more neighbors and surrounding themselves with forces, but, above all, of engaging in a legitimate organizational form, capable of disputing the circulation of the then "president" of the villa through its streets.

As a tragic reversal, in 2005 one of these processions, dedicated to the mulatto Peruvian Señor de los Milagros, ended up being the site of a massacre owing to a confrontation between different disputing drug groups.[30] The massacre took place a year after the end of the body of delegates, the end of its moment as a popular and plurinational institutional experiment. Between one festival and another, a striking change in authorities took place in the territory: from the neighborhood presentation of the body of delegates to drug gangs, whose attempt to settle their scores ended in a massacre.

CHAPTER 6

Between Populism and the Politics
of the Governed

Governmentality and Autonomy

The *politics of the governed* is, for Partha Chatterjee, a way of immersing the Foucauldian perspective on governmentality within a discussion about popular politics. With this move, this political lexicon changes its meaning to a certain extent: the governed do politics; they are not simply the passive targets of techniques directed at them. Michel Foucault's theorizations are thus challenged from another perspective, questioned from subalternity. Along this line, the category of population, a key name in this conceptual framework, is opposed to that of citizens, as a form that has more affinity with what occurs in the postcolonial territories of India in this case but that can be expanded to all those places that are not strictly organized by images of modern Western politics. The art of governing denominated as governmentality thus proposes the population as a counterpoint to the idea of "popular sovereignty and granting equal rights to citizens" (Chatterjee 2004, 37). The language of the population and of the governed thus abandons the more majestic constellation of sovereignty and universal rights to ground politics in a series of mundane everyday transactions.

In this perspective, the population becomes a way of naming the inhabitants of the colonial metropolis less abstractly and universally—less "morally," the author says—than the notion of citizenship does. Its *descriptive and empirical* character is useful for refuting, from within, the notion of popular sovereignty, which corresponds with the postrevolutionary nation-state imaginary that Chatterjee critiques. But, unlike Foucault, Chatterjee gives the notion of population and its synonym, *the governed*, a popular valence, turning it into the name for a pragmatic popular *potencia*. In this way, he reconceptualizes the democratic regime from a different political theory: "Governance . . . is the body of knowledge and set of techniques used by, or on behalf of, those who govern. Democracy today, I will insist, is not government of, by and for the people. Rather, it should be seen as the politics of the governed" (2004, 4).

The governed are not the people, the ideal subject of unitary sovereignty synthesized in the state. They are the ones who know how to deal with— appropriate, reject, negotiate with—the mechanisms of governmentality of which they are the object. Therefore, democracy depends on the political agency of those toward whom the knowledges or techniques of government are directed. Democracy continues to be determined by the practice of governmentality, and thus the deepening of democracy would seem to inevitably be a dispute within that governmentality.

To the extent that the category of citizens, and the type of modern articulation between the state and society that it supposes, is not a comprehensive reality in peripheral (or postcolonial) countries, the state makes itself present through mechanisms of direct negotiation with which people must transact. The management of populations through public policies supposed by governmentality organizes a scenario that replaces, from Chatterjee's (2004, 34) point of view, representation based on citizen sovereignty.

There is a second twist regarding revolutionary political traditions when speaking of the governed: the popular sectors—those from below, if understood according to the common vertical distinction—no longer seek to occupy the government. They have abandoned or lost that possibility and, rather, aim to determine how they want to be governed. The governed assume the context of governmentality described by Foucault, but they modify the political status of what it means to be governed. This analysis has the virtue of being provocative and realistic at the same time: it captures the popular political dynamic beyond the revolutionary hypothesis of taking state power. In that sense, it dignifies a politics of concrete and local conquests in terms of nonmarginal or minor practices of intervention and determination of public policy. In turn, this requires thinking about the public in a new way: beyond modern institutional mediations. Along this line, it dismisses the idealism of a certain revolutionary paradigm as well as that of the interpellation of citizens in strictly formal and normative terms. The active perspective—not as conquests of consolation—with which these concrete struggles are theorized eludes the classic categorization of "reformist," giving them a new quality: their ability to politically appropriate resources and subjectively open up a space that seeks to objectify and pacify them.

At the same time, that realistic reading of the apparatuses of government seems to have a labile border with the outright acceptance of the distinction between the governing and the governed. As subjects of governmentality, the governed give up on contesting the system itself. In this regard, it supposes accepting the place that the governed occupy as such. Could what Chatterjee calls the "politics of the governed" be conceptualized as forms of self-government? Classically the notion of self-government involves a different, more ambitious level of autonomy. However, the politics of the governed seems to propose a paradoxical situation: that it is possible to assume a level of permanent negotiation with apparatuses of government, while also carrying out a reappropriation from below based on the governed's own resources, forms of intervention, and languages.

Is it possible to speak of two hypotheses for understanding the same situation: a politics of the governed (Foucault–Chatterjee) on one hand and, on the other, a greater level of autonomy or self-government?[1] If the first assumes that the subaltern have lost the capacity to govern but are "devising new ways in which they can choose how they should be governed" (Chatterjee 2004, 77), the second is not based on the acceptance of being governed but instead on the reclaiming and problematizing of autonomy. Are there two different ideas of autonomy? Or is a new notion of autonomy achieved from within the apparatuses of *governance* that are being imposed? Does Chatterjee's hypothesis imply that the principle of the multitude, which tends to reclaim rights of entitlement to power, should be cast aside? Or are we seeing a reinvention of the way of obtaining rights?

It is clear that Chatterjee seeks to deliberalize and depacify the discourse of governmentality. He proposes that a simple strategy of governmentality from the perspective of liberal dogma (the articulation of civil society and nongovernmental organizations) is not perceived in the same way by the governed, for whom it can be a practical exercise of democracy. In this sense, he argues that populations, on identifying as refugees, homeless, landless peasants, or the poor, are attributed to "demographic categories of governmentality. That is the ground on which they define their claims" (2004, 59). The language of governmentality itself acquires another meaning in the mouths of those who are believed, as the subaltern, to not be able to speak themselves but to only be able to be spoken about by the language of power. Yet isn't the language of governmentality the language of power?

Speaking becomes a way of subverting the passive voice of the governed and the names that categorize them as populations: the homeless, the unemployed, and so on. Is it a confirmation that the subaltern cannot speak other than through categories that are not their own?

So far we have retained the ambiguity of Chatterjee's position. From my point of view, he accepts the cogency of neoliberalism and its whole technology of government as the space of political dispute for the poor. Although they are governed, the author proposes a phase of resistance that consists of conducting politics within that very rationality. This supposes, as I have been saying, an acceptance of certain limits of what it means to do politics, and, at the same time, it poses the dilemma that those limits can be broken only once they are taken beyond their strictly regulatory content.

Political Society and Civil Society

Aiming to reconceptualize the capacity for popular action, Chatterjee proposes thinking about *political society* in opposition to the liberal figure of civil society, which, in the classic words of Alexis de Tocqueville, functions as the intermediary between individuals and the state. Chatterjee calls it political society because the conquest of rights has been fragmented and because it unfolds as a direct expression of social antagonisms in countries where the liberal sphere of civil society lacks consistency. Furthermore, there is a decisive difference: political society demonstrates the inefficiency of modern political mediation when the figure of the citizens is not operative. In practice, political society, then, replaces universal rights with concrete and particular demands, giving rise to the creation of a "heterogeneity of social rights." Therefore, the politics of the poor is immediately political. And it is so by appropriating the categories that would confine the poor as a population, as noncivil (read *uncivilized*) society. Chatterjee argues, "When the poor in countries like India, mobilized in political society, can affect the implementation of governmental activities in their favor, we must say that they have expanded their freedoms by using means that are not available to them in civil society" (2004, 67). In this regard, civil society and political society conceive of two divergent images of the political subject. Thus, the antinomy that Chatterjee posits between the "political imaginary of popular sovereignty and the mundane administrative reality of governmentality" supposes another antinomy: "*between the homogeneous national and the heterogeneous social*" (36).

Governmentality operates precisely as a knowledge and technology in the face of a heterogeneous social body, which does not reach the ideal of an "equal and uniform exercise of the rights of citizenship" (Chatterjee 2004, 60).

Democratic possibility then finds a place in the politics of the governed, in the form of a political society that knows how to connect itself with procedures of governmentality, a space of pragmatic negotiation dealing with "administrative processes that are *paralegal*" and assuming "collective claims that appeal to ties of *moral solidarity*" (74). Instead of proposing a subsidiary theory of civil society, Chatterjee radicalizes the theoretical and political possibilities for understanding the concrete action of the poor as a complete political subject, without lack.

According to Chatterjee, it is in disputes over property that we can see, "on the terrain of political society, a dynamic within the modern state of the transformation of precapitalist structures and of premodern cultures. It is there that we can observe a struggle over the real, rather than the merely formal, distribution of rights among citizens" (2004, 75). This adds two new twists to liberal political theory: it not based on the assumption of equality nor citizen equivalence, nor does it appeal to the logic of rights. However, this political practice is associated with the persistence of precapitalist and premodern cultures. Here Kalyan Sanyal's (2007) critique is relevant for noting that the end of the "teleological" and "historicist" paradigm of development also supposes the end of the perspective that proposes overcoming the economy's "traditional" and "informal" sectors in favor of "modern and formal" sectors. Instead, he argues, we are faced with a change of paradigm that organizes the heterogeneous and continuous coexistence of development with a very modern poverty.[2] My hypothesis is that this political society, to provisionally use this name, would be more powerful if it were projected beyond a linear and progressive capitalist norm. Its strength lies in dealing with capitalist dimensions and confronting them with noncapitalist dynamics.

Heterogeneous Time

The politics of the governed is a politics that is conducive to dealing with the heterogeneity of the social since "its solutions are always strategic, contextual, historically specific and, inevitably, provisional" (Chatterjee 2004, 22). This means that it does not aspire to an integrating, stable, and universal form of politics. On the contrary, Chatterjee is arguing against a melancholic politics that continues to yearn for "the mythical moment when classical nationalism merges with modernity," asking how the opposition between "global cosmopolitanism" and "ethnic chauvinism" can be avoided (23).

Furthermore, governmentality knows how to read the discrepancy between the utopian dimension of the homogeneous time of modern capitalism and heterogeneous time. This tension unfolds especially when narrating the nation, as Chatterjee shows by tracing it in the literary fictions produced by nationalism. What Josefina Ludmer (2010) calls postnational fictions in Latin America could be read as a counterpoint: how fiction constructs another genre of territories, subjectivities, and times based on the here and now of our continent—and, as Ludmer insists, creates other forms of public imagination.

The time of politics is transformed. The popular conquests and their duration assume a temporal precarity. Additionally, on no longer being utopian, they become *partial*. How so? A reduction is necessarily produced by recognition from government bodies, and there is always a communitarian excess that cannot be realized in terms of demands.

However, a perspective of ungovernability as an insubordinate space remains more diffuse or diluted. This ungovernability is capable of reformulating the very apparatuses of government and, above all, of overflowing or overriding them. Additionally, the productive character of the governed, as informal social workers and/or the temporarily unemployed, seems to be made invisible in this language to a certain extent. The emphasis on their status as governed seems to dismiss their social participation as worker-consumers. Finally, we are left with a question to develop further: can a popular elaboration of *buen vivir* counter the techniques of governmentality?

Populism and Postcolonialism: From the People to the Population?

The authors speaking of subalternity seek to reclaim a political confidence in the subaltern as a way of defying the Eurocentric theory that privileges a proletarian subject that functions as the criterion of universal adaptation. As Dipesh Chakrabarty comments, "Subaltern Studies's populism was more intense and more explicit than any earlier expression of that perspective" (2009, 155). Populist and postcolonial perspectives thus share a fundamental struggle: both think of the popular subject based on heterogeneity in opposition to the aspiration of an ideal proletariat (that is, *European, masculine, white*), and they seek to explicitly show the rationality of a popular movement that does not coincide with the strict contours of the working class.

These theories declare that they do not fear the masses. What Chakrabarty (2009) notes about subaltern studies could also be said for Ernesto Laclau's perspective. Hence, it is possible to name them as modes of populism.[3] This issue refers us to one of the most brilliant Latin American Marxists, José Aricó, who, in line with Antonio Gramsci and José Carlos Mariátegui, asks, how did Karl Marx pose the analysis of colonial reality so that its propositions and its lack of interest in Latin America would be possible? According to Aricó, this "misunderstanding" becomes relevant insofar as it inaugurates a series of misunderstandings to the point of defining Marxism in Latin America as "a grammatical expression of a real historical difficulty" (2013, 4).[4] It was a mistaken grammar, that of Marxism with Latin America, that attributed predicates that did not name it to the continent, whether for the rigidity of a nonexistent subject, or for the stubbornness of conditions that are never completed. Beyond the quick and easy, well-known label of Eurocentrism, Aricó tries to reconstruct—from within Marx's own thought—the conditions in which the German understood colonial realities, in particular based on the "strategic shift" in his analysis of the Irish situation. Aricó was especially interested in proving—and this is another one of the novel elements of his investigation—that the image of Marx's Eurocentrism is the product of the "official" version of the "Marxist *intelligentsia*," which marginalized Marxian texts referring to Spain, Russia, or Ireland as being written "under the circumstances." It is a permanent game of returns and reconstructions: if Marx undergoes a shift following his analysis of the Irish colonial situation and elaborates a program of action (self-government and independence, an agrarian revolution, and trade protections), Aricó asks why those points were not taken up by the Second International or socialist movements in dependent countries. Aricó's thesis avoids the label of Eurocentrism to conclude that the "essentially statist" character, or the construction "from above," of Latin American nations is what politically blocked Marx's comprehension of the continent's singularity. This is his blind spot: replacing the "real movement" of the Latin American social forces with the figure of Simón Bolívar, while not recognizing an "autonomy of the political" in the essentially statist character of its national formations, which appears as backward in his perspective.

The dynamic of subaltern politicization proposes a clear counterpoint to the logic of an evolutionary politicization that tends to characterize the subaltern as prepolitical. This was the reading of English Marxism—from Edward Palmer Thompson to Eric Hobsbawm—that influenced, as a perspective from below, subaltern studies but that subaltern studies scholars distanced themselves from since the English Marxists situate the urban proletariat as the ultimate unfolding of a developmentalist temporality. The origin of this point of view, Chakrabarty says, analyzing the Indian school, is a mix of Mao and Gramsci: but a Mao that eludes party leadership and a Gramsci that did not consider the critiques of spontaneity. This same point will be taken up again as the anchor of the subaltern studies school's dialogue with Latin America.

What type of relationship can be traced between this conception of populism and the populist reason that Laclau (2005a) puts forth for Latin America based on conceptualizing the equivalential articulation of demands as the constitutive axis of a popular identity? Can the paradigm of governmentality within which Chatterjee moves be compared to the structure of popular demands articulated as the people? Are there similarities in the uses of Gramsci underlying both theories? What differentiates the analysis of the politics of *the governed* from the *popular identity* referred to by populist reason?

The principal defenders of populism in Latin America fight against those who consider the people to be irrational.[5] In this regard, the idea of a populist reason dismantles the traditional distinction between a sentient and illiterate people and theories of enlightened government elites. However, in this case, I am proposing a radically different argument: I want to problematize and debate the unicist rationality that is attributed to popular life as the need for identitarian articulation. Laclau's (2005a) statements on social movements as dispersion without a focal point in opposition to the leadership of progressive heads of state in the region are a continual point of debate and discrepancies.

For Laclau, the heterogeneous emerges as the plurality of demands. His political preoccupation is focused around the articulation of that heterogeneity, through the always contingent combination of the logic of equivalence and the logic of difference. Two elements are decisive in this composition: naming and affect. What is needed, according to Laclau, is "a social cement" capable of uniting heterogeneous elements. Insofar as this unity is not provided by "any logic of articulation (functionalist or structuralist)" (2005a, x) *affect* becomes key in social constitution. It is that affect inherent to populism as "a way of constructing the political" that tends to associate it with a "dangerous excess" (x–xi), an excess that connects the community and irrationality—hence also the vagueness of populism's referents. The theory enters into an impasse when it has to think about populism, Laclau argues, and systematically avoids defining it. Populist theory proposes, without prejudice, to take those features that have always been considered negative qualities of populism—vagueness, indefinition, simplification, a moment of transition, the centrality of rhetoric, and so on—and designate them as indexes of "a social reality itself being, in some situations, vague and undetermined" (17). The hypothesis is that "populism is the royal road to understanding something about the *ontological constitution of the political as such*" (67; italics added). However, what begins as affect for Laclau, as the social cement or equivalence, ultimately becomes the logic of language.

Laclau returns to Gustave Le Bon, also taken up by Sigmund Freud, to demonstrate how the crowd allows itself to be influenced by images that behave as words, beyond their meaning. The crowd operates according to a logic of perverting language. Le Bon (1995) says that it arbitrarily associates words and images, manufacturing a whole series of "illusions." What does Laclau take from this description of *group psychology*? A fragile relationship between words and images is a precondition for any politically significant discursive operation (Laclau 2005, 22). He positively assesses what Le Bon believes to be a perversion to show that "associative networks" are essential to language, differing from each other owing to their performativity. What Le Bon wants to underscore as the source of a total lack of logic and rationality in the masses' actions, Laclau posits as a specific form of action, dismantling the assumptions of its inconsistency. For example, citing Hyppolite Taine, he spells out the idea behind that supposed collective irrationality: that rationality belongs to the individual, and "the individual experiences a process of social degradation by becoming part of a group" (2005, 29).[6]

Le Bon's suggestion, as part of that collective sentimentality and as a form of emotional contagion, takes another turn with Gabriel Tarde and his theorization of "social action at a distance," which he says will be the form of the social bond of the future, replacing physical contact and, therefore, replacing the multitudinous collective with the *publics* (as Maurizio Lazzarato [2006] would later argue). For Laclau, Tarde's idea includes plurality and novelty within the collective subject in a way that becomes central for his theorization of populism: it is a "purely spiritual collectivity" of scattered individuals, yet capable of an inclusive international unity thanks to the media and transportation suitable for expanding its influence in an intensive and lasting way.[7] Here Laclau draws on Freud's analysis in *Group Psychology and Analysis of the Ego* ([1921] 1990) about the model of identification as the libidinal key of the social bond and its investment in the figure of the leader, to ultimately end with Gramsci and his notion of hegemony. This process, Laclau says, is centered around the "progressive theoretical renegotiation of the duality between social homogeneity (or indistinctness) and social differentiation" (2005a, 61).

In other words, Laclau tracks the equivalential moment capable of functioning as "social cement," to use his expression, in what is encoded for each one of these authors. According to Laclau, in Freud there is a relationship of unification between both terms of the first dualism between homogeneity and difference (mass and individual) through mechanisms of identification that regulate the relationship between the leader and members of a social group.

But how is that collective understood? Laclau's unit of analysis is the demand (which always implies the possibility of a transition: from a request into a claim and demand [2005a, 73]). The possible articulations between demands constitute social identities with different levels of universalization of their claims. The objective of the constitution of the people as a historical actor depends on the form of structuration of demands into a "stable system of signification" (74). The Lacanian assumption is key: the people-subject is always a subject of lack; "it always emerges from an asymmetry between the (impossible) fullness of the community and the particularism of sites of enunciation" (26).

Laclau states that "equivalence *does not attempt to* eliminate differences" (79). There is a relation of insoluble tension between the two logics with the social as its *locus* (70). However, populism is the privileging of equivalential logic over difference. This means that totalization will be carried out by a partial element (the people) that aspires to be conceived as the only legitimate totality (82). The people is the partiality with the will to function as the totality of a community. Thus, the communitarian space is constituted based on what Laclau calls a radical *exclusion*. The counterpoint in Laclau's analysis is the institutionalist totality, where "all differences are considered equally valid within a wider totality" (82).

In Laclau, there is a phenomenology of democratic politics whose sequence is initiated when people feel that their demands are not being heard, much less satisfied. If it remains an isolated demand, he calls it a *democratic demand*. In their plurality, articulated under a logic of equivalences, they constitute *popular demands*. The act of making popular demands has a double value. It collects and projects the discontent of those who are making the demands in respect to the institutional order, through coordinating a series of dissatisfactions that are placed in equivalence with the most dissimilar demands. The base term is then the demand with two possible positions: fulfillment or unfulfillment. The latter, however, is distinguished because it is the start of a radicalization that culminates in the claim, the protest, and, if conditions mature, a populist phenomenon.

When are the people weakened? This happens when demands disintegrate and *popular demands* become a plurality of specific *democratic demands*, which lessens their logic of equivalence. The dissolution of the people supposes that individual demands are absorbed by the dominant system, and therefore their capacity of repercussion and translation with other demands is weakened. The "pattern of disintegration of the 'people,'" Laclau says, starting from an analysis of the English Chartists, is due to a "crisis in the ability of the 'people' to totalize at all—either the identity of the enemy or its own 'global' identity" (2005a, 92).

Then what relationship does he posit between the heterogeneous and the people? There are two meanings of the heterogeneous in Laclau. First, heterogeneity occurs when the demand exceeds the system's ability to satisfy it (here heterogeneity is equivalent to the Lacanian real): that which lacks "differential positions within the symbolic framework of society" (2005a, 86). Later, heterogeneity arises from the relationship among different demands, whose only common feature is the exhibition of the institutional system's failure. In any case, unity takes place through the social productivity of naming. The names of the people, Laclau will say, give unity to the heterogeneous while it is difficult to limit or provide the demands that unify and those that remain excluded.

Laclau associates his conception of the people with Jacques Rancière's. He cites *Dissensus* when Rancière says that "the people appropriate the common quality as their own. What they bring to the community strictly speaking is contention" (quoted in Laclau 2005a, 94). How is that partiality reclaimed and transformed into totality? The hegemonic operation implies that "popular identity functions as a tendentially empty signifier" (96). It is that emptiness and not a partiality or concrete content that enables its equivalential articulation. It is, the author summarizes, a performative operation that traces the chain of equivalence as such. Above all, that chain has a nominal consistency: "An assemblage of heterogeneous elements kept equivalentially together only by a name is, however, necessarily a singularity" (100).

The revolution, as such, does not appear to be a problem for the populist dynamic as the logic always operates at the level of recognition, whether vertical recognition (produced by institutions or not) or horizontal recognition (flowing from antagonism). That is, populism, on radicalizing the pressure on institutions, opens them up to the chains of equivalence forged in democratic struggle. The process does not culminate in a decisive central point since the hegemonic struggle is constantly renewed.

In the hegemonic process, a class content that would essentially vary with the resolution—even if partial—of antagonism is not emphasized. The category of the governed, I believe, is better supported by a dual model, like that of classes, and a suspension or arrest of the political dialectic that puts subjects in circulation and competition for power. From this point of view, Laclau's model is more fluid, although anchored in a heavy formalism, giving a type of original consistency to the idea of radical democracy, founded on rules of the connection and dissolution of demands—liberal atomism—by institutions. Meanwhile, the model of the governed remains "frozen" in a strict dualist dimension, emphasizing a type of dissatisfaction that promotes a double and simultaneous bond as a key point in the constituent process: a horizontal bond, between those who as the governed possess "common demands," and a vertical one, as the common demand becomes a claim directed upward, toward the top, for new rights. The common constituent character of antagonist subjectivity is the essential element in this model, while for Laclau this possibility is diluted in an excessively weak formalism.

There is a second important point: the people operate over a lack, as an always failed unity. In this sense, heterogeneity for Laclau is not equivalent to multiplicity, since it is defined as "deficient being" or a "failed totality" (2005a, 70). This supposes that there is not a positive element in heterogeneity but rather the presence of an absence, which opens space for articulation and hegemony. The tension from which the people emerge is the tension between the particularity of popular demands and the aspirations of totalization that it deploys.

If the first perspective abandons the idea of the people as a concept associated with an ineffective citizen norm of the nation-state in postcolonial countries, the second proposes a revival of this same notion from the equivalential articulation that is able to produce popular identity through operations of naming and affection. The first assumes the political as an intrinsic dimension of the daily management of specific demands, particularized in population categories, and thus derives its ability to create rights, while the second wagers that those demands, the less specific the better, coagulate into a unitary identity that is constituted into the people insofar as that naming is founded on an *empty* or floating signifier. Thus, for Laclau, in the origin of politicization, people are perceived as owners of unrecognized rights. In Chatterjee, it has to do with entitlement to rights, based on the recognition of positions of fact, for those who perceive themselves as not having rights, for those who do not feel incorporated into any rhetoric that names and represents them as citizens or the people. In respect to the political logic: while Chatterjee's discourse is postrevolutionary, since taking state power is not the horizon of the governed, in Laclau the revolutionary claim is sublimated in favor of the current form of condensed popular hegemony of the region's progressive governments.

A possible compatibility between the model of the governed and populism remains to be demonstrated. An ad hoc argument in favor of the latter can be explained in the following way. Laclau formalized a theory whose ultimate referent is Peronism in Argentina.[8] Peronism operates as a model of a unity of multiplicities that are not explained solely by a class dynamic. This reference remains implicit in Laclau as his theoretical development exposes logical models applicable to any situation, with the indicated formalist effects of its formulation. However, it suffices to remember this implicit Peronist in order to highlight a final argument excluded by right of his political philosophy: those who make the demands belong to a historical cycle and actively benefit from its memory. They do not perceive themselves as lacking rights but rather as bearing unrecognized rights. They do not address the state as a faraway or unreachable body but rather as an entity whose function is commonly recognized as satisfying their demands; as the effective owners of those demands, they want to be received, taken into account. To what extent is it legitimate to attribute this type of inspiration to Laclau at the expense of the model of the governed, modeled after the history of India, with its entrenched castes and colonial powers?

The only solution to this problem, which ends up reducing political images and concepts to mere national-historical conditions, is to ask whether appealing to the national space is sufficient for understanding and accounting for the ongoing politicization of the social. It is necessary to read both models in their global aspiration: in relation to the global (but not for that reason indifferent to the social composition of each nation, region, or subregion) effects of trans-postnational political and economic dynamics capable of accounting for fractures within national history, mutations of global capitalism, migratory phenomena, and the effects on those same institutions that propelled resistance in recent decades.

Yet an important issue is highlighted in this point. Populism rehabilitates the logic of friend versus enemy. It is a binary that, drawing from Carl Schmitt (Mouffe 2005), portrays society as agonist. It is not exactly an antagonism but the idea of a society with conflict as its nature and settled on a space of disputes over hegemony. In essence, what emerges is an *autonomy of the political* as the privileged *locus* of social action. But that autonomy of the political is the logic of the production of a hegemonic and unitary subject. For Laclau, diversity revitalizes the national-popular identity to the point of being able to revive national sovereignty. The notion of the governed—beyond its attribution as precapitalist, which I have already critiqued—allows us to understand its political dimension without the need for mediation.

From the political philosophy at stake, it could be said that Chatterjee's theory places its trust in the same plane where the governed do politics, while Laclau places his trust in the projection of a transcendent authority from the struggles. Laclau accuses Slavoj Žižek as well as Hardt and Negri (2000) of immanence: Žižek since, for him, the central political actor is class, which leads to a "logical immanence" (of the Hegelian type), while Hardt and Negri wager, according to Laclau, on a radical immanentism, that is, a "spontaneous and underlying universality," that would be opposed to a "politically constructed partial universality" (2005b, 298). His critique of immanentism is that it does not imply any particular political mediation. The unity that, for Laclau, requires a "hegemonic articulation" would suppose, for the followers of radical immanence (of the Spinozist-Deleuzian type), a "gift from the sky" (2005b, 299), which means trusting in a sort of "a priori of rebellion" (conatus).

As I stated previously, Laclau instead proposes a "failed transcendence," where "transcendence appears within the social as the presence of an absence" (2005a, 244). Now, through the necessity of establishing a political mediation, Laclau rehabilitates a politicism (autonomy of the political) that displaces popular agency onto the state and popular leaders as they are the figures who enable the failed totalization of the people. Then, it is those instances of mediation that guarantee the projection of popular unity. The autonomy of the political becomes Laclau's a priori. Despite his declarations, would we not be faced with a new—undoubtedly sophisticated—way of situating the social as prepolitical again?

If, in Laclau, there is no articulation without mediation, in Spinoza and Gilles Deleuze the collective potencia is spun in a game dominated by reciprocal determination (the plane of immanence) that is not regulated in advance by a symbolic order but rather is desiring or constituent.

Finally, an immanentist precision: as Spinoza reasons in his *Political Treatise* (2000), the body politic, as seen in the state, supposes a material, affective dimension of common habits that determines the space of the political-juridical: that movement or plane of composition is named "pre" by the "politicist" perspectives that deny the productivity of the collective conatus since its origin. Said perspectives (counterculturalists, convinced that the dynamic structure of the collective body can be substituted by a moral body of pure linguistic meanings) attribute agency, which configures the collective whole, to the juridical state level. On the contrary, efforts to think about the micropolitical dimension following the 1960s reveal the impulse to redetermine, in a material sense (where words are articulated to the dynamism of affections of a body), this productive relation between the genesis of a collective body and the juridical-political dimension.

People and Population

According to Foucault, the *people* appear in opposition to the population, who behave "as if they were not part of the population as a collective subject-object, as if they put themselves outside of it, and consequently the people are those who, refusing to be the population, disrupt the system" (2007, 43–44). The people are the counterfigure to the population: "those who resist the regulation of the population, who try to elude the apparatus by which the population exists, is preserved, subsists, and subsists at an optimal level" (44).

Allow me to problematize this opposition a bit. If the people require a level of homogeneity that is provided only by the national-popular amalgam (peripheral or not) of states, what other modes arise for naming political subjectivity? Does the notion of the community today allow us to go beyond ideas of population and the people? How has community been redefined confronted with the neoliberal dynamic? Capitalism's need to expand required the destruction of communities and their replacement by nation-state rule. Confronted with the crisis of nation-state authority in contemporary global capitalism (see for instance Bonefeld and Holloway 1994), the community reemerges but in a new way, plagued with ambivalence and, above all, escape points.

Chatterjee maintains that the community offers a space of agency for the subaltern. However, the discourse of the community—he adds—is only "moral varnish" that allows population groups to move within governmentality. For Chatterjee, the political action of the governed aims to "seek and find recognition as a population group, which from the standpoint of governmentality is only a usable empirical category that defines the targets of policy" (2004, 57). According to Chatterjee, the governed's self-construction as a singular population also implies the self-attribution of a "moral character" to the community itself. For the case analyzed by Chatterjee, the community is built from nothing using metaphors linked to the family that refer not to biological belonging but rather to a "shared experience." However, the community also functions as a counterpoint to governmentality understood as a pure apparatus of submission: "The categories of governmentality were being invested with the imaginative possibilities of community, including its capacity to invent relations of kinship, to produce a new, even if somewhat hesitant, rhetoric of political claims" (60). However, the community seems to be even more ambiguous than Chatterjee suggests, especially when it emerges as an experience of crisis.

The Crisis as a Locus

The crisis is a privileged *locus* for thinking because there is a cognitive porosity; concepts are set in motion, and sensibilities express the commotion and reorganize the thresholds of what is considered possible and how it is enunciated. One of the poisoned legacies of liberalism is the projection of the social as a space made from above, without its own consistency or potencia. This has its counterpart in the definition of the crisis: it is experienced as barbarism, as a noncivil, prepolitical stage.

Therefore, this definition of the crisis conspires in a restoration of the political, in which the social does not exist but is produced by the political, understood according to its traditional institutions: political parties, the state, unions (the core of Hobbesian theories and of the dissemination of Laclau's theory). However, the crisis of 2001 in Argentina does not fit this image. In the crisis, a properly political dynamic of experimentation carried out by the social was deployed (or, in other words, a new social protagonism began). The celebrated "return of politics" starting in 2003—the date marking the beginning of the decade of Kirchnerist government—clearly risks strengthening that schism and freezing the social as that which is merely managed, as the territory of "bare life" that returns as new social conflicts.

The social, when understood as an instance of demands to be satisfied, repaired, and mended, reduces the self-organized collective dynamics to a passive, directly victimist position, denying their immediately productive condition. The consolidation of a (politicist) reading from above ends up failing in two ways. First, on denying the form of the political elaborated from below, it misses information, a sense of opportunity, and even possible paths. Second, it is not effective in creating the illusion of an impossible consistency: the image of an omnipotent "above" for the state is, more than anything, nostalgia.

Neoliberal Reason

The title of this book was imagined following different modes of investigative work. This book has arisen from the montage of what were originally parts of a doctoral thesis, its rewriting in fragments for different articles, and, above all, the rhythm and force adopted by the arguments as they were distilled, rearticulated, and transformed in collective exchange.

Thus, as the book was refined, it became clear that its main axis centered around understanding neoliberalism differently from how its cycle is usually thought about in Latin America. I attempted to highlight the complexity of contemporary neoliberalism, even when debate on the continent can be framed, from various perspectives, within a postneoliberal horizon.

The method of temporal unfolding that becomes fundamental for certain arguments developed here about the multiplication of labor, geographies, and new proletarian trajectories is also the key to a nonlinear temporality for thinking about neoliberalism: simultaneously contemporary and contested, reinterpreted and innovated.

In this regard, neoliberal reason is a formula for exposing neoliberalism as a rationality—in the meaning that Foucault has given the term: as the very constitution of governmentality—but also for presenting it as a counterpoint to how that rationality is appropriated, destroyed, relaunched, and altered by those who, it assumes, are only its victims. But that reappropriation occurs not only from the point of view of direct antagonism, as the more or less traditional geometry of conflict would suppose, but rather through the multiple forms in which neoliberalism is appropriated and suffered based on recombination and contamination with other logics and dynamics that pluralize even the notions of rationality and conflict themselves.

From this perspective, I attempted to make two arguments: first, that neoliberalism does not come only from above and is not embodied only by major actors who supposedly could be commonly described as being antistate and pro-market (the basis of populist theory as the "autonomy of the political"); and, second, that neoliberalism must be characterized by its polymorphic ability to recuperate many libertarian principles, while that polymorphism is also challenged and defied by (commercial, affective, productive) economies, forms of doing and calculating, that use neoliberalism tactically, putting it into crisis in an intermittent but recurring way. Based on these tensions, I formulate the notion of a neoliberalism from below.

The *baroque* logic, of heterogeneous composition, is the expressive dynamic of the contemporary social-political-economic moment that uses long-term memories while proving to be unabashedly flexible for making the city, businesses, and politics. Thus, a dispute unfolds about the idea of *progress* itself, in its purely accumulative and linear meaning. Those *baroque* logics are the material, affective, and expansive fabric that I analyzed in certain popular economies and require us to recategorize what we understand as the productive forces in Latin American metropolises.

As a second term, the popular pragmatic as a vitalist pragmatic refers to the exasperation of a type of logic of calculation that does not exactly coincide with the *homo œconomicus* fantasized about and fulfilled by the liberal imagination and its doctrinaires. Calculation becomes, according to this argument, a *conatus*: a way of conquering space-time in conditions where the popular fabric is confronted with increasingly fast-paced and violent dispossessive, extractive, and expulsive logics. It is in this passage that calculation as conatus becomes transindividual.

Pragmatics is presented as a political mode in opposition to the moralization of popular classes. Moralization (in its diverse versions: solidarity, victimization, criminalization, and/or judicialization) proposes confrontation with the informal (in the strictly *constituent* meaning that I give the term) and plebeian dynamism. Pragmatics therefore attempts to highlight an immanent dynamic of the capture of opportunities under relations of force marked by (post)neoliberal conditions.

Finally, there is the urgent question running through the text of defining how the common—that territory that appears plagued with ambivalence and, at the same time, is permanently expanding—functions. The flexible declinations of the community become a point for rearticulating knowledges and technologies, as well as an attribute of valorization in very diverse economies. Its power to construct poststate urban infrastructure is fully apparent and is what makes popular life possible in the metropolis. Even so, the common, as a space that bypasses the binary between the public and the private, is also converted into a dynamic territory of struggles and conflicts.

NOTES

Introduction

1 The ordoliberal model represents an attempt to agree on a space of rules in which competition would follow a rationale for all the actors and from which the state itself would be reconstructed. Foucault (2008) analyzes it in detail to locate one of the doctrinal origins of neoliberalism.

2 It must be remembered that in the middle of the crisis, following the run on the banks, diverse local currencies were used. Some stemmed from experience with barter clubs, with municipal recognition, while others were notes issued by different provincial governments to pay their employees.

3 The report is available at https://ustr.gov/sites/default/files/2014%20Notorious%20 Markets%20List%20-%20Published_0.pdf.

4 For a discussion of renationalization in the Bolivian case, see Gutiérrez Aguilar and Mokrani Chávez (2006).

Chapter I. Between the Proletarian Microeconomy and the Transnational Network

1 In 2014 the newspaper *La Nación* returned multiple times to the North American classification in this regard; see the articles "La Salada, el principal mercado negro de la región, para EE.UU" [La Salada, the largest illegal market in the region, for the USA], February 12, 2014; and "Estados Unidos se quejó de la 'ausencia de voluntad política' del gobierno argentino para combatir los productos 'truchos'" [USA complains about the Argentine government's "absence of political will" to fight "fake" products], April 30, 2014.

2 In a series of complex unfoldings, expansions, and competitions, the birth of the markets can be recounted as follows: the Virgin of Urkupiña began in 1991 under the leadership of the (then married) Bolivian couple René Gonzalo Rojas Paz, who died in prison under highly suspicious circumstances in November 2001, and Mery Natividad Saravia Rodríguez, along with the Argentine Quique Antequera. In 1994 Ocean was opened, an expansion carried out at first with Rojas as the administrator; later, "by a coup d'état," it came into the hands of another Bolivian, Manuel Remonte. In 1999 Punta Mogotes, administered by the Argentine Jorge Castillo, was founded in open competition with the existing markets (Girón 2011; Hacher 2011).

3 At the height of the crisis, approximately two million people participated in thousands of barter clubs across Argentina, which were organized into national networks using alternative currency notes.—Trans.

4 This perspective is reflected, for example, in Javier Auyero and María Fernanda Berti's book *In Harm's Way* (2015). Their work, interesting in how it locates the problem of violence without compartmentalizing it in order to investigate its interconnections, reiterates the classic locus of violence as an anomie, exacerbated by conditions of poverty.

5 Patricia Barral, "La Salada vende más que los shoppings" [La Salada sells more than shopping malls], *Perfil*, May 9, 2010, http://www.perfil.com/economia/La -Salada-vende-mas-que-los-shoppings-20100509-0009.html.

6 By "communitarian capital," I am referring to a series of practices and knowledges that specifically function as an accumulation capable of being initiated and taken advantage of within the circuits of labor exploitation while simultaneously constituting a force that overflows that capitalist definition of capital.

7 For a study of migrant organization through networks in the horticultural sector, see Benencia (2012).

8 The Spanish equivalent of "under the table" is *en negro* (in black), a term that adds an extra racial connotation to the informal economy.—Trans.

9 Starting with Néstor Kirchner's inauguration in 2003, the Kirchner governments have made reiterated calls for building a "serious country," associated with normalcy, economic growth, and development and implying that the 2001–3 period and the movements active during that time were not serious.—Trans.

10 The title of a newspaper article referring to the art world is striking: "The Louvre in La Salada." The article projects the polemic around La Salada in relation to art: "copyright, copy and paste, and the new rules that demand access to art in the world of corporations and web 2.0." Claudio Iglesias, "El Louvre en La Salada," *Página 12*, April 15, 2012, https://www.pagina12.com.ar/diario/suplementos/radar/9-7866-2012 -04-15.html.

11 During the 2014 World Cup, Adidas launched an advertisement in which an amateur soccer team plays wearing the brand's clothing, but over time you see the shirts shrink and the shoes break. The screen goes dark, and the words appear: "Fake clothing doesn't make you look very good. If it's illegal, it's produced under bad working conditions and with low quality materials." However, these working conditions are the same as those under which "nonfake" clothing is made.

12 They chanted, "What shit, what shit, on Santa Fe you pay a lot, for the same sold in La Salada!" This refers to Santa Fe Avenue, which is lined with expensive boutiques and brand-name shops.

13 The case of Lacoste versus the Wachiturros is emblematic in this sense. Lacoste allegedly offered the *cumbia* band money to stop "discrediting it" by wearing its clothing, and the cumbia singers defended their right of use. *Clarín*, January 18, 2012, http://www.clarin.com/economia/Polemica-relacion-Lacoste-Wachiturros _0_SkCmbIOhPmx.html.

14 For this debate see Curcio and Özselçuk (2010) and Reyes (2010) in a special issue of *Rethinking Marxism* on the common and forms of the commune.

15 It is not clear whether this is produced in the same way in Bolivia: La Salada would need to be compared with what happens in the Uyustus or 16 de Julio markets.

16 The assemblage is first characterized by *relations of exteriority* in opposition to the relations of interiority of organic totalities. By relations of exteriority De-Landa understands the following: (1) A component of an assemblage can be disconnected or disarticulated and plugged into a different one, where its inter-actions will be different. Therefore, it implies a certain autonomy of terms. (2) Components' properties can never explain the relations that constitute a whole, although the whole can be caused by the exercise of the components' capacities. (3) The relationship between components is only *contingently obligatory* (and not *logically necessary*). (4) The heterogeneity of components is an important char-acteristic. DeLanda advises, "I will not take heterogeneity as a constant property of assemblages, but rather as a variable that can take different values" (2006, 11).

17 It should be clarified that the expressive pole cannot be reduced to language and symbols since there are nonlinguistic social expressions.

18 DeLanda defines a flat ontology as follows: "An ontology in which there are only individual singularities is in that sense flat. This is what Deleuze calls the actual plane or the plane of organization. Additionally, we need another plane, the plane of the virtual (or the plane of immanence), constituted by universal singularities. This type of plane would be the 'other side' or the reverse of the first, immanent to the actual plane, never forming a transcendent dimension. It is in this sense that the ontology is flat" (2008, 83).

19 If the notion of assemblage reopens the idea of scale, feminist perspectives are crucial because they introduce scale as the effect of a struggle, of a subjective par-tiality, as we will see later. Speaking about the city, Gerda W. Wekerle (2005, 96) states, "Central to the narratives of the neoliberal city is the concept of scale. This is deeply gendered and associated with masculinist discourses of global compe-titiveness articulated at the scale of the city, national, and global capital flows. A feminist politics of scale, on the other hand, is portrayed as based on the active and strategic use of multiscalar political strategies that acknowledge the interlock-ing and mutually constituted relationships of the body, household, neighborhood, city, national and global scales." She adds, "Erik Swyngedouw (1997) argues that we need to focus on the struggles through which scales are produced in sociospa-tial power struggles. He urges greater attention to the ways that social movements contest the rescaling and glocalization processes and the ways in which move-ments seek to jump scales and link them. According to Swyngedouw (1997, 142), 'Clearly, social power along gender, class, ethnic or ecological lines refers to the scale capabilities of individuals and social groups'" (Wekerle 2005, 97).

20 It must be remembered that in the middle of the crisis, after the run on the banks, diverse local currencies were in operation, some coming from the barter

experiences, with municipal recognition, while others were notes issued by different provincial governments to pay their employees.

21 However, this modality of labor is extended to other areas, especially in the agricultural sector. In the summer of 2011, several allegations came to light over the conditions of "slave labor" in which hundreds of rural workers contracted by multinational corporations, such as DuPont and Nidera, were found. See the report published by *Página 12*: "Campo fértil para la explotación laboral" [Fertile ground for labor exploitation], by Darío Aranda, February 14, 2011, http://www .pagina12.com.ar/diario/elpais/1-162314-2011-02-14.html.

22 Alfonso Prat Gray, "En defensa de La Salada y de sus emprendedores" [In defense of La Salada and its entrepreneurs], *Clarín*, March 31, 2009, http://edant.clarin .com/diario/2009/03/31/opinion/o-01888029.htm.

23 Their succinct and clear text states, "We strongly reject the claims of Dr. Prat Gay, published in the *Clarín* on March 31, 2009, that justify the smuggling, tax evasion, counterfeiting, and extreme informality that are practiced in La Salada. Organized trade and industry believe that excluded social groups—which today are used by strong illegal interests—should be offered productive options to integrate themselves. The European Community itself categorized La Salada as the largest illegal market in the world." See http://www.redcame.org.ar/images /noticias/volante_lasalada2009.jpg.

24 Osvaldo Cornide, "La venta clandestina no es un 'emprendimiento'" [Clandestine sales are not an enterprise], *Clarín*, April 1, 2009, http://edant.clarin.com /diario/2009/04/01/opinion/o-01888814.htm.

25 Cornide, "La venta clandestina."

26 "La Salada is the consequence of a profound social weakness that persists in Argentina. But we must monitor what is sold there, regulate it, and find out how to uncover those who run those markets, who the large and powerful economic mafias are. We must seek options for excluded social groups. But those of us who believe in a productive country, in a country where dignity is a right for all, we resist seeing La Salada as an alternative. Underdevelopment is not overcome with more underdevelopment, and vulnerability is not fought with more vulnerability. Needy families deserve opportunities. Let's not settle for the available options; let's make better options available for them." Cornide, "La venta clandestina," *Clarín*, April 1, 2009.

27 According to the legend, the Virgin of Urkupiña appeared, with her child in her arms, to a girl shepherdess in Quillacollo, Cochabamba, whom the saint spoke to directly in Quechua. She was named by the phrase with which the girl announced the Virgin's arrival to the town: "Ork'hopiña, Ork'hopiña," which in Quechua means "she's already in the hills."

28 "In short, as the festivals are ruled by the calendar and the calendar served to form, if not the concrete notion of duration, at least the abstract notion of time, it can be seen how the system of festivals and the notion of time are simultaneously

elaborated thanks to the collective work of generations of societies" (Mauss and Hubert 2010, 61).

29 See the interview with Raquel Gutiérrez Aguilar, "La lengua subalterna I," You-Tube video, 18:42, posted by Lectura Mundi Program, Universidad Nacional de San Martin, June 28, 2013, https://www.youtube.com/watch?v=M7Uuu8DT878.

30 A dialogue between Italian post-*operaismo* theory and Bolivian theory in particular and Latin American theory in general allows this intersection to occur. This is especially developed in the political anthropology cited in *Commonwealth* (Hardt and Negri 2009).

31 This comparison emerged in conversation with Silvia Rivera Cusicanqui.

32 As Althusser states, "the whole that results from the 'taking hold' of the 'encounter' does not precede the 'taking-hold' of its elements, but follows it; for this reason, it might not have 'taken hold,' and, a fortiori, 'the encounter might not have taken place'" (2006, 197).

33 For another interpretation, see Ossona (2010).

Chapter 2. Between La Salada and the Workshop

1 While the first program (Plan Jefes y Jefas de Hogar) focused on subsidizing the heads of households considered to be temporarily unemployed, the second is based on subsidizing cooperative forms of work that are recognized as quasi-permanent. The beginning of these programs, however, marks a milestone because it was the most massive social program in Argentina's history and the threshold signaled a change of era: the social programs were here to stay.

2 Judith Butler develops this idea from Luce Irigaray in her book *Gender Trouble* (1999).

3 This presence of the feminine as the other of the one-subject is in the very origin of Western mythology, at least in its Judeo-Christian version, through the figure of Lilith, the first woman, who was created with Adam from the earth's dust and who refused to lie beneath him in sexual intercourse. Lilith escapes with an angel, and God solicitously creates Eve from Adam's rib. According to this myth, collected in religious texts for centuries, this is the meaning of Adam's phrase in Genesis, when God creates Eve, "This time you are flesh of my flesh." Lilith, in turn, would acquire a spectral presence. She will return, threatening, hovering over the bed in which a couple is having sex and seek the newborn in order to take them. For a documented version of the features of Lilith in Judeo-Christian mythology see Colodenco (2006).

4 The idea of unproductiveness can also be expanded. On one hand, one can differentiate nonrecognized labor that is primarily domestic-feminine labor that remains productive, that produces value, while it is also invisibilized. On the other hand, unproductiveness could be spoken of as the mode of a feminized economy that shuns accumulation and possession and that could be characterized according to certain

traits: (1) the possession of a multiple, heterogeneous, and limited code; and (2) the capacity to introduce fragments in fragmentation.

5 Eugen Fink explains the Nietzschean association between woman and eternity: "The turn towards the world is, however, always a love for infinity for Nietzsche, however not an infinity of the world of the itself. All seven seals conclude thus: 'O how would I lust for eternity and the wedding ring of marriage—the ring of eternal return. I have not found the woman who I love, with whom I would like to have children, unless it is this woman, who I love; because I love you, O eternity.' The love for infinity is compared to erotic love. Infinity is a woman; the ring of eternal return is a wedding ring" (2003, 101).

6 An interesting debate has been developed around this topic in a special issue of *Rethinking Marxism: The Common and the Forms of the Commune*, vol. 22, no. 3, July 2010, edited by Anna Curcio and Ceren Özselçuk.

7 "There is an element of racism implicit in official Marxism, if only because of the notion of history as a teleological progression. It was evident when (white) Marxists resisted the Marx-inspired thesis of the Jamaican-born Eric Williams in *Capitalism and Slavery* (1944)—seconded by the Marxist historian, Trinidad-born C. L. R. James in *The Black Jacobins*—that plantation slavery was a quintessentially modern institution of capitalist exploitation" (Buck-Morss 2009, 57).

8 The *mita, encomienda,* and *pongo* are different systems of forced labor used by colonial regimes to extract labor from indigenous populations in the Americas, especially for mining gold and silver.

9 This same distinction in the modes of disjunction could be thought for the relationship between voice and writing.

10 Kristeva states, "It is very possible that a society dominated by technology and profit may reduce women to being merely the possessors of 'zoological' life and will not in any way favor the inquiry or spiritual restlessness that constitutes a 'destiny': a 'biography.' When I proposed this exchange regarding 'women and the sacred,' I particularly had that danger in mind: the new version of 'soft' totalitarianism that, after the famous 'loss of values,' erects life as the 'supreme value,' but life for itself, life without questions, with wives-and-mothers supposed to be the natural executors of that 'zoology'" (in Clément and Kristeva 2003, 13–14).

11 Regarding the ambiguity of the term *subaltern* for the argument I am considering, Gayatri Chakravorty Spivak's reading of the Subaltern Studies Group, trying to bring them closer to deconstruction, is interesting: "Our own transnational reading of them is enhanced if we see them as strategically adhering to the essentialist notion of consciousness, that would fall prey to an anti-humanist critique, within a historiographic practice that draws many of its strengths from that very critique. . . . It is in this spirit that I read *Subaltern Studies* against its grain and suggest that its own subalternity in claiming a *positive* subject-position for the subaltern might be reinscribed as a strategy for our times" (1998, 15–16). The "strategic essentialism" that Spivak proposes seems to go against the "bi-frontal" or "schizophrenic" narratives that Cornejo Polar theorizes for thinking about

migration. However, some feminists, such as Chela Sandoval, make both strategies or "technologies" compatible in a postmodern "differential oppositional consciousness" of Third World feminism that brings together "a facultad (a semiotic vector), the 'outsider/within' (a deconstructive vector), 'strategic essentialism,' (a meta-ideologizing vector), la conciencia de la mestiza, 'world traveling' or 'loving cross-cultures' (differential vectors), and 'womanism' (a democratizing, moral vector)" (2000, 180).

12 Here it is interesting to compare Michel Foucault's analysis of the countercon-ducts of female prophets and mystics in convents (between the eleventh and seventeenth centuries), since these women propose another game of visibility than that ruled by the Christian ministry. This alternative game is based on a series of ambiguous experiences, motivated by a body-to-body communication and confidence in immediate sensory experience; in these, rebellion also supposes the resource of writing (see Foucault 2007).

13 However, this atheism proposes a nonreligious relationship to the sacred. Kristeva—following her inquiry into woman as "being on the borderline"—puts it this way: "What if the sacred were not the religious *need* for protection and omnipotence that institutions exploit but the jouissance of that *cleavage* [always on the borderline between nature and culture, the animalistic and the verbal, the sensible and the nameable]—of that power/powerlessness—of that exquisite lapse?" (in Clément and Kristeva 2003, 27).

14 The major finding of his book, in his own words, was to discover "the importance of political cycles and the long-term historical connections in the Andean region" (2006, 15).

15 The concept of community carries multiple accusations, especially from the European Left "as something that mystified the concrete articulations of exploitation, hiding them in a figure in which the associative set of subjects was given by the unity of function rather than by the contradictory articulation of associative and productive process" (Negri 1997). Antonio Negri reinvents the concept of community as a way of thinking about a new transition to communism through the construction of "an autonomous social community" that is no longer defined by its opposition to the state but by "the definition of the times and forms in which the reappropriation of productive functions by the community could occur" (139).

16 "Andean communities rose up almost coincidentally with insurgents in North America and shortly before the *sans culottes* in France and 'black Jacobins' in Saint Domingue (Haiti). Three decades later, creole Spaniards launched the wars that finally achieved independence from Iberian political authority. Given the simultaneity of these movements, it is interesting to note that the pan-Andean insurrection has received scarce mention in the conventional Western historiography of the Age of Revolution. . . . There is next to no evidence that the pan-Andean insurrection was inspired by French *philosophes* or prompted by the success of North American creoles. Nor was it provoked by British secret agents

hostile to the Spanish crown. Unlike the Haitian revolution, which was developed in close connection with multilateral political dynamics in the Americas and Europe, the Andean case here again falls outside the conventional paradigm of the revolutionary Atlantic" (Thomson 2002, 6).

17 Foucault takes up and expands the opposition between the Platonic weaver and the figure of the shepherd in *Security, Territory, Population* (2007).

Chapter 3. Between Servitude and the New Popular Entrepreneurship

1 The most widely circulated information claims that there are five thousand workshops in the city of Buenos Aires and another fifteen thousand in the greater metropolitan area. The former Bolivian consul J. Alberto González maintains this calculation in an article in the Bolivian newspaper *Los Tiempos* (September 7, 2009), saying, "In that case, we would be talking about nearly twenty thousand unauthorized workshops. If you estimate that there are an average of five workers per workshop, the number of people working in this scheme would be around one hundred thousand." But he clarifies that these are only estimated figures. See http://www.lostiempos.com/diario/actualidad/nacional/20090907 /100-mil-bolivianos-esclavos-en-talleres_35452_58150.html. The Demonstrative Center of Clothing estimates that there are seventeen hundred clandestine workshops in the city of Buenos Aires and thirty-five hundred in the Conurbano. The Ombudsman's Office estimates that there are twelve thousand clandestine workshops in the country as a whole and at least thirty-five hundred in the federal capital. The Union of Sewing Workers (La Unión de Trabajadores Costureros) has alleged that in the province of Buenos Aires alone "more than 150,000 sewing workers are enslaved in the 15,000 workshops scattered throughout the district." But their clandestine nature itself obviously hinders accurate official measurements. Alfredo Ayala, leader of ACIFEBO, when asked if there are fifteen thousand workshops in the city and ten thousand in the Conurbano, assures that the number is even greater: "Those are minimum figures, I would say. There are more than that. And in each workshop there are an average of ten or twenty people. Nearly 80 percent of the Bolivians that live here are involved in the textile sector" (Colectivo Simbiosis and Colectivo Situaciones 2011, 50).

2 For a broader view of the industry's trajectory, see Isidro Adúriz, "The Textile Industry in Argentina: Its Evolution and Labor Conditions" (Buenos Aires: INPADE [Instituto para la Participación y el Desarrollo], 2009), available at http://www .foco.org.ar/documentos/Documentos%20de%20trabajo/La%20industria%20 textil%20en%20Argentina.pdf.

3 A report presented in May 2011 by the United Nations special rapporteur on trafficking in persons, Joy Ezeilo, who visited Argentina in September 2010, compiles information about the existence of textile workshops in the province and city of Buenos Aires "where migrant workers are exploited." She recounts

that "the workshops provide services to both national and international large commercial brands. Workers are obligated to work and live on the premises, where their documents are retained and their freedom of movement is totally controlled." Based on information provided by La Alameda, she argues that this organization "has identified around 600 clandestine workshops in the country that work for more than 103 brands" and that they also "reported cases in the poultry industry and in various forms of farming labor in different regional economies." See https://laalameda.wordpress.com/2011/06/29/lapidario-informe-de-la-onu-sobre-trata-y-trafico-de-personas-en-argentina/.

4 See Carlos Rodríguez, "Centro clandestino, esta vez de confección" [Clandestine center, this time for manufacturing], *Página/12*, March 31, 2007, http://www.pagina12.com.ar/diario/elpais/1-82598-2007-03-31.html.

5 An article by Lucila Anigstein, in the newspaper *Renacer*, reported that various Bolivians were detained or disappeared in Automotores Orletti: "According to data provided by FEDEFAM (the Latin American Federation of Associations of Family Members of the Detained-Disappeared, or Federación Latinoamericana de Asociaciones de Familiares de Detenidos Desaparecidos), there are thirty-five documented cases of disappeared Bolivians in Argentina, and more than one hundred cases of disappeared people in northern Argentina, mostly very poor people who did not report it. It is known that many of them were taken to the Automotores Orletti clandestine detention center, located on 3519 Venancio Flores Street on the corner of Emilio Lamarca street in the Floresta neighborhood." See Anigstein, "Experiencia boliviana en la lucha del Movimiento Villero" [The Bolivian experience in the struggle of the villero movement], *Renacer*, http://www.renacerbol.com.ar/edicion173/sociedad01.htm.

6 See Jorge Vargas, *Renacer*, http://www.renacerbol.com.ar/edicion160/sociedad01.htm.

7 For the Bolivian migrant population, we can refer to the enumeration by the former consul himself, José "Gringo" González: "Bolivians are working in incredible situations, for example, in fish cleaning. We have had the opportunity to speak with compañeras, we have gone to a fish cleaner, a cooperative, where the system of the textile workshops is repeated. They make them think that they are cooperativists, when, in reality, there is one owner who exploits everyone. They call them 'cooperativist brothers and sisters.' That's a lie, they are employees. They call it a cooperative, but it is a business where there is an owner of the means of production and the others work there. Compañeros who lived in Potosi, who had never seen a fish in their whole lives, cleaning fish, specialists, at a hallucinating velocity. Comrades making bricks, mostly around Neuquén. The best bricks in Argentina are produced in that area, where the workers' situation is dramatic, because these are family businesses where little children start working as soon as they can walk. However, I believe that the worst conditions are experienced in the workshops because there people are enclosed, and that is what is perverse. In brick production at least they see the sun, they see the stars at night, they breathe

the air. It's very painstaking work, very demanding. They don't want to take out documents, because they don't have fingerprints, because they work with clay and it erases their fingerprints. The solution for immigration control is that they stop working for two months, because the skin regenerates in two months. But what do they live off of for those two months? They never answered us. So they continue without being able to register" (personal interview).

8   "—*Did they produce for their brand, or did they work for other brands too?*—They had their own brand. They only worked for their own brand. It was girl's clothing: T-shirts, tank tops, and simple little things that would come out at once and were easy to make.—*They would go to the stall in La Salada, and they would sell every-thing . . .*—Yes. They had a fixed stall that they had bought, and they rented another two. Everything was sold there. They had a good entry. They even had some vendors who were Argentine women who they paid twenty pesos per market or something like that. They also accused those women of robbing them. But we always had to put up with it because we didn't have anywhere else to go. And the guarantee that we had was the document that she had. And without your document you can't do anything" (Colectivo Simbiosis and Colectivo Situaciones 2011, 67–68).

9   Alfredo Ayala, a leader of the workshop owners and head of ACIFEBOL (Aso-ciación Civil Federativa Boliviana), gave the following description of the inter-mediaries' role:

ALFREDO AYALA (AA): The brands today have something like front men. There are intermediaries. The brands themselves are not the ones who make the contracts. The intermediaries are the ones who negotiate prices between the brands and the workshop owners. They are the ones who put them-selves out there and distribute.
COLECTIVO SIMBIOSIS (CS): Is the intermediary legal?
AA: They are also illegal. They don't even have an invoice with which to respond. The workshop owner has the receipt, and the brand obtains it through the intermediary.
CS: Do you call for the embassy to promote legalization?
AA: Of course, because if not we are always going to be in the same situation.
CS: Would the brands stop being interested in the workshop economy if it were legalized?
AA: No, no, I don't think it would be like that. On the contrary, it would make it so that many people could obtain work directly.
CS: In any case, intermediaries exists because they guarantee cheap labor for the brand . . .
AA: Not only cheap labor but also freedom from paying taxes. They have to pay social security for the workers. The brand saves millions of pesos.
CS: Are the intermediaries normally Argentines or Bolivians?
AA: Most are Argentine, but there are also some Bolivians.
CS: And what legal figure does the brand use to issue invoices?

AA: As a workshop owner. Even if you don't have a workshop, you represent various small workshops. And those guys control the workshops. I heard about one case, where the intermediary didn't want to pay the workshop, and they couldn't demand anything because there was no documentation.

CS: In other words, the future of Bolivian business is either for it to be legalized here or for it to return to Bolivia and export from there to Argentina or Brazil . . .

AA: Yes. The first of the possibilities you describe would be what we want to happen. We are fighting for legalization. Because many people are tired of working like criminals, hiding from the police and inspectors. There are even fake inspectors who are criminals that take advantage of this situation.

(Colectivo Simbiosis and Colectivo Situaciones 2011, 54)

10 An anonymous interviewee told me, "The issue is that Bolivia is very traditional. There has always been help within families, and working with your mom or your aunt is not considered work. It's not work, it's helping, it's sharing with the family. So they use this a lot to bring people. I found out about a woman from a small town who goes every year to pick up girls between twelve and fourteen years old to work in sewing. In the village, she is seen as the most caring person because she takes the girls to Argentina. And the people of the town trust her because she is from there, like one of the family. . . . It is for this reason that there are almost entire towns from Bolivia here. In Parque Avellaneda, there are soccer tournaments of towns against towns" (personal interview).

11 Paraphrasing Sinclair Thomson (2002, 41), when he characterizes the seventeenth-century chiefs based on their privileged access to land and the communitarian labor force.

12 For more on this interesting debate see Baud et al. (1996), and for another perspective, see Comaroff and Comaroff (2009).

13 Oscar Olivera, "La oposición en tiempos de Evo," *Desinformémonos*, August 1, 2010, http://desinformemonos.org/oscar-olivera-la-oposicion-en-tiempos-de-evo/.

14 According to María D'Ovidio, "for analytical reasons, it is important to differentiate the textile sector from the apparel industry. The industrial textile sector is not directly connected to the problem of slave labor in the workshops, as this is the area where yarn and fabric are manufactured to make the textiles that the apparel sector later uses to produce garments. This industry is characterized by a greater degree of formality because of the requirements for a large amount of capital and the type of machinery being used. However, the problem does not escape its orbit, and the sector has demonstrated its concern with addressing it, since it is what provides raw materials to the rest of the value chain, and hence there is a direct link to those workshops" (2007, 33).

15 —Say a factory needs to make a thousand garments. One thousand garments can be made in less than three days, depending on their complexity; now if they need

them in one or two days, the outsourcer is not going to only give them to one workshop because they know it will take the workshop three days. They give the orders to three workshops so that each one makes an effort, telling each of them that they are being given the order so that they will complete it in one day. Then, each workshop stops what they had been doing to work on that order.

—See that the logic of the small workshop also makes sense for this, right?

—Absolutely. This is why I say that it doesn't matter if you call them small or family workshops, or craft manufacturers or whatever. What matters is how they function.

(Anonymous, personal interview)

16 "Explotación, esa 'costumbre ancestral'" [Exploitation, that "ancestral" custom], *Página/12*, May 15, 2008, http://www.pagina12.com.ar/diario/sociedad/3-104190 -2008-05-15.html.

17 Prosecutor Evers had charged Nelson Alejandro Sánchez Anterino, Gabina Sofía Verón, and Hermes Raúl Provenzano, legally responsible for the firm Soho, for this crime, "after determining that this company outsourced sewing jobs to at least two workshops where the presence of undocumented foreigners had been detected, who worked twelve hours a day, with salaries between five hundred and nine hundred pesos a month, and lived in a tiny room rented to them by the same workshop owners. 'No business person contracts a sewing workshop without having a minimum amount of previous contact with it, where they guarantee meeting the deadlines and quality norms,' the prosecutor argued in that moment. He added that 'this circumstance of labor exploitation not only cannot be ignored by business owners but rather, on the contrary, indicates that it is consented to and tacitly favored to obtain the most production at the least cost.'" "Explotación, esa 'costumbre ancestral.'"

18 "Explotación, esa 'costumbre ancestral.'"

19 "Explotación, esa 'costumbre ancestral.'"

20 "La explotación no es herencia cultural," *Pagina/12*, June 27, 2008, https://www .pagina12.com.ar/diario/sociedad/3-106763-2008-06-27.html.

21 "Explotación, esa 'costumbre ancestral.'"

22 As Lieutier (2010) points out, there is a reference to the prohibition of slavery in the Argentine Constitution (1853) and in the Legal Code that makes reduction to servitude punishable by law. However, reduction to servitude is difficult to define, requiring reference to the supplementary convention about the abolition of slavery, the slave trade, and analogous practices and institutions adopted by the United Nations in 1956 and ratified by the Argentine government in Law 11,925.

23 One of the testimonies from the employers reverses the calculation in their reasoning; instead of saying these costs are deducted, he describes them as "added" to the income: "You have to consider the following: In most of the workshops the modality of work includes room and board. The Labor Law does not stipulate

either food or housing. If you add food and housing to those who earn 3,500, they would be earning about 5,000" (Colectivo Simbiosis and Colectivo Situaciones 2011, 51).

24 *Cambio*, http://www.cambio.bo/noticia.php?fecha=2010-01-18&idn=13572.

25 Eduardo Videla, "Otro eslabón en la cadena" [Another link in the chain], *Página/12*, March 25, 2010, http://www.pagina12.com.ar/diario/sociedad/3-142617 -2010-03-25.html.

26 *Escraches* (protests in front of the home or workplace of the accused) were originally practiced by human rights organizers in the 1990s as a form of popular justice for crimes committed under Argentina's 1976–83 dictatorship.

27 Silvia Camps, "Rodeado de cartoneros y prostitutas, Bergoglio condenó la 'esclavitud'" [Surrounded by cartoneros and prostitutes, Bergoglio condemned "slavery"], *Clarín*, September 5, 2009, http://edant.clarin.com/diario/2009/09 /05/sociedad/s-01992636.htm

28 Camps, "Rodeado de cartoneros y prostitutas," *Clarín*, September 5, 2009. The religious ceremony had its offerings: "a burlap bag overflowing with folded cardboard boxes, 'what we gathered night and day to feed our children,' a bag made by Bolivian men and women who escaped the clandestine workshops, a piece of clothing made by the La Alameda cooperative."

29 The question of reciprocity, in Émile Durkheim and Bronislaw Malinowski, and especially with Marcel Mauss and Karl Polanyi, becomes a fundamental concept in the social sciences for understanding economies that mix commercial forms with noncommercial forms. According to Ricardo Abduca (2010), the "ubiquitous, nodal, and central character of 'reciprocity,' which combines economic distribution and political and legal justice, is not an invention of the Greeks nor of their readers. We find it, to give only two examples, west of the Bering Strait, as well as in Andean tradition."

30 You can see the film narration of this scene in *Colección Overlock* by Julián D'Angiolillo.

31 *Los Tiempos*, October 7, 2009.

32 "Workshop owners have had to be included, a derivation from home work, whose diffusion has only exacerbated the problem. They are small business owners who make workers manufacture according to merchandise orders that they receive from the givers of work. Paid well below the legal amount, they sacrifice their workers with the implementation of the most unbridled 'Taylorism.' When the small workshop is merged with a private room, exploitation is aggravated by the permanent violation of all the legal protections for workers" (Foundations of Executive Power for Law, quoted in Lieutier 2010, 115). Additionally, the fourth article of the law states, "Intermediaries and workshop owners are considered home workers in relation to the givers of work and as employers subject to the obligations that this law imposes on them and the regulations issued to those who are responsible for work being carried out" (quoted in Lieutier 2010, 119).

33 Lieutier's book was based on his management as the undersecretary of labor, employment, and training of the city of Buenos Aires between September 2006 and December 2007. In it, he points to, with sincerity, the perplexity, disbelief, and confusion of state officials in regard to the dynamic of the clandestine workshops, as well as the attempts at understanding and regulating to which they were obligated following the fire on Luis Viale Street.

34 Is there an inverse but parallel relationship between the state's justification of migration and of colonization? The strongest argument for the latter was often called the "internal solution": a way of getting rid of the "multitudes of unproductive people," as Linebaugh and Rediker (2000) argue. Is migration the state's way of getting rid of people in the context of exclusion and the reduction of social spending? In December 2010, after the massive land takeover in Parque Indoamericano mostly by Bolivian families, Evo called for them to return to their country and stop occupying land, attempting to rhetorically invert the image of a country that expels its population for social and economic reasons. Facing the media impacts of the allegations of slave labor, Gustavo Vera of La Alameda has a different reading of this phenomenon within the Bolivian government: "it is clear that we are not the most important concern for the Bolivian government, but each time the topic is touched upon there is a sort of debate between two tendencies within the government: one principled tendency that says 'this must stopped, by any means possible,' the appointment of this consul was an expression of this, and, on the other hand, a more pragmatic expression that perhaps is more linked to the ministry, that . . . in short . . . let it continue flowing on its own because meanwhile it is less budgetary spending and more remittances, less inversion and more remittances."

35 "After the fire he [Quint] was one of the people who sought to ensure that the structure of this system would not be threatened by overexposure. Several of the survivors felt harassed at different points in the case, in addition to being completely abandoned by the workshop owners' sector. According to the only plaintiff in the case, Luis Fernando Rodríguez, the consul offered him work and money in exchange for silence. 'What do you want? Do you want money? Work? Why are you making such a fuss if your son is already dead and this is already over!'" (Estrada Vázquez 2010, 18).

36 See "La explotación y la promiscuidad sexual son moneda corriente," *Pagina/12*, October 26, 2005, http://www.pagina12.com.ar/diario/sociedad/subnotas/58447 -19286-2005-10-26.html. Later he was also investigated for illegally buying luxury cars as a state official. See "For Corruption and Other Crimes, Evo Calls for 'Cleaning' the Foreign Service," *Diario Hispano Boliviano*, January 31, 2008.

37 The feminization of both economies is clear. In the case of the migrant economy, Aihwa Ong indicates that "ethnicized production networks depend on disciplinary institutions of ethnic enclaves, factories, and families to instill feminine values of loyalty, obedience, and patience, and to mold docile labor." According to Ong, the disciplinary mechanisms of government govern in an ethnicized manner,

providing "an ethnicizing connection to the agile and entrepreneurial managers who shape the horizontal space of markets." She adds, "The combination of latitudinal citizenship and ethnicized disciplinary regimes can undermine territorialized rights of citizenship" (2006, 124).

Chapter 4. Between the Workshop and the Villa

1 Antonio Negri proposes a different thesis in respect to movements' *potencia* of "passing through while distancing" themselves from state institutions. See Verónica Gago, "Cambio de paradigmas" [Change of paradigms], *Página/12*, December 12, 2007, https://www.pagina12.com.ar/diario/elpais/1-94094-2007-11-04 .html.

2 Foucault notes that this implies a whole array of utilitarian philosophy and the ideology of sensuality.

3 Can a sort of parallel be traced with the so-called postneoliberal situation in Latin America? The exercise would be to say that in the 1980s and 1990s the free market was abruptly and violently introduced to weaken the state's Fordist-interventionist modality and in postneoliberalism a state is invented that assumes neoliberalism as its basis at the same time as it reinvents interventionism in another form.

4 For a paradigmatic case, such as that of the microfinancier Gran Poder, see Verónica Gago, "El consumo como marca de época" [Consumption as the sign of the era], *Le Monde Diplomatique*, Edición Cono Sur, October 2013.

5 To see family trajectories in Brazil similar to what I have discussed in relation to Argentina, see Cássia Almeida, Cristiane Bonfanti, Flávio Ilha, Letícia Lins, Roberta Scrivano, and Victor Furtado, "Alta na renda, no consumo e nas dívidas marca o ano das famílias," *O Globo*, December 14, 2013, http://oglobo.globo.com /economia/alta-na-renda-no-consumo-nas-dividas-marca-ano-das-familias -11073212. I would like to thank Eduardo Viveiros de Castro for this reference.

6 For more on the reconfigurations of the state that I am referring to, see Gago et al. (2014).

7 The drift of the discussion in Argentina regarding the notion of the destituent/ constituent potencia of the movements in 2001 to their conversion into a threat to the state and democratic institutionality is paradigmatic of this shift from the axis of invention to that of conservation, whose operation is due to the perspective of populism as state reason. For the term "destituent power," see Colectivo Situaciones 2011.

8 Horacio Verbitsky, "Conurbanos," *Página/12*, December 8, 2013, http://www.pagina12 .com.ar/diario/elpais/1-235202-2013-12-08.html.

9 By "street negotiations" (*paritarias callejeras*), I am referring to the mode of direct action in which people press for an increase in their benefits and informal wages through marches, protests, and even looting. As a mechanism, it shifts from the traditional space of union negotiation to unregulated street action. This takes

place in the context of a monetary scheme that is being squeezed by those who control the currency market, which translates into inflation, the police strike as a wage claim, and the explosion of media and financial scandals related to the connections between sectors of the police and the drug economy.

Chapter 5. Between Postnational Citizenship and the Ghetto

1　On the dynamic of the inversion of high and low that produces a city, see Colectivo Situaciones (2005).
2　See Verónica Gago, "Punto de vista: Buenos Aires según Beatriz Sarlo" [Point of view: Buenos Aires according to Beatriz Sarlo], *Página/12*, April 10, 2009. https://www.pagina12.com.ar/diario/suplementos/las12/13-4846-2009-04-16.html.
3　María Carman formidably analyzes this contrast between nature and culture as the distribution of legitimacies in a city in two of her books: *Las trampas de la naturaleza* (2011) and *Las trampas de la cultura* (2006).
4　Saskia Sassen, "Articulaciones ocultas entre la ciudad global y la villa global" [Hidden articulations between the global city and the global villa], *Página/12*, August 10, 2012, http://www.pagina12.com.ar/diario/suplementos/las12/subnotas/7428-797-2012-08-10.html.
5　This figure is from a report published by the General Syndicate of the City in 2007, after a census of the living conditions in fourteen villas, fifty-seven precarious settlements, and sixteen municipal neighborhoods or housing complexes.
6　For a history of the successive attempts to eradicate the villas during the dictatorship, see Blaustein (2001).
7　Also the report published by the General Syndicate of the City in 2007, "Looking at the age group of twenty- to twenty-nine-year-olds shows that 85 percent of them are foreigners, supporting the hypothesis of this change in migration in Argentina, since they are recent arrivals."
8　More than 140,000 migrants settled in the Buenos Aires villas receive social assistance from the main assistance programs of the city's Ministry of Social Development. This implies that foreigners make up 46 percent of the beneficiaries of the *Ciudadanía* program and that nearly 120,000 of them obtain a welfare card for purchases of basic food items or school materials, with individual amounts ranging from two hundred to a thousand pesos. Foreigners also represent 70 percent (nearly twenty thousand out of twenty-six thousand) of the beneficiaries of the social tickets given to mothers of households in situations of poverty, which consist of a check for 150 pesos for buying food. These assistance programs are compatible with other aid given to the same people by the national government. These figures are summarized in the article "Hay mayoría de extranjeros en las villas" [There is a majority of foreigners in the villas] by Daniel Gallo, published in *La Nación*, September 6, 2010, http://www.lanacion.com.ar/1301797-hay-mayoria-de-extranjeros-en-las-villas.

9   Law 403, like other laws of urbanization of the villas, is still in effect, but its dead-
    lines have expired. The lack of response from the executive board turned into
    legal procedures that did not result in material progress either.
10 For a history of the *villero* (slums) movement, see Dávalos, Jabbaz, and Molina
    (1987). For a detailed and updated history of organizations in the villa, see Cra-
    vino (2006, 62–80).
11 All of the testimonies cited in this chapter are part of a still-unpublished book
    that compiles interviews with former delegates of Villa 1-11-14. The interviews
    were carried out by Frida Rojas, Hernán Fernández, Diego Sztulwark, and Verónica
    Gago.
12 "Red zone" indicates a dangerous zone or an area for sex workers.
13 "They called upon the legislature to make and approve a law so that people in
    Villa 1-11-14 would begin paying for electricity, begin paying for water, sewage.
    Or, rather, we requested it as an organization, as the body of delegates, we have
    asked for it because it was a way to introduce the city government to the social
    problems of the villa. Even so, the government has not taken action in that case.
    I don't know why the government today still has that vision of subsidizing all of
    those costs, something that the citizens today deny. I feel that they refuse because
    they pay taxes, pay all of their obligations, and that money could certainly be
    used for other, more concrete benefits. Because we have seen that Villa 1-11-14
    is in a condition to be able to comply with those obligations." Every year, the
    issue of subsidies for consumption of services returns to the public debate, but,
    inversely, what it indicates is that the wealthy are also generously subsidized.
14 Pablo Tomino, "Alto consumo de electricidad en villas" [High electricity con-
    sumption in villas], *La Nación*, March 20, 2011, http://www.lanacion.com.ar
    /1358848-alto-consumo-de-electricidad-en-villas.
15 *Diccionario de la lengua española*, 23th ed., s.v. "baldío"
16 Quoted in Laura Rocha, "Son 163.000 las personas que viven en las villas porte-
    ñas" [There are 163,000 people living in the villas of Buenos Aires], *La Nación*,
    December 18, 2010, http://www.lanacion.com.ar/1334700-son-163000-las-personas
    -que-viven-en-villas-portenas.
17 Laura Rocha, "El 6% de la población porteña se congrega en 30 asentamientos"
    [Six percent of the population of Buenos Aires is congregated in thirty settle-
    ments], *La Nación*, October 5, 2011, http://www.lanacion.com.ar/1411968-el-6-de
    -la-poblacion-portena-se-congrega-en-30-asentamientos.
18 Ismael Bermúdez, "La población en las villas creció por más del 50 por ciento"
    [The population of the villas grew by more than fifty percent], *Clarín*, Septem-
    ber 7, 2011, http://www.clarin.com/capital_federal/poblacion-villas-crecio-ciento
    _0_550145018.html.
19 For an overview of various methodological and theoretical questions about these
    changes, see "Las fiestas en el ámbito urbano" (The festivals in the urban sphere)
    in Néstor García Canclini's (2005) book *La antropología urbana en México*.

20 Another point to keep in mind is how these festivities have been recognized by the national and municipal governments, how they have been taken into the center of the city (Avenida de Mayo), and what modes of dialogue and organization they have given rise to.

21 For further discussion about citizenship, see Mellino (2009).

22 Delegates running parallel businesses are also looked on with suspicion, for example, a delegate who has her own construction business.

23 These types of nominations can be found, for example, in the sociological perspective of G. Mauger, who analyzes the revolts of the youth in Parisian suburbs, as well as in different interpretations of social movements in Argentina. Perhaps one common element would be the Bourdieusian framework of these analyses.

24 This idea is developed in another way in relation to the movement of the unemployed in MTD de Solano and Colectivo Situaciones (2002).

25 The prerogatives attributed to the state also depend on this debate: a politicist argument for the "relative autonomy of the state" is constructed along a Gramscian line around the Miliband-Poulantzas debate that is confronted by the perspectives of Autonomist Marxism and Open Marxism starting in the 1970s.

26 Butler's critiques of Agamben's notion of *bare life* go in this direction: on one hand, it rescues the category of sovereignty (bare life as the ultimate decision of the sovereign) and, on the other, it maintains that the *jettisoned* life is "saturated with power precisely at the moment in which it is deprived of citizenship" (in Butler and Spivak 2007, 40). She adds, "These are not undifferentiated instances of 'bare life' but highly juridified states of dispossession" (42).

27 For a discussion about the right to the city in Argentina, see Oszlak (1991).

28 Several priests who have worked in the villas of Buenos Aires have debated, via a public document, the logic of urbanization as a logic that is external to the villa. For example, see the interview with Father Pepe Di Paola de Carmelo Paredes: "El verdadero urbanizador es el villero" [The true urbanizer is the villero], *Revista Zoom*, August 20, 2008, http://revista-zoom.com.ar/articulo2534.html.

29 *Diccionario de la lengua española*, 23th ed., s.v. "anticresis."

30 For more about this episode, see Cristian Alarcón's (2010) notable account.

Chapter 6. Between Populism and the Politics of the Governed

1 Perhaps Antonio Negri's hypothesis of a multitude in Spinozist terms is shaped along these lines.

2 In any case, as Sandro Mezzadra and Gigi Roggero indicate in the introduction to the Italian edition of Sanyal's book, the notion of a "subsistence economy" that Sanyal theorizes is complicated by intertwining the action of the movement of the poor and governmental apparatuses as spaces "external to capital."

3 Chatterjee has published a new book, *Lineages of Political Society: Studies in Postcolonial Democracy* (2011), in part bringing together the debates in the book I cite here, *The Politics of the Governed: Reflections on Popular Politics in Most of the*

World (2004). Here he cites *On Populist Reason* (Laclau 2005a) several times as a related line of argument as it refers to the development of democratic forms that are often disregarded—or categorized as perverted forms—by modern theories.

4 In my book *Controversia* (Gago 2012), I develop the thesis of this "misencounter" between Marx and Latin America that Aricó proposes.

5 There are two different types of remarks on the issue. From a sociological perspective, the studies of Javier Auyero (2011) and Denis Merklen (2005) are relevant for Argentina. From a global philosophical perspective, the question of the poor and poverty is also addressed in *Multitude* (2004) and *Commonwealth* (2009) by Michael Hardt and Antonio Negri.

6 The analogy between crowds and women is also highlighted by Laclau, who points out that as fear of crowds increased at the end of the nineteenth century, descriptions of women as pathological beings became more violent (34, 35). On this point, it is also worth adding that women remain clearly excluded from the idea of the individual.

7 It should be noted that Lazzarato (2006), returning to Foucault's theorization addressed in the beginning of this chapter and in relation to Tarde, also points to the public as a decisive actor and develops its relation to the notion of the population.

8 See the interview "Pensar la política (Diálogos con Ernesto Laclau)" [Thinking politics (dialogue with Ernesto Laclau)], in the magazine *El Ojo Mocho*, fall 1997. See also Laclau 2008.

REFERENCES

Abduca, Ricardo. 2010. Introduction to *El sacrificio*, by Marcel Mauss and Henri Hupert. Buenos Aires: Las Cuarenta.

———. 2011. "Igualdad y equidad: La unidad de la especie humana como proyecto de autonomía individual. Las problemas de un caso concreto. Los talleres de costura en Buenos Aires." Paper presented at the 10th Mercosur Anthropology Congress, Curitiba, Brazil, July 11.

Agamben, Giorgio. 1998. *Homo Sacer: Sovereign Power and Bare Life*. Stanford, CA: Stanford University Press.

Aglietta, Michel. 2001. *A Theory of Capitalist Regulation: The US Experience*. New York: Verso.

Aira, César. 2001. *La villa*. Buenos Aires: Emecé.

Alarcón, Cristian. 2010. *Si me querés, quereme transa*. Buenos Aires: Norma.

Althusser, Louis. 2006. *Philosophy of the Encounter: Later Writings, 1978–1987*. Translated by G. M. Goshgarian. London: Verso.

Amin, Shahid, and Marcel van der Linden, eds. 1997. "Introduction," in " 'Peripheral' Labor? Studies in the History of Partial Proletarianization." Supplement, *International Review of Social History* 4 (S4): 1–8.

Anzaldúa, Gloria. 2012. *Borderlands/La Frontera: The New Mestiza*. San Francisco: Aunt Lute Books.

Arendt, Hannah. 1998. *The Human Condition*. 2nd ed. Chicago: University of Chicago Press.

Arguedas, José María. 1965. *El sueño del pongo*. Lima: Ediciones Salqantay.

Aricó, José. 2013. *Marx and Latin America*. Translated by David Broder. Leiden: Brill.

Auyero, Javier. 2001. *Poor People's Politics: Peronist Survival Networks and the Legacy of Evita*. Durham, NC: Duke University Press.

Auyero, Javier, and María Fernanda Berti. 2015. *In Harm's Way: The Dynamics of Urban Violence*. Princeton, NJ: Princeton University Press.

Azpiazu, Daniel, and Martín Schorr. 2010. *Hecho en Argentina: Industria y economía, 1976–2007*. Buenos Aires: Siglo XXI.

Balibar, Étienne. 1997. *Spinoza: From Individuality to Transindividuality*. Delft, the Netherlands: Eburon.

———. 2014. *Equaliberty: Political Essays*. Translated by James Ingram. Durham, NC: Duke University Press.

———. 2015. *Citizenship*. Malden, MA: Polity.

Barrancos, Dora. 2013. "Mujeres y crisis en la Argentina: De las Madres de Plaza de Mayo a las piqueteras." In *Los conflictos en los mundos ibéricos e iberoamericanos contemporáneos, de las elaboraciones sociales y políticas a las construcciones simbólicas*, edited by Michel Ralle, 252–76. Paris: Éditions Hispaniques.

Bartra, Armando. 2005. "Dilemas históricos y actuales en las luchas populares en México." In *Bienvenidos a la selva: Diálogos a partir de la Sexta Declaración del EZLN*, edited by Colectivo Situaciones. Buenos Aires: Tinta Limón.

Basualdo, Eduardo. 2000. *Concentración y centralización del capital en la Argentina durante la década del noventa: Una aproximación a través de la reestructuración económica y el comportamiento de los grupos económicos y los capitales extranjeros*. Buenos Aires: UNQui-FLACSO-IDEP.

———. 2006. *Estudios de historia económica Argentina (desde mediados del siglo XX a la actualidad)*. Buenos Aires: Siglo XXI.

Baud, Michiel, Kees Koonings, Gert Oostindie, Arij Ouweneel, and Patricio Silva. 1996. *Etnicidad como estrategia en América latina y el Caribe*. Quito, Ecuador: Abya-Yala.

Benencia, Roberto. 2012. "Participación de los inmigrantes bolivianos en espacios específicos de la producción hortícola argentina." *Política y Sociedad* 49 (1): 163–78.

Benjamin, Walter. 1969. "Theses on the Philosophy of History." In *Illuminations: Essays and Reflections*, edited by Hannah Arendt, translated by Harry Zohn, 253–64. New York: Schocken Books.

Bialet Massé, Juan. (1904) 2010. *Informe Sobre el Estado de las Clases Obreras Argentinas*. Buenos Aires: Ministerio de Trabajo de la Provincia de Buenos Aires.

Biscay, Pedro. 2015. "El control del sistema financiero como garantía de protección de los derechos humanos." Paper presented at the conference "Los derechos humanos a la luz de las transformaciones económicas y financieras," Banco Central de la República Argentina, Buenos Aires, March 25. http://web2.bcra.gob.ar/Pdfs /BCRA/ddhh/Desgrabacion_Seminario_DDHH25_03_15.pdf.

Blaustein, Eduardo. 2001. *Prohibido vivir aquí: Una historia de los planes de erradicación de villas de la última dictadura*. Buenos Aires: Comisión Municipal de la Vivienda-GCBA.

Bloch, Ernst. 1995. *The Principle of Hope*. Translated by Neville Plaice, Stephen Plaice, and Paul Knight. Cambridge, MA: MIT Press.

Bonefeld, Werner, and John Holloway, eds. 1994. *¿Un nuevo estado? Debate sobre la reestructuración del estado y el capital*. Mexico City: Cambio XXI.

Bové, Laurent. 2009. *La estrategia del conatus: Afirmación y resistencia en Spinoza*. Madrid: Tierra de Nadie.

Braidotti, Rosi. 2011. *Nomadic Subjects: Embodiment and Sexual Difference in Contemporary Feminist Theory*. 2nd ed. New York: Columbia University Press.

Brand, Ulrich, and Nikola Sekler. 2009. "Postneoliberalism: Catch-All Word or Valuable Analytical and Political Concept? Aims of a Beginning Debate." *Development Dialogue*, no. 51, 5–13.

Brighenti, Maura, and Verónica Gago. 2013. "L'ipotesi del meticciato in America latina: Dal multiculturalismo neoliberale alle differenze come forme di contenzioso." *Scienza & Politica* 25 (49): 81–106.

Brown, Wendy. 2015. *Undoing the Demos: Neoliberalism's Stealth Revolution*. Brooklyn, NY: Zone Books.

Buck-Morss, Susan. 2009. *Hegel, Haiti, and Universal History*. Pittsburgh, PA: University of Pittsburgh Press.

Butler, Judith. 1999. *Gender Trouble: Feminism and the Subversion of Identity*. New York: Routledge.

Butler, Judith, and Gayatri Chakravorty Spivak. 2007. *Who Sings the Nation-State? Language, Politics, Belonging*. London: Seagull Books.

Cabezón Cámara, Gabriela. 2009. *La virgen Cabeza*. Buenos Aires: Eterna Cadencia.

Carman, María. 2006. *Las trampas de la cultura: Los "intrusos" y los nuevos usos del barrio de Gardel*. Buenos Aires: Paidos.

———. 2011. *Las trampas de la naturaleza: Medio ambiente y segregación en Buenos Aires*. Buenos Aires: Fondo de Cultura Económica and CLACSO (Consejo Latinoamericano de Ciencias Sociales).

Carmona-Rodríguez, Antonio, Giovanna Ferrufino, Juan Manuel Arbona, and Nico Tassi. 2012. "El desborde ecónomico popular en Bolivia: Comerciantes aymaras en el mundo global." *Nueva Sociedad*, no. 241: 93–105.

Chakrabarty, Dipesh. 2009. *El humanismo en la era de la globalización*. Buenos Aires: Katz.

Chang, Hsiao-hung. 2004. "Fake Logos, Fake Theory, Fake Globalization." *Inter-Asia Cultural Studies* 5 (2): 222–36.

Chatterjee, Partha. 2004. *The Politics of the Governed: Reflections on Popular Politics in Most of the World*. New York: Columbia University Press.

———. 2011. *Lineages of Political Society: Studies in Postcolonial Democracy*. New York: Columbia University Press.

Cielo, Cristina, Lisset Coba, and Ivette Vallejo. 2016. "Women, Nature, and Development in Sites of Ecuador's Petroleum Circuit." *Economic Anthropology* 3 (1): 119–32.

Clastres, Pierre. 2010. *Archeology of Violence*. Translated by Jeanine Herman and Ashley Lebner. Los Angeles: Semiotext(e).

Clément, Catherine, and Julia Kristeva. 2013. *The Feminine and the Sacred*. New York: Columbia University Press.

Colectivo Simbiosis and Colectivo Situaciones. 2011. *De chuequistas y overlockas: Una discusión en torno a los talleres textiles*. Buenos Aires: Tinta Limón.

Colectivo Situaciones. 2005. *Mal de altura: Viaje a la Bolivia insurgente*. Buenos Aires: Tinta Limón.

———. 2011. *19 & 20: Notes for a New Social Protagonism*. Translated by Nate Holdren and Sebastián Touza. New York: Minor Compositions, Common Notions, and Autonomedia.

———. 2009. *Conversaciones en el impasse: Dilemas políticos del presente*. Buenos Aires: Tinta Limón.

Colectivo Situaciones and Movimiento de Trabajadores Desocupados de Solano. 2002. *Hipótesis 891: Más allá de los piquetes*. Buenos Aires: De mano en mano.

Colodenco, Daniel. 2006. *Génesis: El origen de las diferencias*. Buenos Aires: Lilmod.

Comaroff, John L., and Jean Comaroff. 2011. *Ethnicity, Inc*. Chicago: University of Chicago Press.

Connell, Raewyn, and Nour Dados. 2014. "Where in the World Does Neoliberalism Come From?" *Theory and Society* 43 (2): 117–38.

Cornejo Polar, Antonio. 1996. "Una heterogeneidad no dialéctica: Sujeto y discurso migrantes en el Perú moderno." *Revista Iberoamericana* 62 (176–77): 837–44.

Cravino, María Cristina. 2006. *Las villas de la ciudad: Mercado e informalidad urbana*. Buenos Aires: Universidad de General Sarmiento.

Curcio, Anna, and Ceren Özselçuk. 2010. "Introduction: The Common and the Forms of the Commune." *Rethinking Marxism* 22 (3): 304–11.

Curcio, Anna, Ceren Özselçuk, Étienne Balibar, and Antonio Negri. 2010. "On the Common, Universality, and Communism: A Conversation between Étienne Balibar and Antonio Negri." *Rethinking Marxism* 22 (3): 312–28.

Dalla Costa, Mariarosa, and Selma James. 1972. *The Power of Women and the Subversion of the Community*. Bristol, UK: Falling Wall.

D'Angiolillo, Julián, dir. 2010. *Hacerme feriante*. El Nuevo municipio & Magoya Films.

Dardot, Pierre, and Christian Laval. 2013. *The New Way of the World: On Neoliberal Society*. New York: Verso.

Dávalos, Pablo. 2012. *Democracia disciplinaria: El proyecto posneoliberal para América latina*. Santiago de Chile: Editorial Quimantú.

Dávalos, Patricia, Marcela Jabbaz, and Estela Molina. 1987. *Movimiento villero y estado, 1966–1976*. Buenos Aires: Centro Editor de América Latina.

Davis, Mike. 2007. *Ciudades muertas: Ecología, catástrofe y revuelta*. Madrid: Traficantes de Sueños.

De Andrade, Oswald. (1928) 1997. "Anthropophagite Manifesto." In *The Oxford Book of Latin American Essays*, edited by Ilan Stavans, 96–99. New York: Oxford University Press.

De Vito, Christian G. 2012. Introduction to *Global Labour History: La storia del lavoro al tempo della "globalizzazione."* Verona: Ombre corte.

DeLanda, Manuel. 2006. *A New Philosophy of Society: Assemblage Theory and Social Complexity*. New York: Continuum.

———. 2008. "Hacia una nueva ontología de lo social: Manuel De Landa en entrevista." By Ignacio Farías. *Persona y Sociedad/Universidad Alberto Hurtado* 22 (1): 75–85.

Deleuze, Gilles. 1992. "Postscript on the Societies of Control." *October* 59:3–7.

———. 2014. *El poder: Curso sobre Foucault.* Buenos Aires: Cactus.

Deleuze, Gilles, and Félix Guattari. 1987. *A Thousand Plateaus: Capitalism and Schizophrenia.* Translated by Brian Massumi. Minneapolis: University of Minnesota Press.

Derrida, Jacques. 1992. *Given Time: I. Counterfeit Money.* Chicago: University of Chicago Press.

Didi-Huberman, Georges. 2006. *Ante el tiempo: Historia del arte y anacronismo de las imágenes.* Translated by Antonio Oviedo. Buenos Aires: Adriana Hidalgo Editora.

Domingos Ouriques, Nildo. 2013. "La crisis del neodesarrollismo y la teoría marxista de la dependencia." *Argumentos* (Mexico City) 26 (72): 129–40.

Donzelot, Jacques. 1979. *The Policing of Families.* New York: Pantheon Books.

D'Ovidio, María. 2007. "Quién es quién en la cadena de valor del sector de indumentaria textil." Buenos Aires: Fundación El Otro. https://www.mpf.gov.ar /Institucional/UnidadesFE/Ufase/trata/Recoleccion/Quien_es_quien.pdf.

Dufy, Caroline, and Florence Weber. 2009. *Más allá de la Gran División: Sociología, economía y etnografía.* Buenos Aires: Antropofagia.

Dumont, Louis. 2001. *Homo Aequalis.* Madrid: Taurus.

Echeverría, Bolívar. 2000. *La modernidad de lo barroco.* Mexico City: Ediciones Era.

Escobar, Arturo. 1995. *Encountering Development: The Making and Unmaking of the Third World.* Princeton, NJ: Princeton University Press.

Estrada Vázquez, Juan Carlos. 2010. *No olvidamos.* Buenos Aires: Retazos.

Federici, Silvia. 2004. *Caliban and the Witch: Women, the Body, and Primitive Accumulation.* New York: Autonomedia.

———. 2012. *Revolution at Point Zero: Housework, Reproduction and Feminist Struggle.* Oakland, CA: PM Press.

Feldman, Germán. 2013. "Créditos para el consumo: Análisis del fenómeno socioeconómico y su impacto en los sectores populares." Informe de la Procuraduría de Criminalidad Económica y Lavado de Activos (PROCELAC). Buenos Aires: Ministerio Público Fiscal, República Argentina.

Fink, Eugen. 2003. *Nietzsche's Philosophy.* New York: Bloomsbury Academic.

Fiorini, Leticia Glocer, and Graciela Abelin-Sas Rose, eds. 2010. *On Freud's "Femininity."* London, England: Karnac Books.

Foucault, Michel. 1978. *The History of Sexuality.* New York: Pantheon Books.

———. 1995. *Discipline and Punish: The Birth of the Prison.* Translated by Alan Sheridan. New York: Vintage Books.

———. 2001. *Power.* Edited by James D. Faubion. Translated by Robert Hurley. New York: New Press.

———. 2007. *Security, Territory, Population: Lectures at the Collège de France, 1977–78.* Translated by Graham Burchell. New York: Palgrave Macmillan.

———. 2008. *The Birth of Biopolitics: Lectures at the Collège de France, 1978–79.* Translated by Graham Burchell. New York: Palgrave Macmillan.

Freud, Sigmund. [1921] 1990. *Group Psychology and the Analysis of the Ego.* Edited by James Strachey. Rev. ed. New York: W. W. Norton.

Fujita, Jun. 2015. "Jyosei ka no Seiji Tesugaku: Diego Sztulwark to no Taiwa" [Political philosophy under the conjuncture: Conversation with Diego Sztulwark]. In *Boryoku Kaikyu toha Nanika* [What is the class of violence?], 282–307. Tokyo: Koshisha.

Gaggero, Alejandro, Martín Schorr, and Andrés Wainer. 2014. *Restricción eterna: El poder económico durante el kirchnerismo.* Buenos Aires: Futuro Anterior.

Gago, Verónica. 2012. *Controversia: Una lengua del exilio.* Buenos Aires: Biblioteca Nacional.

———. 2015. "Contra el colonialismo interno." *Revista Anfibia*, August 16. http://www.revistaanfibia.com/ensayo/contra-el-colonialismo-interno/.

Gago, Verónica, and Sandro Mezzadra. 2015. "Para una crítica de las operaciones extractivas del capital: Patrón de acumulación y luchas sociales en el tiempo de la financiarización." *Nueva Sociedad*, no. 255 (February): 38–52.

Gago, Verónica, Sandro Mezzadra, Sebastián Scolnik, and Diego Sztulwark. 2014. "¿Hay una nueva forma-Estado? Apuntes latinoamericanos." *Utopía y Praxis Latinoamericana.* Revista Internacional de Filosofía Iberoamericana y Teoría Social 19 (66): 177–84.

Galindo, María. 2010. "Prólogo." In *La pobreza: Un gran negocio. Un análisis crítico sobre oeneges, microfinancieras y bancas,* by Graciela Toro. La Paz: Mujeres Creando.

García Canclini, Néstor. 2005. *La antropología urbana en México.* Mexico City: Fondo Cultura Economica.

García Linera, Álvaro. 1995. *Forma valor y forma comunidad.* La Paz: Chonchocoro.

———. 2001. "Sindicato, multitud y comunidad. Movimientos sociales y formas de autonomía política en Bolivia." In *Tiempos de rebelión,* by Álvaro García Linera, Felipe Quispe, Raquel Gutiérrez Aguilar, and Luis Tapia. La Paz: Comuna and Muela del Diablo.

———. 2012. *Geopolítica de la Amazonia.* La Paz: Vicepresidencia del Estado Plurinacional.

———. 2014. *Plebeian Power: Collective Action and Indigenous, Working-Class and Popular Identities in Bolivia.* Leiden: Brill.

Gibson-Graham, J. K. 2005. "Building Community Economies: Women and the Politics of Place." In *Women and the Politics of Place,* edited by Wendy Harcourt and Arturo Escobar, 130–57. Bloomfield, CT: Kumarian.

Giorgis, Marta. 2004. *La virgen prestamista: La fiesta de la Virgen de Urkupiña en el boliviano Gran Córdoba.* Buenos Aires: Antropofagia y Centro de Antropología Social del Instituto de Desarrollo Económico y Social.

Girón, Nacho. 2011. *La Salada: Radiografía de la feria más polémica de Latino-américa*. Buenos Aires: Ediciones B.

González Rodríguez, Sergio. 2002. *Huesos en el desierto*. Mexico City: Anagrama.

Gramsci, Antonio. 1971. "Americanism and Fordism." In *Selections from the Prison Notebooks*, edited by Quintin Hoare and Geoffrey Nowell Smith, 277–318. New York: International Publishers.

Grosso, José Luis. 2007. "El revés de la trama: Cuerpos, semiopraxis e interculturalidad en contextos poscoloniales." *Arqueologia Suramericana* 3 (2): 184–217.

Guattari, Félix. 2004. *Capitalismo mundial integrado y revoluciones moleculares*. Madrid: Traficantes de Sueños.

Gudynas, Eduardo. 2015. *Derechos de la naturaleza: Ética biocéntrica y políticas ambientales*. Buenos Aires: Tinta Limón.

Gunder Frank, Andre. 1972. *Lumpen-Bourgeoisie and Lumpen-Development: Dependency, Class and Politics in Latin America*. New York: Monthly Review Press.

Gutiérrez Aguilar, Raquel. 1999. *Desandar el laberinto: Introspección en la feminidad contemporánea*. La Paz: Muela del Diablo.

———. 2011a. "Modernidades alternativas: Reciprocidad y formas comunitarias de reproducción material."

———. 2011b. *Palabras para tejernos, resistir y transformar*. Mexico City: Pez en el árbol.

———. 2014. *Rhythms of the Pachakuti: Indigenous Uprising and State Power in Bolivia*. Translated by Stacey Alba D. Skar. Durham, NC: Duke University Press.

Gutiérrez Aguilar, Raquel, and Dunia Mokrani Chávez. 2006. "¿Reformar o refundar el estado?" Agencia Latinoamericana de Información, June 30. http://www.alainet.org/es/active/12090.

Hacher, Sebastián. 2011. *Sangre salada*. Buenos Aires: Marea.

Hall, Stuart, and Miguel Mellino. 2011. *La cultura y el poder: Conversaciones sobre los cultural studies*. Buenos Aires: Amorrortu.

Haraway, Donna. 1991. *Simians, Cyborgs, and Women: The Reinvention of Nature*. New York: Routledge.

Harcourt, Wendy, and Arturo Escobar, eds. 2005. *Women and the Politics of Place*. Bloomfield, CT: Kumarian.

Hardt, Michael. 2008. "Políticas y multitud." In *Imperio, multitud y sociedad abigarrada*, by Toni Negri, Michael Hardt, Giuseppe Cocco, Judith Revel, Alvaro García-Linera, and Luis Tapia, 87–102. La Paz: Vicepresidencia de la República, Consejo Latinoamericano de Ciencias Sociales (CLACSO), and Muela del Diablo.

Hardt, Michael, and Antonio Negri. 2000. *Empire*. Cambridge, MA: Harvard University Press.

———. 2004. *Multitude: War and Democracy in the Age of Empire*. New York: Penguin.

———. 2009. *Commonwealth*. Cambridge, MA: Belknap Press of Harvard University Press.

Harvey, David. 1989. *The Condition of Postmodernity: An Enquiry into the Origins of Cultural Change*. Cambridge, MA: Blackwell.

———. 2003. *The New Imperialism*. Oxford: Oxford University Press.

Hegel, G. W. F. 1977. *Phenomenology of Spirit*. Translated by A. V. Miller. Oxford: Oxford University Press.

Heidegger, Martin. 1982. *The Question Concerning Technology, and Other Essays*. New York: Harper Collins.

Hirsch, Joachim. 1996. *Globalización, capital, estado*. Mexico City: UAM-Xochimilco.

Hirschman, Albert O. 2013. *The Passions and the Interests: Political Arguments for Capitalism before Its Triumph*. Princeton, NJ: Princeton University Press.

Hubert, Henri, and Marcel Mauss. 1964. *Sacrifice: Its Nature and Functions*. Chicago: University of Chicago Press.

Instituto de Investigación y Experimentación Política (IIEP). 2015. "Realismo de la potencia: por una nueva imagen de la organización política." *Lobo Suelto*, April 14. http://anarquiacoronada.blogspot.com.ar/2015/04/realismo-de-la-potencia-por-una-nueva.html.

Irigaray, Luce. 1985. *Speculum of the Other Woman*. Translated by Gillian Gill. Ithaca, NY: Cornell University Press.

Jaguaribe, Beatriz. 2007. *O choque do real: Estetica, midia e cultura*. Rio de Janeiro: Rocco.

Karakayali, Serhat, and Özge Yaka. 2014. "The Spirit of Gezi: The Recomposition of Political Subjectivities in Turkey." *New Formations* 83 (winter): 117–38.

Karsenti, Bruno. 2009. *Marcel Mauss: El hecho social como totalidad*. Buenos Aires: Antropofagia.

Kim, Jihye. 2014. "Looking at the Other through the Eye of a Needle: Korean Garment Businesses and Inter-ethnic Relations in Argentina." *Asian Journal of Latin American Studies* 27 (1): 1–19.

Klossowski, Pierre. 2012. *La moneda viva*. Madrid: Pre-Textos.

Laclau, Ernesto. 2005a. *On Populist Reason*. London: Verso.

———. 2005b. *La razón populista*. Buenos Aires: Fondo de Cultura Económica.

———. 2008. *Debates y combates*. Buenos Aires: Fondo de Cultura Económica.

Larrea, Carlos. 2004. *Pobreza, dolarización y crisis en el Ecuador*. Quito, Ecuador: Abyayala.

Lazzarato, Maurizio. 2006. *Políticas del acontecimiento*. Buenos Aires: Tinta Limón.

Le Bon, Gustave. 1995. *The Crowd*. New Brunswick, NJ: Transactions Publishers.

Lefebvre, Henri. 1996. *Writings on Cities*. Selected, translated, and introduced by E. Kofman and E. Lebas, Oxford: Blackwell.

Lévi-Strauss, Claude. 1966. *The Savage Mind*. Chicago: University of Chicago Press.

———. 1992. *Triste Tropiques*. New York: Penguin.

Lieutier, Ariel. 2010. *Esclavos: Los trabajadores costureros de la ciudad de Buenos Aires*. Buenos Aires: Retórica.

Limas Hernández, Alfredo. 2004. "Minorías postnacionales en la globalización: El feminicidio en Juárez del 2002. Minorización de categorías culturales, el sentido del capital multinacional." In *Las muchas identidades: De nacionalidades, migrantes, disidentes y géneros*, edited by Mónica González. Mexico City: Quimera.

Linebaugh, Peter, and Marcus Rediker. 2000. *The Many-Headed Hydra: Sailors, Slaves, Commoners, and the Hidden History of the Revolutionary Atlantic.* Boston: Beacon.

Lins Ribeiro, Gustavo. 2008. "El sistema mundial no-hegemonico y la globalizacion popular." *Alambre: Comunicación, información, cultura,* no. 1.

Lonzi, Carla (1971) 1991. "Let's Spit on Hegel." In *Italian Feminist Thought: A Reader,* edited by Paola Bono and Sandra Kemp, 40–59. Cambridge, MA: Blackwell.

Ludmer, Josefina. 2010. *Aquí América latina.* Buenos Aires: Eterna Cadencia.

Macpherson, Crawford B. 1962. *The Political Theory of Possessive Individualism: Hobbes to Locke.* Oxford: Clarendon Press.

Mailhe, Alejandra. 2010. "Imágenes del otro social en el Brasil de fines del siglo XIX: Canudos como espejo en ruinas." *Prismas: Revista de historia intelectual* no. 14: 37–56.

Marazzi, Christian. 2008. *Capital and Language: From the New Economy to the War Economy.* Los Angeles: Semiotext(e).

———. 2011. *Capital and Affects: The Politics of the Language Economy.* Translated by Giuseppina Mecchia. Los Angeles: Semiotext(e).

Marshall, Thomas H. 1950. *Citizenship and Social Class, and Other Essays.* Cambridge University Press.

Marx, Karl. (1885–1867) 1977. *Capital.* Vol. 1. Translated by Ben Fowkes. New York: Vintage Books.

———. 1993. *Grundrisse: Foundations of the Critique of Political Economy.* Translated by Martin Nicolaus. Reprint edition. New York: Penguin Classics.

Marx, Karl, and Friedrich Engels. 1998. *The German Ideology.* Amherst, NY: Prometheus Books.

Massidda, A. L., J. d'Angiolillo, M. Dimenstein, M. di Peco, J. P. Scarfi, P. Torroja, A. I. Guérin, and C. Molíns. 2010. "Feria La Salada: Una centralidad periférica intermitente en el Gran Buenos Aires." In *Argentina: Persistencia y diversificación, contrastes e imaginarios en las centralidades urbanas,* edited by Margarita Gutman, 169–206. Quito, Ecuador: Olacchi-Flacso Ecuador.

Matellanes, Marcelo. 2003. *Del maltrato social.* Buenos Aires: Ediciones Cooperativas.

Mauss, Marcel. 1999. "Review of Hubert's Essay on Time." In *Essay on Time: A Brief Study of the Representation of Time in Religion and Magic,* by Henri Hubert, translated by Robert Parkin and Jacqueline Redding, 93–96. Oxford: Berghahn Books.

———. 2002. *The Gift: The Form and Reason for Exchange in Archaic Societies.* Translated by W. D. Halls. New York: Routledge.

Mauss, Marcel, and Henri Hupert. 2010. *El sacrificio.* Buenos Aires: Las Cuarenta.

Mellino, Miguel. 2009. "Ciudadanías postcoloniales como símbolo y alegoría del capitalismo postcolonial." *La Biblioteca* (Buenos Aires), no. 8, 82–92.

Merklen, Denis. 2005. *Pobres ciudadanos: Las clases populares en la era democrática (Argentina, 1983–2003)*. Buenos Aires: Gorla.

Mezzadra, Sandro. 2008. *La condizione postcoloniale: Storia e politica nel presente globale*. Verona, Italy: Ombre corte.

———. 2011. "Bringing Capital Back In: A Materialist Turn in Postcolonial Studies?" *Inter-Asia Cultural Studies* 12 (1): 154–64.

Mezzadra, Sandro, and Brett Neilson. 2013a. *Border as Method, or, The Multiplication of Labor*. Durham, NC: Duke University Press.

———. 2013b. "Extraction, Logistics, Finance: Global Crisis and the Politics of Operations." *Radical Philosophy*, no. 178: 8–18.

———. 2015. "Operations of Capital." *South Atlantic Quarterly* 114 (1): 1–9.

Mezzadra, Sandro, and Gigi Roggero. 2010. "Ripensare lo sviluppo capitalistico." Introduction to *Ripensare lo sviluppo capitalistico. Accumulazione originaria, governamentalità e capitalismo postcoloniale: il caso indiano*, by Kalyan Sanyal. Firenze: La Casa Usher.

Monsiváis, Carlos. 2006. *A ustedes les consta: antología de la crónica en México*. México: Era.

Morales, Bruno. 2006. *Bolivia construcciones*. Buenos Aires: Sudamericana.

———. 2010. *Grandeza Boliviana*. Buenos Aires: Eterna Cadencia.

Moreno, María. 2011. *La comuna de Buenos Aires*. Buenos Aires: Capital Intelectual.

Mouffe, Chantal. 2005. *On the Political*. New York: Routledge.

Moulier Boutang, Yann. 2006. *De la esclavitud al trabajo asalariado*. Madrid: Akal.

Mujeres Creando. 2007. "Las exiliadas del neoliberalismo." http://www
.mujerescreando.org/pag/articulos/2007/ponenicasexiliadas.htm.

Nápoli, Bruno, Celeste Perosino, and Walter Bosisio. 2014. *La dictadura del capital financiero: El golpe militar corporativo y la trama bursátil*. Buenos Aires: Peña Lillo and Ediciones Continente.

Negri, Antonio. 1991. *Marx beyond Marx. Lessons on the Grundrisse*, translated by Harry Cleaver. New York: AK Press.

———. 2006. Preface to *De la esclavitud al trabajo asalariado*, by Yann Moulier Boutang. Madrid: Akal.

———. 2007. "El monstruo político: Vida desnuda y potencia." In *Ensayos sobre biopolítica: Excesos de vida*, edited by Gabriel Giorgi and Fermín Rodríguez, 93–139. Buenos Aires: Paidos.

Negri, Antonio, and Felix Guattari. 1997. *Las verdades nómadas y general intellect*. Madrid: Akal.

Nichols, Walter J., and Justin Beaumont. 2004. "The Urbanisation of Justice Movements? Possibilities and Constraints for the City as a Space of Contentious Struggle." *Space and Polity* 8 (2): 119–35.

Nietzsche, Friedrich. 1974. *The Gay Science: With a Prelude in Rhymes and an Appendix of Songs*. Translated by Walter Kaufmann. New York: Vintage.

Ong, Aihwa. 2006. *Neoliberalism as Exception: Mutations in Citizenship and Sovereignty*. Durham, NC: Duke University Press.

Ossona, Jorge Luís. 2010. "El shopping de los pobres: Anatomía y fisionomía de La Salada." http://www.unsam.edu.ar/escuelas/politica/centro_historia_politica /publicaciones/JorgeOssona/EL_SHOPPING_DE_LOS_POBRES.pdf.

Oszlak, Oscar. 1991. *Merecer la ciudad: Los pobres y el derecho al espacio urbano.* Buenos Aires: CEDES/Hvmanitas.

Pashukanis, Evgeny. 2001. *The General Theory of Law and Marxism.* New Brunswick, NJ: Transaction Publishers.

Pateman, Carole. 1988. *The Sexual Contract.* Stanford, CA: Stanford University Press.

Peck, Jamie. 2013. "Explaining (with) Neoliberalism." *Territory, Politics, Governance* 1 (2): 132–57.

Plato. 2002. *Plato: Statesman.* Translated by J. B. Skemp. 2nd ed. Bristol: Bristol Classical Press.

Polanyi, Karl. 1944. *The Great Transformation: The Political and Economic Origins of Our Time.* Boston: Beacon Press.

Prebisch, Raúl. 1970. *Transformación y desarrollo: la gran tarea de América Latina.* Mexico City: Fondo de Cultura Económica.

Precarias a la deriva. 2004. *A la deriva por los circuitos de la precariedad femenina.* Madrid: Traficantes de Sueños.

Rama, Ángel. 1996. *The Lettered City.* Translated by John Charles Chasteen. Durham, NC: Duke University Press.

Rancière, Jacques. 1999. *Disagreement: Politics and Philosophy.* Translated by Julie Rose. Minneapolis: University of Minnesota Press.

———. 2004. *The Philosopher and His Poor.* Edited by Andrew Parker. Translated by Corinne Oster and John Drury. Durham, NC: Duke University Press.

———. 2011. *The Emancipated Spectator.* Reprint ed. London: Verso.

———. 2012. *Proletarian Nights: The Workers' Dream in Nineteenth-Century France.* 2nd ed. Translated by John Drury. New York: Verso.

Reyes, Alvaro. 2010. "Subjectivity and Visions of the Common." *Rethinking Marxism* 22 (3): 498–506.

Rich, Adrienne. 1994. *Blood, Bread, and Poetry: Selected Prose, 1979–1985.* New York: W. W. Norton.

Rivera Cusicanqui, Silvia. 1996. *Bircholas. Trabajo de mujeres: explotación capitalista y opresión colonial entre las migrantes aymaras de La Paz y El Alto.* La Paz: Editorial Mama Huaco.

———. (1984) 2003. *Oprimidos pero no vencidos: Luchas del campesinado aymara y quechua, 1900–1980.* La Paz: Aruwiyiri.

———. 2009. "La contradicción/suplementación entre cultura y desarrollo." Paper presented at the seminar "Cultura y Desarrollo," Prince Claus Foundation, the Hague, the Netherlands, February 28.

———. 2010a. *Ch'ixinakax utxiwa: Una reflexión sobre prácticas y discursos descolonizadores.* Buenos Aires: Retazos and Tinta Limón.

———. 2010b. *Principio Potosí: Reverso.* Madrid: Museo Nacional Centro de Arte Reina Sofía.

Rivera Cusicanqui, Silvia, and Rossana Barragán (eds.). 1997. *Debates postcoloniales. Una introducción a los estudios de la subalternidad.* La Paz: SEPHIS, Historias, Aruwiyiri

Rolnik, Suely. 2001. "Deleuze esquizoanalista." *Revista Campo Grupal*, no. 23 (April).

Rozitchner, León. 1996. *Las desventuras del sujeto político.* Buenos Aires: El Cielo por Asalto.

———. 2001. *La cosa y la cruz: Cristianismo y capitalismo (en torno a las Confesiones de San Agustín).* Buenos Aires: Losada.

Samaddar, Ranabir. 2009. "Primitive Accumulation and Some Aspects of Work and Life in India." *Economic and Political Weekly* 44 (18): 33–42.

Sandoval, Chela. 2000. *Methodology of the Oppressed.* Minneapolis: University of Minnesota Press.

Sanyal, Kalyan. 2007. *Rethinking Capitalist Development: Primitive Accumulation, Governmentality and Post-colonial Capitalism.* New Delhi: Routledge.

Sarlo, Beatriz. 2009. *La ciudad vista.* Buenos Aires: Siglo XXI.

Sassen, Saskia. 1999. "Cracked Casings: Notes toward an Analytics for Studying Transnational Processes." In *Sociology for the Twenty-First Century: Continuities and Cutting Edges*, edited by Janet L. Abu-Lughod, 134–45. Chicago: University of Chicago Press.

———. 2003. *Contrageografías de la globalización.* Madrid: Traficantes de Sueños.

———. 2005. "The City: Its Return as a Lens for Social Theory." In *The Sage Handbook of Sociology*, edited by Craig Calhoun, Chris Rojek, and Bryan S. Turner, 457–70. London: Sage.

———. 2007. *Sociology of Globalization.* New York: W. W. Norton.

———. 2008. *Territory, Authority, Rights: From Medieval to Global Assemblages.* Princeton, NJ: Princeton University Press.

Segato, Rita Laura. 2013. *La escritura en el cuerpo de las mujeres asesinadas en Ciudad Juárez.* Buenos Aires: Tinta Limón.

Spinoza, Benedict de. 2000. *Political Treatise.* Translated by Samuel Shirley. Indianapolis, IN: Hackett Publishing

———. 2005. *Ethics.* Translated by Edwin Curley. New York: Penguin Classics.

Spivak, Gayatri Chakravorty. 1988. "Can the Subaltern Speak?" In *Marxism and the Interpretation of Culture*, edited by Cary Nelson and Lawrence Grossberg, 271–313. Urbana: University of Illinois Press.

———. 2013. *En otras palabras, en otros mundos.* Buenos Aires: Paidos.

Svampa, Maristella, and Sebastián Pereyra. 2003. *Entre la ruta y el barrio: La experiencia de las organizaciones piqueteras.* Buenos Aires: Editorial Biblos.

Swyngedouw, Erik. 1997. "Neither Global nor Local: 'Glocalization' and the Politics of Scale." In *Spaces of Globalization: Reasserting the Power of the Local*, edited by Kevin R. Cox. New York: Guilford.

Tapia, Luis. 2008a. *Política salvaje.* La Paz: Consejo Latinoamericano de Ciencias Sociales (CLACSO), Muela del Diablo, Comuna.

———. 2008b. "Multitud y sociedad abigarrada". In *Imperio, multitud y sociedad abigarrada*, by Alvaro García Linera, Judith Revel, Giuseppe Cocco, Michael Hardt, Antonio Negri, and Luis Tapia. La Paz: Vicepresidencia de la República, Clacso, and Muela del Diablo.

Thomson, Sinclair. 2002. *We Alone Will Rule: Native Andean Politics in the Age of Insurgency*. Madison: University of Wisconsin Press.

———. 2006. "'Cuando sólo reinasen los indios': Recuperando la variedad de proyectos anticoloniales entre los comuneros andinos (La Paz, 1740–1781)." *Argumentos* (Mexico City) 19 (50): 15–47.

Toro, Graciela. 2010. *La pobreza: Un gran negocio. Un análisis crítico sobre oeneges, microfinancieras y banca*. La Paz: Mujeres Creando.

Virno, Paolo. 2004. *A Grammar of the Multitude: For an Analysis of Contemporary Forms of Life*. Translated by Isabella Bertoletti, James Cascaito, and Andrea Casson. Los Angeles: Semiotext(e).

———. 2008. *Multitude between Innovation and Negation*. Translated by Isabella Bertoletti, James Cascaito, and Andrea Casson. Los Angeles: Semiotext(e).

———. 2015a. *When the Word Becomes Flesh: Language and Human Nature*. Translated by Giuseppina Mecchia. South Pasadena, CA: Semiotext(e).

———. 2015b. *Déja Vu and the End of History*. Translated by David Broder. Brooklyn, NY: Verso.

Viveiros de Castro, Eduardo. 2014a. *Cannibal Metaphysics*. Translated by Peter Skafish. Minneapolis: Univocal.

———. 2014b. "El consumo no evita la queja." Interview by Verónica Gago and Mario Santucho. *Revista Ñ*, June 16. http://www.revistaenie.clarin.com/ideas/consumo-evita-queja_0_1156684344.html.

Wekerle, Gerda. 2005. "Domesticating the Neoliberal City: Invisible Genders and the Politics of Place." In *Women and the Politics of Place*, edited by Wendy Harcourt and Arturo Escobar, 86–99. Bloomfield, CT: Kumarian.

Wilkis, Ariel. 2013. *Las sospechas del dinero: Moral y economía en la vida popular*. Buenos Aires: Paidós.

Williams, Eric. (1944) 1994. *Capitalism and Slavery*. Chapel Hill: University of North Carolina Press.

Zavaleta Mercado, René. 1982. *Lo nacional-popular en Bolivia*. Mexico City: Siglo XXI.

———. 1990. *El estado en América latina*. La Paz: Editorial Los Amigos del Libro.

———. 2009. *Lo Nacional-Popular en Bolivia*. La Paz: Plural.

Zibechi, Raúl. 2003. *Genealogia de la revuelta: Argentina, la sociedad en movimiento*. La Plata, Argentina: Letra Libre.

———. 2010. *Dispersing Power: Social Movements as Anti-state Forces*. Translated by Ramor Ryan. Oakland, CA: AK Press.

INDEX

accumulation, fractal, 46–48, 122
aesthetics, realist, 43
ALBA Summit, 141–42
aleatory proletariat, 66–67
alliance, the (theory), 152
ambivalence, 17–18
anachronism, 73–75
anticréticos, 212–13
Argentina: crises, 1, 3, 6, 82, 153,
238n3; economic recovery, 6–7, 166;
foreign capital in, 26; Home Work
Act, the, 146; informal economies,
6–7; neoliberal governmentality,
158–59; neoliberalism in, 158–60;
slavery laws, 248n22; textile industry, 81–82. *See also* La Salada; textile
workshops; villas
assemblages: De Landa's theory,
51, 239n16; Delueze's theory, 9;
and denationalization, 49–50;
La Salada as, 30, 48, 51; ontology
of, 50–51; as relational, 50; textile
workshops as, 118
autonomy: and communitarianism,
44–45; during crises, 82; and difference, 20; the leftist problematic,
18; in motley societies, 63–64; and
perserverance, 149; of the political,
153, 158, 203, 224, 230–31; as preserving *potencia*, 149; problematizing,
220; productive and reproductive,
165; regional, 22–24; of the state,
19, 254n25; of the subject, 13; textile

economy, 130, 136; of villas, 183–85.
See also Villa 1-11-14: delegates,
political
ayllu, 126–28
ayni, 135, 137, 210

"bare life," 4, 233, 254n26
baroque logics, 22, 235
baroque modernity, 14, 70, 118–19
Bergoglio, Jorge (Cardinal), 133
bodies, 150–51, 157–58
Bolivia: ALBA Summit, 141–42; baroque
modernity and, 14, 70, 118–19; communitarianism, 79, 137, 210–12; crisis
(2003), 4; expatriate relations, 145,
147; informal economies in, 6–7;
microfinance in, 51; money, attitude
toward, 175; as motley society, 63;
neoliberal reforms, 119; resistance
movements, 2–3, 63, 99–100; and
textile workshops, 108–9, 137–41,
244n2–3; as traditional, 247n10;
workshop recruitment in, 130.
See also migrant workers
borders, 30, 37–38, 96. *See also*
migrant workers
border zones, 24, 30–31, 139
brands: authenticity, 38–39, 41; and
workshops, 40–41, 118, 122, 244n3.
See also forgery
Brazil, 23, 43, 169
Brukman (factory), 112
Buen Vivir, 25, 223

calculation: of affective-domestic labor, 162; as conatus, 142–43, 161, 163–64, 235; government, 200, 206; Heidegger on, 161–62; in informal economies, 6; migrant, 117, 119, 134–37; monstrosity of, 6, 160, 175; and neoliberalism, 154, 160, 163; and rationality, 163; urban, 21, 109–10, 135; as vitalist pragmatic, 20, 160–64

cannibalism (political theory), 151–52

capital, 26–27, 45–48, 79, 110, 121, 238n6; the state, relation to, 26–27

Castillo, Jorge, 42, 53

children, 192–93

ch'ixi, 61–62, 65, 138–39

cities, 36–37, 70, 179. *See also* urban spaces; villas

citizenship: via consumption, 159, 168–70; and migrants, 145, 166, 184; and neoliberalism, 10; versus population, the, 218; and statelessness, 201–3; and villas, 187–88, 192–93

Ciudad Juárez, 109–10

civil society, 221–22

clandestine spaces, 114, 245n5

clandestine textile workshops. *See* textile workshops

Colectivo Simbiosis, 134

common places (theory), 96

communitarianism: and autonomy, 44–45; capital, 45–48, 79, 238n6; critiques of, 243n15; culturalist argument, 126–29; and deterritorialization, 100; dynamics of, 80–82; economies of, 85–86; entrepreneurship, 119–122; exploitation of, 109–10; feminist perspectives, 88–90; flexibility of, 79, 99–101; and irony, 86–88; as job attribute, 110–11, 116–17, 125; and migration, 130–32; overview, 44–45; persistence of, 78–79; textile workshops, 144–46; in transnational economies,

79; in villas, 198–99, 209–13; "webs" of, 111–12

communities: as capital, 121; and crisis, 80; as flexible, 99–101; and governmentality, 233; and morality, 232–33; motley, 101–2; and nation-states, 232; unions as, 121–22

conatus, 8–10, 142–43, 161, 163–64

consumption: citizenship via, 159, 168–70; and finance, 175; mass, 169, 174

contemporaneity of the noncontemporaneous, 73–75

conversion ideology and villas, 205–6

convertibility, 26

counterfitting. *See* forgery

credit: anticréticos, 212–13; and democratization, 169; and looting, 174–75; *pasanakus* as, 211–12; post-crisis, 166, 168

crisis: autonomy during, 82; and community, 80; definition of, 3–4; neoliberalism, reflecting on, 21–22; social productivity, 8; as thought locus, 233

crowd, the. *See* populism

deferred reciprocity, 134–37

delegates, of Villa 1-11-14, 183–85, 199–201, 206, 214–17

demands, 227–29

democracy, 219–20

democratization, 169–71, 183

deproletartianization, 19, 33, 111

deterritorialization, 100

dictatorship, 1, 28, 132

difference, 143, 150–51

differential of exploitation, 119, 137, 148

domestic knowledges, 82

domestic labor, 82, 85, 89, 91, 93, 162

domination, legitimate, 136–37

economic difference, logic of, x, 85

economic rationality, 203, 213

economic recovery, Argentina, 6–7, 166
economic strategies, workers', 7–8
economies, baroque: La Salada as,
    69–71; resistance in, 20; theoretical
    framework, 12–15, 19
economies, community, 85–86
economies, diverse, 84–85
economies, informal: Argentina,
    52, 76, 167; in cities, 36–37; and
    citizenship, 170; definition, 5–6; and
    domestic sphere, 82; La Salada as,
    68; post-crises, 6–7; rationality in,
    9; in villas, 209–13
economies, microproletarian, 19
economies, migrant, 8, 165, 250n37
economies, popular: as baroque, 70;
    in crises, 6; moralization of, 15–18;
    as neoliberal, 11, 176; and previous
    labor modes, 46; rationality in, 2,
    142; as victimizing, 7, 18
economies, rentier, 3, 26–27, 61
economy, workshop, 117, 145–48
Ecuador, 3, 7, 25
entrepreneurship: and La Salada,
    34–35, 38, 53; micro, 15, 17, 21, 36,
    175; popular, 6, 164–65; self, 6, 20;
    and textile workshops, 119–22
equivalence, logic of, 227–28
escraches, 132, 249n26
eternal feminine, the, 86–88, 242n5
ethnicization of difference, 121
exiles of neoliberalism, 131
exploitation, differential of, 119, 137, 148
extractivism, 25, 159, 171–74. See also
    neoextractivism

fakes. See forgery
feminine voice, the, 95, 97–98
festivals: as market consolidation,
    57–60; and migrants, 139–40; as po-
    litical integration, 141–42; in villas,
    17, 194–96, 215–17
finance, 164–69, 175

fire, Luis Viale workshop, 147,
    250n35
flat ontology, 51, 239n18
forgery: and borders, 37–38; cam-
    paigns against, 238n11; as hetero-
    topia, 41–42; and La Salada, 38–39,
    41, 69
fractal accumulation, 46–48, 122.
    See also brands

Gay, Alfonso Prat, 52–53
gifts, 213
global rationality, 22
governed, the: definition, 218–19; dual
    model of, 229; and governmental-
    ity, 219–21, 223; politics of, 220, 222;
    versus populism, 230–31; self-
    construction of, 232–33
governmentality, 2, 12, 153, 219–21
governmental rationality, 10
governments, progressive: cycle of,
    4, 27; and extractivism, 24–25, 171;
    and financial mediation, 27; and
    neoliberalism, 5, 158

Hacerme feriante, 56–57
heterogeneous time, 222–23
heteronomy, 129, 149
heterotopias, 41–42
Home Work Act, the (Argentina), 146
homo economicus, 10, 13–14, 160,
    213, 235
hybridity, 62

immanence, 8, 231
incommensurability, 15
indigenous peoples, 60–61, 93, 101–2,
    141, 151
individual rationality, 226
industrialism, 162
inflation, x, 175
informal economies. See economies,
    informal

informality, 15, 33, 52–54, 145
institutional rationality, 91
intensive spaces, 180
invisibilization, 43

La Alameda, 132–34, 145
labor: changes over time, 21, 74; in crises, 80–81; feminine, 83–86, 93–95; history of, 72; in La Salada, 34–35
labor, slave: as foreign, 129; migrants as, 42; versus wage, 91–93; versus women's, 81–82
language, 96, 193–95, 226
La Salada: and 2001 crisis, 31–32; accumulation in, 46–48; as Argentinian, 42, 52–53; as assemblage, 30, 48, 51; as border zone, 30–31, 69–70; cartography of, 54–56; communitarianism, 44–47; and entrepreneurship, 34–35, 38, 53; festivals in, 57–60; and forgery, 38–39, 41; growth of, 35, 42–43, 237n2; *Hacerme feriante*, 56–57; as heterotopia, 41–42; labor, 34–35; market dynamism, 36; as motley space, 67–69; overview, 16–17, 29–30; as proletarian microeconomy, 32–34, 68; regulation debate, 53; and villas, 180
life, regulation of, 148–49
Limachi, Edgar, 138
literature, of migrants, 95–96
logistical urbanism, 55
looting, 174–75

maquilas, 109–10
market, the world, 71
markets, as heterotopias, 41–42
market-state dichotomy, 153
Marxism, 25, 224–25, 242n7, 254
microentrepreneurship, 15, 17, 21, 36, 175

microfinance, 51
migrant economies, 8, 165, 250n37
migrant workers: and communitarian capital, 110; communities of, 79; in crises, 80–81; exploitation of, 119, 245n7; and festivals, 139–40; as labor force, 34–35; and neodevelopmentalism, 115–16; political representation of, 145; and pragmatics of the self, 20, 35; rationality of, 8, 35, 165; and reproletarianization, 111; as slave labor, 34, 42, 129–30, 150; in textile workshops, 109, 114–15, 118; victimization of, 36, 130, 133, 150; and villas, 180–81; visibility of, 124–25
migration: community, 98; as family strategy, 131–32; of labor forms, 118–19; and literature, 95–96; as neoliberal exile, 147; state reactions to, 250n34; textile economy, 103, 116–17
misogony, 106, 110
monstrosity, 6, 160, 175, 179–80, 189–91
morality, 232–33, 235
Morenada dance, the, 138
motley, the, 63–64, 67–69
multiculturalism, 60, 151
multinaturalism, 151–52

neodevelopmentalism, 3, 22–26, 115–16
neoextractivism, 24, 27, 159–60. *See also* extractivism
neoliberalism: from above, 2, 5–6; in Argentina, 158–59; from below, 2, 6, 10–11, 20, 110, 165–66, 176–77; and calculation, 154, 160, 163; definitions of, 1–2, 5, 160; delegitimization of, 28, 176; as developmental strategy, 27–28; end of, analyzing, 18–19;

exiles of, 131, 147; Foucault on, 154–57; overcoming, 158; pluralization of, 19; as polymorphic, 235; and progressive governments, 5, 158; as rationality, 2, 21, 160, 234; variability of, 170, 176
neoliberal reason, 21–22, 24, 234
No olvidamos, 147–48
noninstrumental rationality, 10

ontology, 50–51, 239n18
ordoliberalism, 156–57, 237n1

pasanakus, 210–12
Peronism, 27, 52, 230
Plan Jefes y Jefas de Hogar, 83, 241n1
planner states, 24–25
political autonomy, 153, 158, 203, 224, 230–31
political society, 221–22
popular economies. *See* economies, popular
popular entrepreneurship, 6, 164–65
popular resistance and rationality, 154, 221, 223
population, 218–19, 232
populism: in crises, 4; and demands, 227–29; versus governed, the, 230–31; Laclau's theories, 225–31; and reason, 225; and rights, 229–30; as state reason, 170; as statism, 18–22
postcolonialism, 75–77, 223
postconvertibility, 26
post-Fordism, 70, 75, 169
potencia: affect as, 162; and autonomy, 149; and communitarianism, 44–45; and conatus, 13; definition, 6; feminine, 84, 86; and historical time, 74; of monstrosity, 191; popular, 218, 231
potential, 74–75
potentiality, 12, 62, 85

poverty: in Argentina, 1; feminization of, 92; language of, 53; moralization of, 124–25; resymbolization of, 43
pragmatics, 20, 35, 235
precarity, 17, 72, 113–14, 215, 223
present, the, 73–75
production of social relations, 72
progress: in baroque economies, 20, 22, 235; and migrants, 69–70, 110, 119; producing villas, 191–92; and self-management, 18; Virgin of Urkupiña, the, 58
progressive governments. *See* governments, progressive
proletarianization, 111–12
proletarian microeconomies, 32–34, 68
promiscuity, 54, 64–65, 164, 177, 195
public assistance, 82–83, 241n1

Quint, Álvaro González, 147, 250n35

radio, 43, 123, 130, 143–44
rationality: and calculation, 163; economic, 203, 213; global, 22; governmental, 10; individual, 226; institutional, 91; and migrant workers, 8, 35, 165; of necessities, 175; neoliberalism as, 2, 21, 160, 234; and neoliberalism from below, 5–6, 20, 110, 177; noninstrumental, 10; in popular economies, 2, 142; and popular resistance, 154, 221, 223; of progress, 134; strategic, 3, 9; unicist, 225
realism, aesthetics of, 43
reciprocity, 44–45, 134–37, 249n29. *See also ayni; pasanakus*
regional autonomy, 22–24
rent: *anticrético* system, 207, 212; as control, 167; as growth, 28–29; in neodevelopmentalism, 23–24
rentier economies. *See* economies, rentier

reproduction, 91–93, 204
reproletarianization, 111, 115
resistance, 9, 19, 91, 100–101

scale, 239n19
self, pragmatics of, 20
sex work, 93, 150, 186, 253n12
slave labor. See labor, slave
social, the, 4, 24, 83, 230–31, 233.
    See also populism
social benefits, 166–67, 171, 252n8
social factory, the, 88–91
sovereignty, 155, 157, 202–4, 218–19, 231
state, the, 26–27, 96, 153–54
statelessness, 87–88, 96, 201–3
state-market dichotomy, 153
statism, 18–22
strategic conatus, 8–10, 13
strategic rationality, 3, 9
strategy, 9, 121, 131–32
street negotiations, 175, 251n9
subaltern, the: and community,
    232; and Eurocentrism, 223; and
    feminization, 94, 97; and govern-
    mentality, 220–21; as mute, 42–43,
    134, 194; politicization of, 224–25;
    as victim, 95
subaltern studies, 223–25, 242n11
suburbs, 57, 179

temporality, nonlinear, 234
territorial transposition, 127
territories, 49–50
textile economies, 102–3, 116–17,
    247n14
textile workshops: in Argentina, 108–
    9, 244n2, 244n3; as assemblages,
    118; and ayni, 137; and brands, 118,
    246n9; characteristics of, 113–14,
    122–24; as ch'ixi, 138–39; communi-
    tarian character, 144–46; culturalist
    perspective on, 126–29; as depoliti-
    cized, 113; and entrepreneurship,

119–22; as foreign, 132–33; legal
    perspective on, 129–32; as maquilas,
    109; migrant workers in, 114–15, 118,
    124, 130, 148; and migration, 116–17;
    moral perspective on, 132–34; as
    oppressive, 112; owners of, 146–47,
    248n17, 249n32; slavery question,
    129–36; and villas, 180
trademarks. See brands
transindividualness, 13–14, 235

unions, 121–22
unproductiveness, 87–88, 241n4
urban calculation, 21, 109–10, 135
urbanization, 208–9
urban space, 7, 13, 68, 179, 205–7

Venezuela, 2–3, 7
Vera, Gustavo, 132–33
victimization, 18, 36, 102, 130, 133, 150
Villa 1-11-14: as a city, 189; delegates,
    political, 183–85, 199–201, 206,
    214–17; as exceptional, 186–87;
    internal discrimination, 187; map-
    ping, 197–98; overview, 178, 181–82;
    property logics, 206–7; and ser-
    vices, 185–89, 253n13
villas: children in, 192–93; and citizen-
    ship, 187–88, 192–93; and the city,
    178–79, 188–89; communitarianism
    in, 198–99, 209–13; conversion ide-
    ology, 205–6; festivals in, 194–96,
    216–17; growth of, 191–92, 207–8; as
    insecure, 205; as intensive spaces,
    180; as monstrous, 189–91; as trans-
    national, 196–97; urbanization of,
    208–9; verticality of, 178
Virgin of Urkupiña, the, 58, 240n27
vitalist pragmatics: calculation as, 20,
    160–64; and migrants, 35–36; and
    neoliberlaism from below, 6, 14–15,
    18, 21; popular pragmatics as, 235
voice, the feminine, 95, 97–98

weaving, 102–7
"webs" of communitarianism, 111–12
welfare production, 47
women: as communal goods, 91–93;
  in crises, 83–86; and crowds, 255n6;
  in informal economies, 7; and
  irony, 86–88; labor of, 81–83, 89,
  91; in maquilas, 110; and migrants,
96–97; in textiles, 103; and weaving,
105–7
workers' economic strategies.
  See economic strategies,
  workers'
workplaces, control of, 71–72
workshop economy, 117, 145–48
world market, the, 71